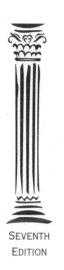

ECONOMICS
IN PERSPECTIVE

CHANGING TIMES—EVOLVING PRINCIPLES

CURRENT ISSUES & PROBLEMS

SEVENTH
EDITION

ELBERT V. BOWDEN
APPALACHIAN STATE UNIVERSITY

JUDITH HOLBERT BOWDEN

Previously entitled:
Economics in Historical Perspective © 1973 by author.
Economics Through the Looking Glass © 1974 by Canfield Div., Harper & Row
Economic Evolution © 1981, 1985 by South-Western.
Economics in Perspective © 1990 by South-Western.

Copyright © 1997, 2000 by Elbert V. Bowden and Judith H. Bowden

ISBN 0-7872-6869-0

Library of Congress Catalog Card Number: 00-101056

Printed in the United States of America
10 9 8 7 6 5 4 3 2 1

CONTENTS

BOOK ONE: THE EVOLUTION OF IDEAS AND EVENTS FROM ANCIENT TO MODERN TIMES

PART TWO—THE SLOW EVOLUTION OF TRADITIONAL ECONOMIC LIFE—ANCIENT TIMES THROUGH THE MIDDLE AGES

PART THREE—THE EMERGENCE OF NEW ECONOMIC CONDITIONS, IDEAS, AND THEORIES—THE INDUSTRIAL REVOLUTION (1750s–1850s)

BOOK TWO: THE RAPIDLY CHANGING WORLD AND CONFLICTING THEORIES OF MODERN TIMES

PART SIX—RECENT DEVELOPMENTS AND CURRENT CONTROVERSIES IN ECONOMIC THEORY

PREFACE

This book is for anyone who wants to understand the economic conditions and crisis issues of the modern world, and the conflicting economic theories being offered to explain them. In this book you will see how these changing conditions and conflicting theories have evolved—as a part of the rapid sweep of historical change. Also you will gain insight into the far-reaching, basic changes which are occurring in modern times.

There's quite a lot of economics—principles, and theory—in this book, because there *must* be. You can't understand what has been happening without understanding the *economic forces* at work. So as the book explains the evolution of events and ideas it also explains and integrates the economic principles involved.

Even before you begin this rapid trip through time, you need to understand some basic economics. So the first two chapters give an introduction to basic economic concepts and principles. The explanations are written in such a way that you will have no difficulty understanding them. The writing style in those chapters, as throughout this book, reflects our personal convictions:

- that the easier the reading, the more it will be read and the better it will be understood—that the task at hand is tough enough without compounding it by couching the explanations in unfamiliar language;
- that scholarly prose is not an efficient medium for the transmission of basic thoughts to students—there's no idea so deep, no theory so rigorous that it can't be explained in simple English;
- that one of the reasons students don't see the *flow* of history is that they spend so much time memorizing details and stumbling over scholarly vocabulary and syntax.

In short, we believe that learning can be (and whenever possible *should* be) fun. In this book we have tried to make it that.

This book has but one purpose: to explain the economic realities of today—the conditions, problems, and ideas—in historical perspective and thereby to provide better awareness and understanding of the present, and insight into the future. There isn't much *historical detail* in this book. The flow of thought moves rapidly from one period to another and from one developer of ideas to another, touching the highlights, gathering the threads and pulling them all together.

The facts of history, once learned, are easily forgotten. But an awareness of the flow of history, once gained, is never lost. And an awareness of the importance of *economic forces* in influencing history, once gained, is never lost. All of us can gain this awareness—can learn to see ourselves and our world as a part of this evolutionary sweep through time. We have tried to design this book to enable the reader to gain this awareness.

We would like to acknowledge the significant debt which this book owes to Robert Heilbroner. Our ideas about how to conceptualize and synthesize the history of economics and the economic history of the world have been greatly influenced by his *The Worldly Philosophers* and *The Making of Economic Society*. Also, we acknowledge Alvin Toffler, author of *Future Shock*, whose influence on our thinking about the speed and impact of change is evident at various places throughout the book.

Our sincerest appreciation to Professors Maryanna Boynton, Ann N. P. Fisher, Warren L. Fisher, Kanji Haitani, Richard K. Hay, Kenneth M. Parzych, Mike Shields, and Charles Spruill, whose suggestions have resulted in significant improvements; and to Mary Ann Burgess, Lois G. Eggers, Sandy Hicks, Dinah Lanning, Laura Page, and Betty Webb whose secretarial skills and cooperation have made the preparation of this edition and previous editions of this book much more pleasant than we had any right to expect.

Elbert V. Bowden

Judith Holbert Bowden

# INTRODUCTION

Here we are in the beginning of the 21st century. And how are things in the U.S. and world economy? Unbelievably good, as compared with a few short years ago.

Back in the early 1980s there was a "near crisis" environment. All of those problems weren't entirely economic problems. But you can be sure that economics was playing a very important role in most of them. Let's take a look.

THE WORLD'S ECONOMIC CRISES OF THE EARLY 1980S

At home we were faced with serious inflation and serious unemployment—and with the energy crisis which was playing an important role in both of these. The Chrysler Corporation was near bankruptcy, as were a few major banks, and a few of the large cities. Angry taxpayers were fighting for relief while government spending cuts threatened the anti-poverty programs.

Some people feared that the Social Security program was in danger of being unable to meet its commitments. Many people couldn't afford to buy homes because of the high interest rates—which also were creating serious problems in the nation's financial markets, and for many financial institutions.

Productivity growth in the economy had slowed down. This was contributing to inflation and bringing declining standards of living to many people. Foreign producers were out-producing American industry in many fields and out-selling American products in many markets, both in this country and worldwide. Environmental destruction was a serious problem, while attempts to contain it were adding to production costs and holding down the growth of productivity.

There had been a continual worsening of the competitive position of the United States in the world economy. The high price of imported oil together with the high and increasing volume of imported foreign products contributed to a series of dollar crises in the foreign exchange markets.

Among the less developed countries (LDCs) where the great majority of the world's population lives, many of the non-oil-producing ones were facing a near-hopeless situation. In addition to their chronic problem of historically low levels of production and consumption and the problem of exploding population, they were facing an impossible balance of payments situation. Their meager receipts from their exports and from foreign aid and all other available sources couldn't possibly pay the high price of the oil required to permit their economic development to proceed.

CONFLICTING ECONOMIC IDEAS

In the midst of all these crisis and near-crisis conditions, you might expect that the economists of the United States and the world would have been providing clear guidance for remedial action. But nothing could be further from the truth. Disagreement was so widespread among economists that from the outside looking in it must have appeared to be a situation of total confusion.

Academic economists were in wide disagreement among themselves, as were government economists, Federal Reserve economists, business economists, labor economists, news media economists, and all others. There was strong disagreement between the monetarist economists and the Keynesian economists—and the radical economists were taking positions against both of them. But that wasn't the end of it. There was conflict and disagreement within each group—within each "school of thought"—and from economists whose ideas didn't fit neatly into any of the "schools."

IMPROVED CONDITIONS SINCE THE EARLY 1980S

Several of the near-crisis conditions of the early 1980s had been overcome or much improved by the mid-1980s. The inflation rate had slowed to where it was no longer a serious problem. The economy was rapidly recovering from its serious recession, and unemployment (although still high) was coming down.

Then in the remainder of the decade of the 1980s unemployment continued to come down, from a high of 10.7% in January of 1983 to 5% of the labor force in 1989. The inflation rate remained low—less than 4% most of the time. Huge improvement!

As we came to the end of the 1990s we were experiencing what some economists were calling a "Storybook economy." We had the lowest rate of inflation (<2%), the lowest rate of unemployment (4.0% of the labor force), and the most rapid rate of growth of both productivity and gross domestic product (GDP) in several decades. And in January of 2000 the economy broke all records for the longest uninterrupted economic expansion ever. Fantastic!

THE NEW "ONE-WORLD" ECONOMY

The new technologies and the telecommunications and computer revolution were bringing dramatic changes. The world was becoming a global market place, with worldwide financial markets and instantaneous transactions between New York, London, Tokyo, Frankfurt, and just about anywhere else! By the beginning of the new millenium we really had entered into a new world of finance and economics. You'll be reading about all this later.

IN THE ECONOMY, WHAT CAUSES WHAT?

What about all those conflicting theories?—Those serious disagreements among economists? Had economists finally come to agree about what's happening? And why? And what public policies should be followed to achieve the best results for the society? Don't you believe it!

For everything that happens in the economy, there are different possible explanations of why—of what causes it to happen that way. Some economists will explain it one way. Others, another. And there's no clear way to prove whose explanation is right and whose is wrong.

By the time you get to the end of this book you'll understand much better what all of this means. And, more important, you'll have a basic understanding of the principles of economics—of the theories which explain so much of what's happening in our individual and family lives, in our nation, and in our world.

A BACKWARD GLIMPSE THROUGH TIME

For more than ten thousand centuries people have been roaming around on various parts of the earth. That's right—more than ten thousand centuries! All this time these people have been struggling to make it, trying to choose the best ways of using their limited resources to meet their needs, to satisfy their wants, to achieve their objectives—that is, trying to solve their "basic economic problem."

It is only in the fleeting moments of recent history that people have been making progress in improving their economic conditions. Once this progress began it turned out to be cumulative. Each step forward was building on the previous progress. As time went on, the rate of change became explosive.

And you who are lucky (or unlucky?) enough to be living today were born right into the middle of this explosion.

Much that will happen during your lifetime will be incomprehensible to you unless you have some awareness and understanding of this explosive change we're all caught up in. In just your short lifetime you have observed rapid changes in so many things. We have new attitudes toward acquiring wealth and toward the environment. Our feelings have changed about authority, freedom, poverty, marriage, sex, education, music, dancing, purpose in life—just about everything!

You have seen so many new ways of doing things—new productive processes, new technology, the computer and telecommunications revolution—so many, many changes!

And what about the crumbling of communist economies? And the worldwide resurgence of capitalism? The people in those countries are really being shook up!

The world of today is already a very different place from the world in which you were born. Maybe it's impossible for anyone to fully grasp all of the many effects of such rapid changes in so many aspects of life and society.

Big changes have been going on in economic conditions and in the economic behavior of mankind. And there have been new changes in the ideas and philosophies about economics, and about what has been causing all these changes. It's hard to comprehend. But a thoughtful reading of this book will help you to gain a better perspective on all of this.

HOW RAPIDLY TIME PASSES!

How quickly the years (even the centuries!) go by. You have not yet lived long enough to observe the passing of very much time, so it may be difficult for you to develop an awareness of how rapidly time passes—especially historical time.

If you are twenty years old you have lived one-fifth of a century—perhaps one-fourth of your lifetime. During the other three-fourths of your life, time will seem to go by much more rapidly than during the first one-fourth. And after the other three-fourths go by, all of your time will have passed. You see, a human lifetime isn't very long. Historically speaking, one lifetime, or even one century, is a very short time. After all, you have already "lived up" about a fourth of an average lifetime—about a fifth of a century!

If you can realize the speed at which time passes you may be able to feel the explosive rate of change in our modern-day world. It was only about two centuries ago that the United States was established as a nation. That's less than three complete lifetimes.

It was three centuries before that when Columbus discovered America. But it was ten centuries before that when the Roman Empire collapsed, and some thirty-five centuries before that when the early civilizations were emerging in Babylonia and the Nile Valley. And before that, for how long had human beings already been on the earth? More than ten thousand centuries!

EXPLOSIVE CHANGE IS BEING FUELED BY ECONOMIC FACTORS

Todays explosive rate of change isn't entirely caused by economics. But economic factors are playing a very important role. Without the disruptive influence of adventuresome and acquisitive individuals, breaking free, following the market, struggling to enrich themselves and simultaneously enriching future generations—without all this, the explosive thrust of the modern world wouldn't have developed.

If you are going to understand what is happening to you, to your world, in your lifetime—if you are going to be able to see the explosion in which you are caught and hurtling along—if you are to gain any idea of where all this might be going, and why, and how—then you must be able to see and understand the economic forces at work.

WE CAN'T FORSEE THE FUTURE

It isn't that understanding the economic forces of change will let you see with any certainty where the world is going. It won't. But at least it will help you to understand that you are caught up in a world of explosive change. You will be able to understand a little better what's happening to all of us, and how, and why. And perhaps you'll gain some insight into where it all might be going. If you get all that out of reading this little book, then surely your time and thoughts will have been well spent.

PART ONE

AN INTRODUCTION TO BASIC ECONOMIC CONCEPTS AND PRINCIPLES

The concepts and principles of economics have played a vital role in the evolution of the modern world. These concepts and principles are explained at appropriate places throughout this book. But first, you need a few of the basics right up front. That's what you'll get from Part One.

1

SCARCITY, CHOICE, AND THE PRICE MECHANISM

 KEY TERMS

- the "economic problem"
- scarcity
- limited (scarce) resources
- opportunity cost
- the marginal concept
- the three basic economic questions
- the output question the input question the distribution question

- the three ways to solve them the social process of tradition the political process of command the market process: price mechanism
- productivity principle of distribution
- shortage
- surplus
- distributive share

Soon, this book will begin back in ancient history. Then it will bring you swiftly forward through the changing economic conditions and ideas from one age to another, up to the economic issues and problems of modern times. But first, before you begin this rapid journey through time, there are some basic economics concepts and principles you will need to understand. Otherwise you won't get the full meaning from the historical sweep of events and ideas that follow.

As you read through the chapters of this book, many more economics concepts and principles will be introduced. But you will understand those as you go along because each is explained as it comes up. Then by the time you arrive at the present-day issues and problems and conflicting ideas about economics, you will be able to understand. You will be able to see our current conditions in historical perspective. You'll have a much better feel for where we've come from, and where we are. But first, some basic principles of economics, coming up now.

THE ECONOMIC PROBLEM

The economic problem is the problem of *having to decide how to use the available things.* How does an individual or a family—or even an entire society—decide which ways to use the things they have? Of course they would like to use the things available so as to come out "best."

Every family and society would like to have enough food and clothing and shelter to take care of its people. Then, after these basic needs are satisfied there are all kinds of other things they would like to have—better food, better clothing, better housing, better transportation, more opportunities for music and the arts and recreation, and lots of other things—including more leisure time to enjoy. Definition: The economic problem is the problem of deciding—of choosing among all of the conflicting objectives.

SCARCITY

The "economic problem" of choosing among alternatives is basic to every individual, family, and society. It is forced upon all of us by the natural condition of *scarcity.* Scarcity means that the things available to work with are *limited.* We always have (and probably always will have) less things available to work with than we would like to have.

Throughout history, in most societies there have always been poor and hungry people. This has resulted from the basic fact of scarcity—the limited supplies of the things people want. Chronic poverty also has resulted from the inefficient, primitive methods with which the available resources have been used.

In the modern world, great advances in production technology have made it possible to get a lot more output from our available (scarce) resources. But from ancient times all the way up to recent centuries, production methods remained very primitive. For many centuries there weren't any important technological breakthroughs. But even in the most advanced nations of the modern world, scarcity still exists everywhere. Almost everyone would like to have more and better things and more leisure time to enjoy them.

THE ECONOMIC PROBLEM DEALS WITH SCARCITY

The economic problem is the problem of dealing with scarcity. It's the problem of deciding, given the scarcities of the things we have, exactly how each of the available resources (including natural, human, and capital resources) will be used.

OPPORTUNITY COST

The idea of "opportunity cost" is that "you can't have your cake and eat it too." Opportunity cost results from the basic fact of *scarcity*. It applies to every individual, every family, and every society. The availability of things is always limited. So when you want to use something for one purpose, that means you can't use that same thing for some other purpose.

Each time you choose to use an acre of land to produce wheat, then you give up the opportunity to use that land to produce corn. So the "opportunity cost" of the *wheat* you get, is the *corn* you must give up.

When my daughter spends her allowance on candy bars she gives up the opportunity to go to a movie. So to her, the opportunity cost of the candy bars, is the movie. When any society decides to increase its output of one thing (say, military hardware), then it must give up something else which is also desired (say, better highways, or schools).

When you make—or when the society makes—a choice, the opportunity cost is what must be given up to get what was chosen. You might say: "The opportunity cost is the opportunity lost."

THE MARGINAL CONCEPT

Economists use the term "marginal" to refer to *small adjustments* which individuals, businesses, and societies make as they are trying to "fine tune" their resource choices, seeking to arrive at their "optimum position" of (for the consumer) maximum satisfaction, or (for the producer) maximum profit, or (for the society) maximum "social good"—however the society may choose to define that.

The idea of a "marginal" adjustment is that a small change is made in the way resources are allocated. Then you ask "Is that better than before?" If the answer is yes, then you have moved closer to the "optimum" which you are seeking. Each individual, business, and society is constantly making "marginal adjustments" as they attempt to "optimize."

The marginal concept is very important in economics because it provides a way of describing and analyzing the process of "optimization"—the process of moving small steps, step-by-step, toward the desired optimum position.

THE THREE BASIC ECONOMIC QUESTIONS

As the society works out its "economic problem" there are three basic questions that must be answered:
1. Which products (and how much of each) will be produced? How much food? clothing? shelter? and which kinds of each? And how much of various other things? transportation? education? arts and recreation? etc.? etc.? This is the *output* question: "What to produce?"
2. Which resources (natural resources, work-time inputs, tools, etc.) will be used in the production of each product? And how will the production be organized? Much labor on each small piece of land? Or much land for each worker to till? Many tools of the best-known kinds? Or only a few of the most primitive tools? Will the corn rows be planted one foot apart? Or three feet apart? This is the *input* question: "How will the products be produced?"
3. Which members of the society will get a share (and how big a share) of the output? That is, how will the output which is produced, be distributed (shared) among the members of the society? Will everyone receive an equal share regardless of age, sex, health, strength, "noble birth," political affiliation, or whatever? Or will more of the output go to the "nobles"?— or perhaps to the ones who "need" more?—or to the ones who *produce* more? This is the *distribution* question: "How do we divide up the output among the people?"

All three of these questions somehow must be answered in every society. This has always been true. It probably always will be true. Certainly it will be true as long as *scarcity* exists—as long as people desire more and better things than they have. So the questions must be answered. But how?

THE THREE WAYS TO ANSWER THE BASIC ECONOMIC QUESTIONS

There are three ways—and *only* three ways, or "processes" which can be used—to answer the three basic economic questions and thereby solve the "economic problem" for the society. This is true for every society—ancient or modern, primitive or advanced. The three ways or "processes" are: (1) the social process, (2) the political process, and (3) the market process.

THE "SOCIAL PROCESS" OF "TRADITION"

Tradition can answer all three of the questions. This means that all three questions can be answered in the "traditional" way—all the answers are the same as they always have been in the past. The people produce the same products, use the same kinds of resource inputs and production techniques, and then share the outputs among themselves in the same way that their parents, grandparents, and all their other ancestors did for as far back as anyone can remember.

Tradition played the most important role in solving the economic problem in ancient times and, in fact, throughout most of history. It still plays a very important role in some of the less developed countries of the world. Its influence still can be seen even in modern society in such things as the economic relationships among family members.

THE "POLITICAL PROCESS" OF "COMMAND"

The power of *government* can be used to decide the answers to the three basic economic questions. Government can decide which products will be produced, which inputs and production techniques will be used, and how much of the output each person will get.

As you read the following chapters you will see that *command* has played an important role in solving the economic problem in various societies from time to time throughout history. In the modern world there have been several major nations in which command has played the most important role in making the economic choices. That's been true of the former USSR, the People's Republic of China, Castro's Cuba, and some other nations.

Even in the "capitalist" countries such as the United States, the political process makes many of the production and distribution choices. You can see it in the development of highways and education, in the welfare and social security programs, in the armed forces, in urban renewal, and in many other government programs, federal, state, and local.

THE "MARKET PROCESS" AND THE "PRICE MECHANISM"

The idea of the "market process" and the "price mechanism" is that people produce things, not because that's what their ancestors did and not because the government directs them to do so, but because they think they can *sell* what they produce and *earn income.*

When the market process is in charge of working out the choices, people produce things for "the market." Whatever people are demanding most and are willing to pay the highest prices for, those are the things which producers will produce. That solves the "output" question for the society automatically without anyone having to "decide."

The "input" question is also solved automatically by the market process and the "price mechanism." Every producer will carefully conserve those inputs which are most scarce and therefore most valuable—the ones that have the highest prices. Producers will always try to use the most plentiful, lowest-priced inputs and the lowest-cost production techniques. That's how they can earn the most *income,* or *profit.*

So when the market process is answering the basic questions, each producer responds to *prices* and tries to produce the most demanded (highest priced) things and to produce them using the most plentiful (lowest priced) inputs and the most efficient production techniques.

The third basic question also is answered automatically. The people who produce the most valuable, most demanded things and do it most efficiently will earn the most income. With their income they "claim their share" of the society's output. This is called the "productivity principle of distribution"— the "distributive share" which each person receives is determined by the value of what that person produces. The more valuable the *productive contri-bution* the greater the income and the greater the "distributive share" of the output received.

The "productivity principle of distribution" didn't have very much influence in the traditional societies of ancient times. Each person's production was meant to be shared with others. The political process of command sometimes used the productivity principle. But mostly governments in those days stimulated people to produce by the threat of punishment—not by the promise of "rewards for productivity."

OF SPECIAL INTEREST . . .

IN THE MODERN WORLD THE "PRODUCTIVITY PRINCIPLE" PLAYS AN IMPORTANT ROLE IN DETERMINING EACH PERSON'S INCOME— EACH PERSON'S "DISTRIBUTIVE SHARE" OF THE SOCIETY'S OUTPUT. IT ALSO PLAYS THE IMPORTANT ROLE OF STIMULATING PEOPLE TO BE MORE PRODUCTIVE—TO TRY TO WORK TO GET AHEAD. THE PRODUCTIVITY PRINCIPLE OF DISTRIBUTION HAS PROVED TO BE A VERY EFFECTIVE METHOD FOR STIMULATING PEOPLE TO PRODUCE MORE.

THE POWERFUL PRICE MECHANISM*

The market process works through the "price mechanism." The price mechanism works automatically, responding to changes in demand and supply. It encourages the production and discourages the consumption of higher-priced goods.

When people for whatever reason begin demanding *more* of something, that causes *shortages* in that market and the price is forced up. The higher price stimulates more production of this item. It attracts new producers to enter this market. But when people begin demanding *less* of something, *surpluses* develop and the price is forced down. The lower price discourages the production of that item and producers shift into the production of something else—something that brings them more income.

Businesses, and workers too, shift from producing one thing to another, from one place to another, from one kind of production technique to another, all in response to the "signals" of the price mechanism. Why? Because that's how they can increase their incomes and their "distributive shares" of the output.

The price mechanism exerts a powerful, almost irresistible force. And it works automatically, almost like magic. When the price of something goes up very much, if you will wait awhile, you almost always will see more of this item being produced and less of it being consumed. That's what happened in the world's oil markets in the 1980s in response to OPEC's high oil prices.

---

* In Chapter 12 you will see how supply and demand curves can be used to explain how the market process works through the operation of the price mechanism. If you want to, you can jump ahead and read that chapter now.

When you get to the chapter on the Industrial Revolution you'll see the great power and influence of the price mechanism in directing and influencing the economic choices.

REVIEW QUESTIONS

1. Explain what is the basic economic problem, and who faces this problem. Be sure to include the concepts of scarcity, opportunity cost, and marginal adjustments in your explanation.

2. What are the three basic economic questions that each society must answer? How does the concept of scarcity influence these basic questions?

3. Explain how the three basic economic questions are solved automatically by the market process and the price mechanism.

4. Explain how the price mechanism works automatically in the economy. Use the concepts of surplus and shortage in your explanation.

2 PRODUCTION, DISTRIBUTION, AND DEFINITIONS OF ECONOMICS

KEY TERMS

- market structure
- pure (perfect) competition
- economic growth, economic progress
- future production vs. present consumption
- the definitions of economics
- political economy
- microeconomics
- macroeconomics
- John Maynard Keynes
- Keynesian economics
- factors of production
- inputs
  land
  labor
  capital
- capitalist
- entrepreneur
- economic system
- capitalism
- pure capitalism
- laissez-faire

The *inputs* which are used to produce outputs, are called "factors of production." There are hundreds of different factors of production, of course. But for convenience and to simplify economic analysis, economists usually group these factors under three different headings: land, labor, and capital.

FACTORS OF PRODUCTION

LAND. All natural resources—the "free gifts of nature"—are grouped together and called "land."

17

LABOR. All human effort, whether it be physical effort or mental effort, highly skilled effort or unskilled effort, is grouped together and called "labor."

CAPITAL. All tools, equipment, factories, and everything else which has *already been produced,* and which is to be used *to assist in further production,* are grouped together and called "capital."

Be careful to note that as economists use the term "capital" it does not mean "money." It means the physical things which have been produced and are going to be used in further production. Much of the process of economic growth consists of building more and better *capital.* But economic growth also results from improving the abilities and skills of the society's *labor.* Improving the ability and skills of the labor force is sometimes referred to by economists as "building human capital."

CAPITALIST. The reason the owners of big businesses are called "capitalists" is because they are the ones who own most of the capital—the buildings and machines and equipment and other things—needed in the production process. And the reason some economic systems are referred to as "capitalist systems" is to emphasize the importance of "the capitalist" in the functioning of these economic systems.

THE ENTREPRENEUR. Economists sometimes define the *entrepreneur* as a fourth factor of production, separate from the other three. Ideally, the "entrepreneur" is the enterprising person who sees the opportunity to bring together some capital, labor, and land and produce a product which people will buy. The entrepreneur who succeeds in producing products which are in high demand and who produces the products efficiently (at low cost) will make a lot of profit—and then will reinvest the profit in more capital and generate even more profit. The entrepreneur is responsible for increasing the productivity and growth of the economy.

In a "market-process-oriented" economic system, it is necessary for the "entrepreneurial function" to be performed. Otherwise the economy will not keep going, and growing. In the modern world, this function is performed mostly by big business organizations, not by one individual—an "entrepreneur." But as you will see in the following chapters, during the period of the industrial revolution and the rapid industrialization which occurred between the mid 1700s and the early 1900s, the individual entrepreneur played a vital role.

ECONOMIC SYSTEM

The term "economic system" is used to refer to the kind of arrangement which exists in a society for solving the "economic problem"—for working out the answers to the three basic economic questions: What to produce? What inputs and production techniques to use? and How to distribute (share) the output among the people?

In all economic systems in the world today there is some mixture of all three processes—social, political, and market—for working out the answers to these questions. In all present-day economic systems, some of the economic choices are made in each of the three ways: some by tradition, some by command, and some by the price mechanism. But the *importance* of the role which each of these decision-making processes plays, differs greatly from one economic system to another.

In some systems, tradition is most important. We see this in some of the less developed countries. In some other systems, *command* plays the most important role. We have seen this in the so-called "Communist" countries. And in still other systems—including those of the United States, Canada, Western Europe, Japan, Australia, and several others—we see the *price mechanism* as most important. But in all economic systems, all three processes are at work to some extent. As you read through the following chapters you will find that throughout most of history, the social process of *tradition* has been most important in most places, most of the time.

CAPITALISM

Capitalism is a form of economic system in which the market process and the price mechanism are left free to work out the answers to the three basic economic questions. "Pure capitalism" would operate with no government interference, and with no restrictions from "tradition."

When the people are free to follow the influences of the price mechanism, to produce whatever they think will be profitable, to produce it in the ways they think will be most efficient, and to earn and keep as much income or profit as they can—that's "capitalism." It is a system of "laissez-faire" (hands-off by government) and competition, where each person has an equal right to get into any market, to produce anything which looks profitable, to out-sell and under-sell the other producers—and "let the devil take the hindmost."

In a system of "pure capitalism" the people who are highly productive get high incomes; the people who do not produce anything do not get any incomes at all. This kind of harsh, dog-eat-dog, unrestricted capitalism doesn't exist anywhere in the world today. But a somewhat modified and tempered version of capitalism does exist in the United States, in the countries of Western Europe and Japan, and in several other places in the world.

MARKET STRUCTURE AND PURE COMPETITION

Pure competition (also called "perfect competition") is a kind of "market structure" in which there are many buyers and many sellers of the product. Pure competition means no seller or buyer has any "monopoly power." Because of the large number of buyers and sellers for the product, no buyer or seller can do anything but accept the price as it exists in the market.

In a market structure of pure competition, the only time the price would go up is when many buyers are all trying to buy more, or many sellers are all offering less of the product for sale. Any *one* of the many buyers could buy two or three times as much and it wouldn't noticeably influence the price. Any *one* seller could stop producing and selling this product altogether, and it wouldn't noticeably influence the price.

In markets of "pure competition" the price is set by the "impersonal forces" of demand and supply. This kind of market structure (or something which results in approximately the same conditions) is necessary for the "pure market forces" to work as they are described in the "pure market model" developed by some of the economists you will be reading about soon. You will find out that one of the important reasons for disagreement among economists in modern times stems from their basic disagreement about the extent to which modern-world economic systems work the way a market system of "pure competition" would. It's a question of whether or not the monopoly power (the lack of pure competition) which exists in most real-world markets does (or does not) prevent real-world economic systems from working more or less as the "pure competition model" specifies.

ECONOMIC PROGRESS, OR ECONOMIC GROWTH

Economic growth is the process which results in *increasing output* per person. With economic growth, the average worker produces more, so in the end there is *more total output* to be shared among the members of the society. As economic growth proceeds, it softens some of the harshness of "opportunity cost"—the idea that when you get more of one thing, that "costs you" the opportunity of having more of something else.

With economic growth, a society can to some extent lessen the limitations imposed by opportunity cost. Over time, if better techniques of production can be introduced, or if more and better agricultural land can be discovered and/or developed, then that society will be able to have more of some things without having to give up something else. That's the great appeal of "economic progress" or "economic growth."

Economic growth comes about mostly from the discovery of better techniques of production, and the development of more and better tools and machines. With more and better equipment, each worker can produce more output per day, week, or year.

But here's the problem with trying to generate economic growth. When everybody is already busy producing the food needed to keep the people from starving, who has the time to do what's necessary to bring economic growth? Economic growth requires that energies and resources be directed toward developing new techniques, building tools, clearing new land, and doing other things that will increase worker productivity in the future. Who is going to do this?

THE DILEMMA: PRESENT CONSUMPTION? OR FUTURE GROWTH?

The energies and resources which are aimed toward increasing *future production* are not adding any output for *present consumption*. If the society can only produce enough to just barely get by on, what happens when some of its energies and resources are shifted out of food production and directed toward economic growth? You know what happens. The output of food goes down and some of the people starve! That's the opportunity cost of economic growth. But if everything currently produced is aimed toward current consumption, then there is no economic progress—no economic growth.

So the society faces a dilemma. If resources are diverted from consumption and aimed toward increasing *future* output, then some people will go hungry. And in a society where *tradition* locks everyone into their "proper role" in the production-distribution circle, there isn't much chance for anyone to break loose and strike out for economic progress. As you read the following chapters you will be able to understand why so little economic progress occurred for so many, many centuries.

THE DEFINITION(S) OF ECONOMICS

Now that you understand some of the most basic concepts and principles of economics, you know what economics is all about. So now you're ready for a definition.

ECONOMICS

Economics can be defined in various ways:

- Economics is the study of how people—individuals, families, businesses, organizations, and societies—work out their economic choices and "solve" their "economic problem."
- Economics is the study of how people (and businesses, societies, etc.) choose (decide) about how to use their available things—land, labor, and capital.
- Economics is concerned with how people (and businesses, societies, etc.) use the things they have to try to get the most of what they want.

You can see that all of these definitions are saying the same thing. Economics is concerned with facing the natural condition of *scarcity,* and choosing which ways to use the available things. It always must deal with the inescapable reality of *opportunity cost.* Every choice to have more of one thing involves the loss of the opportunity to have more of something else. That's *economics.*

POLITICAL ECONOMY

The term "political economy" refers to working out the solution to the "economic problem"—deciding the answers to the three basic economic questions—just as does the term "economics." But the term political economy assumes that *government* will be playing an important role in influencing those choices.

If you want to understand how an economic system can work "on its own," through the operation of the market process and the price mechanism, then you study "economics." But if you want to investigate the operation of an economic system in which government policies are playing an important role in influencing the operation of the economy—trying to re-aim and redirect the economic activities and choices of the people—then you study "political economy."

In the late medieval period and in the early years of the industrial revolution, most economic writers wrote books on "political economy." During that period, government was exerting strong influences on the operation of the economy. A good bit of the emphasis of these early "political economy" books was aimed toward explaining how government policies were interfering with the efficient operation of the economy—holding down production and slowing economic progress in the nation.

Since the late 1800s, most books in the field of economics have been called "economics"—not "political economy." The emphasis of these more recent books has been on explaining how an economic system operates on its own, directed by the forces of the *market process* and the *price mechanism*.

MICROECONOMICS

Microeconomics is that part of the study of economics which is concerned with most of the concepts and principles you have been reading about so far in this chapter. Microeconomics is concerned with how "the economic problem" is solved—with how the three basic economic questions are answered. It is concerned with making *choices* about what to do with the available resources, given the natural condition of *scarcity*.

Microeconomics is concerned with how these questions are answered by the individual, the business, and the total society. Microeconomics is the study of opportunity cost, of substitution, of choosing this or that, of trade-offs, of "deciding (among all of the possible alternatives) which way to use the available resources." The definitions of *economics* which you read a few minutes ago are really definitions of "microeconomics."

MICROECONOMICS, AND "PRICE THEORY"

If you are studying an economic system which is directed by the market process—that is, by the powerful price mechanism—then the study of microeconomics is the study of *price theory*. It's the study of how the resource allocation decisions—the choices about what to do with the available resources—are made automatically in response to changing conditions of supply and/or demand, and as carried out by price changes. It's the study of how prices automatically adjust to shift goods and resources from less desired, less valuable places and uses, to more desired, more valuable places and uses.

MACROECONOMICS

Macroeconomics is a term which has come into use since the Great Depression of the 1930s. *Macroeconomics* is that part of economics which is concerned with understanding the *speed,* or *rate* at which the entire economy will run. It is concerned with *totals:* the total level of production, output, employment, consumer spending, investment spending, government spending, national income, etc.

If you are studying *macroeconomics* you are trying to understand what causes the economy to speed up and slow down—what causes recessions or depressions, and inflation. The term "macroeconomics" has arisen in connection with "Keynesian (KAYN'sian) economics" which was introduced by John Maynard Keynes (KAYns) during the depression of the 1930s.

As you will be finding out in this book, Keynes introduced some new ways of looking *directly* at the question: "What determines the rate at which the economy will run?" As this "new approach" became integrated into the study of economics, it became necessary to have terms to distinguish between this kind of economics, and the other economic theories which had traditionally been "economics." So that's why we now talk about "microeconomics" and "macroeconomics." In this book you will find out how these developments occurred, and you'll find out about the latest theories of both microeconomics and macroeconomics.

REVIEW QUESTIONS

1. Define and explain the three basic factors of production.

2. Sometimes economists define the "entrepreneur" as a fourth factor of production. Who is this "entrepreneur," and what is the "entrepreneurial role" in the economic process?

3. Define an "economic system." Discuss some modern economic systems and how the basic economic questions are answered in each of these systems.

4. Explain how the economic system of capitalism answers the basic economic questions. Can you list any modern real-world examples of pure capitalism? Explain.

5. Define the market structure of pure competition. Be sure your definition answers these questions: (1) How many buyers and sellers are there? (2) How much influence does each buyer and each seller have over price? and (3) How is price determined?

6. Define and distinguish between microeconomics and macroeconomics.

BOOK ONE

THE EVOLUTION OF IDEAS AND EVENTS FROM ANCIENT TO MODERN TIMES

PART TWO

THE SLOW EVOLUTION OF TRADITIONAL ECONOMIC LIFE—ANCIENT TIMES THROUGH THE MIDDLE AGES

After thousands of centuries of very little change, economic forces suddenly trigger an explosion and everyone is caught in the force of the blast.

3

FROM ANCIENT TIMES TO THE MIDDLE AGES

KEY TERMS

- Aristotle's economic philosophy
- religious writings on economics
- St. Thomas Aquinas
- economic morality
- economic progress and the command process
- the Roman Empire and the political force of command
- usury

People have been on earth for more than *ten thousand centuries.* But it was only about fifty centuries ago that "civilizations" began to emerge.

THE CRADLES OF CIVILIZATION

Historians talk about the "cradles of civilization": Mesopotamia, Babylonia, the Nile Valley—all places you have heard about many times. In Asia there were still other early civilizations, some even older and perhaps more advanced than those of the Middle East. In all these places, people always faced their economic problem—how to deal with scarcity, how to choose what to do with the limited things they had: What to use? And what to save? What to make? And who will get to have how much of what?

THE ROLE OF "TRADITION," AND "COMMAND"

Each of the ancient societies had to have some kind of economic system—some way of getting the choices made and the decisions carried out. And what system? Like all economic systems, some mixture of social, political, and market forces or processes. But the choices in the ancient societies were made and carried out mostly by the social force of *tradition*, as influenced and altered in various ways from time to time by the political force of *command*.

Some trade existed, but very little. Trade had almost no influence on the life patterns of the people. Usually, people produced for themselves and shared with their families and leaders. Sometimes the force of command by the ruler—sheik or pharoah or some such—would turn people into slaves and exert a powerful influence on the society's economic choices. (Certainly the pyramids were not built in response to the free wishes of the common people!)

ANCIENT GREECE AND ROME

From the cradles of civilization we can leap forward about twenty-five centuries to the early days of Greece and Rome—at about the time of Confucius and Buddha in Asia, about five centuries before the birth of Christ. And what do we find that was different? Actually, not very much. There had been a good bit of social and political evolution. Specialization and trade were somewhat more developed. People had learned how to do and make a lot more things. But the economic systems were still mostly tradition-bound.

"TRADITION" WAS IN CONTROL

Workers, craftsmen, noblemen, slaves, all followed in the footsteps of their parents—the traditional way. Except when conquerors would come in and take over, and use the force of command to make changes, the economic choices of production and distribution followed the same traditional patterns, century after century.

EARLY CIVILIZATIONS IN THE FAR EAST

This same pattern of "rule by tradition" was followed in the early civilizations of India, China and Japan. Ruling families came and went, kingdoms and empires waxed and waned, but customs and traditions controlled most aspects of people's lives. Economic allocations were determined by the customs of society—that is, by the social system. By tradition.

In the twenty-five centuries between the early civilizations and the rise of the Greek and Roman city-states, the economic systems—the ways of solving the basic economic problem, making the economic choices—really didn't change much. Some changes would occur in one place or another from time to time. But the movement was mostly back and forth. There wasn't much continuous progress—no step-by-step evolution of new and better ways of solving the society's economic problem; no cumulative chain reaction of economic progress from one period to the next.

THE ROLE OF "COMMAND"

From time to time, political control over the economy would be more powerful in one place or another. But as time passed, the rulers (the "government") would change, government directives would be relaxed, and tradition again would take over. Throughout these many centuries the economic choices generally reflected the traditions of the society, but as modified by the waxing and waning of political controls.

Under the early Greek and Roman civilizations there was some economic (as well as social and political) progress. Some markets were developing and expanding. The market forces of demand, supply, and prices were having some influence on the production and distribution choices of the society—but still only very little. Almost all of the choices were either preordained by tradition or ordered by command.

The same was true of the civilizations of the Far East. Societies were essentially agrarian; most people were peasants, earning their subsistence from the land. Many members of the "labor force" were slaves, serving and carrying out the economic choices of their rich and powerful masters; many were soldiers, serving and carrying out the economic choices of those who held the political powers of the state.

EARLY IDEAS ON ECONOMICS

As you know, during the days of ancient Greece and Rome, philosophers were trying to understand and explain things. The most outstanding of them was Aristotle. While Aristotle was becoming "the father" of almost every science—astronomy, chemistry, psychology, biology, medicine, geology, and others—economics did not escape his scrutiny. He expressed some very definite thoughts about economics. Would you believe that Aristotle's ideas about economics set the tenor of Western economic thought for the next *ten centuries?* That's a fact.

Aristotle's Economic Philosophy

Aristotle's economic philosophy was ideal for maintaining stability and harmony and social justice in a tradition-bound society. In such societies, flexibility and change would be disruptive and socially undesirable. But for a society which has broken the bonds of tradition—a society which is responding to the powerful forces of the market—Aristotle's economic teachings would not fit. Yet even today we find fragments of Aristotle's economic thought lingering in the minds of many people in the world. So let's take a minute to look at some of the things he said.

Aristotle considered exchange, and borrowing and lending money to be unproductive activities. Each family should produce what it needs for itself. A person who happens to have a surplus may exchange it or sell it to someone else for a "just" price. But it isn't good for one person to buy something with the idea of selling it to someone else at a profit. The middleman-trader is detrimental to the society because the middleman must be buying for *less* than the "just price" or selling for *more* than the "just price," (or both), otherwise there would be no profit on the deal! So the middleman is a parasite on the society who gains riches at the expense of others. So said Aristotle.

Even worse than the middleman-traders, according to Aristotle, were those who would lend money and charge interest. Interest is *usury*—an unjust charge. Since people can't actually make things with money (as they can with machines and raw materials, etc.) money is not productive. Therefore anyone who lends money should not expect to get back any more than the amount lent.

Early Religious Writings on Economics

Aristotle was not the first to write on economics. There were many before him. Economic thoughts have been included in the writings of most philosophers from the very beginning. The Old Testament and New Testament of the Bible contain much economics, as do the writings of religions other than Christianity. Every religion has been concerned with the issues of the right and wrong economic behavior, and with social choices.

The economic question, "How to do the best for our people with the limited things available," has been an important question for every religion. The

Bible, the Talmud, the Koran, and other sacred scriptures and religious writings contain much economic thought. The concepts of right and wrong in economic matters—of sharing, of "just price," of work and leisure—have been discussed by religious and moral philosophers as far back as recorded history can take us (and very likely even before that).

ONE PERSON'S GAIN IS ANOTHER'S LOSS

The basic ideas of Aristotelian economic thought were reflected in the economic philosophies of early Christianity. The most outstanding economic writer among the many medieval Christian philosophers was St. Thomas Aquinas. His writings on economics emphasize the idea of "just price" and go into great detail on the injustices of lending money for interest, and of trading for profit. The concepts of trading, working to get ahead, acquiring material wealth—all the conditions essential for the market process to operate and to stimulate economic growth—were condemned by the medieval Christian writers.

It was not considered moral to acquire things and to try to enrich one's self. Underlying this anti-acquisitive attitude was the idea that there was only so much of wealth and things around. Any person who worked to acquire more would be forcing others to get by with less. That was bad. A good, moral person would practice "personal denial"—would be charitable and give things to others.

THERE WAS NO ESCAPE FROM POVERTY

It wasn't that the religious (and other) philosophers wanted everybody to be poor and miserable. Not at all! The hard economic facts of life required that almost all of the people be poor almost all of the time, anyway. So, better to be purposefully poor and feel good about it than to be accidentally poor and be miserable! Also, consider this: Poor people (and poor families and poor tribes) never get murdered for their possessions! And there was a lot of that going on in those days.

The highest form of "economic morality" was to live in poverty, consuming very little and leaving almost everything for others. The idea of economic growth—of people working out ways to become more productive; of each person producing more and thereby achieving personal enrichment and also helping to enrich the society—that idea wouldn't be understood and accepted until many centuries later. In the traditional societies and in some religions it still is not accepted, even today.

THE ROMAN EMPIRE

The early civilizations of Greece and Rome began about five centuries before the time of Christ and continued until the Roman Empire took over at about the time of Christ. The Roman Empire continued for about five centuries after Christ. Under the Roman Empire the political force of command took control over many of the economic choices. The government decided about the uses of many resources and about the activities of many people. Many of the social forces of tradition were pushed aside.

Great changes were made in the organization of economic activity and in the choices as to what was to be produced and how it was to be shared among the people. As the Romans spread out over the land, they changed the ways the resources and the energies of the people were used. They redirected and forced increases in productive activities. Using the force of command, they generated increased outputs and held down consumption, created *forced savings* and generated the surpluses needed to support the administrators, the soldiers, and the idle rich, and also to make "investments"—in military equipment, roads, buildings, and whatever else those who held the political power wanted the "savings" to be invested in.

COMMAND GENERATED PROGRESS

Here's an interesting point: Throughout all of ancient and medieval history and until capitalism emerged (only recently), economic progress—savings going into investment and bringing economic growth—rarely occurred except under the impetus of command. In the ancient societies there always seems to have been an elite group running things, living high, and ordering other people around. And always lots of slaves. Most of what we call the advance of civilization—in the arts, in knowledge and philosophy, in buildings, roads, port facilities—all seem to have been brought about by government command, exercised by one or a few forceful rulers.

Traditional systems are designed for survival. Because they seek stability they impede change. So until the force of the market process (only recently) began to wield its influence, progress had to depend on the redirecting influences of powerful political forces. People had to be ordered around. Could it have been otherwise? As long as people follow the social process of tradition, the society is maintained—but that's all. The society remains stationary. All the output is consumed; no economic growth occurs.

Through the force of command the people can be made to produce more and consume less. Surpluses can be generated and economic progress can result. That's the way it happened in the early civilizations, and in the Roman Empire. It is happening that way in several places in the world even today.

 REVIEW QUESTIONS ─────────────────────

1. Explain the economic philosophy of Aristotle. Which of the modern, real-world economic systems are most reminiscent of Aristotle's philosophy? Explain.

2. Discuss and explain the concept of "economic morality" in the writings of St. Thomas Aquinas and other early Christian economic philosophers. What was the basis for this "economic morality" concept?

3. In most societies, from the "cradles of civilization" until the beginning of the Roman Empire, how did their economic systems work? Was the process of tradition or command more important in these societies?

4. Briefly explain why throughout ancient and medieval history, the command process generated more economic progress than did the process of tradition.

4 THE MEDIEVAL PERIOD

KEY TERMS

- feudalism
- the economics of feudalism
- aspirations and the end of feudalism
- enclosures of common land
- John Calvin
- Calvinism
- Protestant Ethic

During the fifth century A.D., the Roman Empire came to an end. The administrative ties—the communications and controls which held all the outlying units of the empire together—weakened and ultimately dissolved. Each of the outlying regions was left free to go its own way. In some localities Germanic peoples took over control from the Romans. But eventually, in most localities the people were just left alone. Without the controls, laws, and productive activities directed (commanded) by the Romans, each little locality slipped back into a traditional, subsistence economic system.

THE EMERGENCE OF FEUDALISM

Little separate, independent socio-economic-political units emerged throughout Europe. As time passed, the ties that held together the larger of the little units, dissolved. The result: more and more smaller and smaller units. Different activities and patterns of behavior emerged in different places. In most places there was a general breakdown of law. People had to figure out their own ways of protecting themselves. There was almost no trade or commerce. Throughout most of Western Europe there evolved the economic, social, and political arrangement we call *feudalism.*

You have already heard many times about feudalism. It took a variety of forms. You know that it was a kind of "mutual responsibility" arrangement. The "lord of the manor" was supposed to protect the people from wandering bands of thieves and plunderers. In exchange, the people had to work to support the manor. The serfs worked the land to produce food and made the implements and other things needed to keep the little economy going. Each person had a job to do and each was allowed a meager share of the output.

The serfs were not exactly slaves. But they weren't free to leave, and they were bound to do the bidding of their lord. Still, customs and traditions placed some limits on the lord's power to run the lives of his serfs. For example, serfs weren't usually bought and sold, and usually they were allowed some land rights and some chance to produce things for themselves. The serfs lived much better on some manors than on others, of course. It depended a lot on the attitude and the wisdom of the one who held the political power—the lord of the manor.

Feudalism Continued for about Ten Centuries

This variety of feudalistic economic-social-political arrangements evolved during the centuries after the end of the Roman Empire and continued to exist for about *ten centuries*—up to about the time Columbus discovered America. Each century saw some change, but usually not very much. Most of the changes were just back and forth—not cumulative, progressive changes. For many centuries there was very little trade and commerce. Usually the obstacles were too great. Some of the Italian trading cities—Venice and Genoa especially—and some cities in Flanders (the present-day Belgium-Holland area) and some elsewhere managed to engage in some successful ventures. But these were the exceptions.

Eventually as the centuries passed, little by little, *cumulative, progressive* change did begin to occur. Very slowly at first, then more rapidly, some chain reactions began to get started. And these changes began to set the stage for the destruction of the stable, tradition-bound feudal way of life. But before going into that you need to know a little more about the economics of medieval times.

WHAT KIND OF ECONOMIC SYSTEM IS FEUDALISM?

Suppose someone asked you what kind of economic system existed in Western Europe during this period of ten centuries—between the time that the Roman Empire fell to pieces and the time that Columbus discovered America. What would you say?

First you would admit that there was much diversity from one place to another and from one time to another. Then you would be quite safe in saying that the thousand-year period was characterized by the existence of many small, tradition-bound socio-political-economic units. As the centuries passed, feudalism became the dominant form of these tradition-bound units.

Feudalism really isn't an economic system. It's a situation in which there isn't any "nationwide" economic system. There isn't any "nation," really—just a lot of little independent units (little socio-political-economic systems), each operating almost entirely on its own.

All these little political-economic systems were scattered over the face of the British Isles and Western Europe. Some were much larger than others, some much more enslaved by ruthless masters than others, some had more ties with the king, or with surrounding feudal estates than others. Each was an individual unit. This was feudalism. It's interesting to note that in much of Asia, especially Japan, similar patterns of feudalism emerged quite independently of what was going on in the Western World.

THE ECONOMICS OF FEUDALISM

How were the economic choices made on each feudal manor? Tradition was the controlling force, but command was important, too. Almost all of the production and distribution choices were determined by the rules of the society, but as interpreted, enforced, and sometimes modified by the lord of the manor. People were bound to the manor where they were born. They produced the things they were supposed to produce—usually the things their family was supposed to produce—and they received their traditionally established "just shares" of the food and other things.

Some trading was going on, to be sure. People bought, sold, and traded things, but usually tradition established the just price for each transaction. The market process—the driving force of demand—was a very minor, almost negligible influence on the production and distribution patterns in the society.

During this period the Roman Catholic Church was a unifying and stabilizing influence. The teachings of the Church emphasized the importance of continuity and stability and of following the established social, economic, and political traditions. No one was supposed to try to break loose, to get ahead. Anyone who did this would only be hurting others. This life was to be accepted. Preparing for the next life was what really mattered.

Somehow, as the centuries passed, change began to creep in. The system began to erode. Ultimately the stage was set for the destruction of this stable socio-economic-political arrangement which had lasted for so many centuries. Without knowing it, the world began preparing itself for the emergence of modern times. How easily feudalism might have lasted for many more centuries! But it didn't.

Except for the cumulative series of events which burst the dike and brought the tidal wave of change, we might all now be living on little feudal estates. Maybe I would be your lord—or maybe you, mine! But under the pressure of change, feudalism began crumbling—slowly eroding away. Finally it was swept away. What happened? What touched off the chain reaction—the cumulative series of events which were to destroy the feudal way of life and bring the end of this stable, tradition-bound world of feudalism?

THE SLOW DEATH OF FEUDALISM

Just as feudalism didn't spring up suddenly, it didn't disappear suddenly. The erosive influences were grinding away at it for several centuries. Near the end, the pace of change was quickening. Various forces for change were reenforcing each other. The chain reaction was beginning. Change was in the wind. Here are some highlights of what happened.

THE CRUSADES

One of the earliest and most continual erosive influences was the Crusades. The Crusades—the "holy wars"—started at the end of the eleventh century and continued, off and on, until about the time Columbus discovered America. (That's *four centuries*—twice as long as the United States has existed as a nation!) The Crusades were going on when Genghis Khan and Kublai Khan were dashing about with their armies, conquering most of Asia, and when Marco Polo made his famous 25-year-long trip to China.

The Crusades had an important "how you gonna keep 'em down on the farm after they've seen Paree" effect. Just as some do now, people then found it easy to live at bare subsistence and to follow custom and tradition if they didn't know of any other kind of life. But some of the people who traveled to different places and saw and experienced new and different things were no longer satisfied with the status quo.

Aspirations and feudalism didn't mix. Just as today, aspirations and the traditional societies don't mix. I suppose if there is any one key to the end of feudalism it would be aspirations—the desire for more and better things, and perhaps for more freedom—and the awareness that such things may be possible.

Today, some economists refer to "the revolution of rising expectations" among the people in the less-developed countries. Aspirations are bringing the rapid destruction of these stable, tradition-bound (semi-feudalistic) societies today, right before our eyes! Even in such advanced nations as the United States, Canada, and those of Western Europe, the urban poor and the people in the depressed rural regions refuse to placidly accept their fate. When people see or hear about better conditions, they *want* better conditions.

FAIRS, TRAVELING MERCHANTS, GROWING CITIES

The Crusades were not the only window to the outside world. There were fairs and traveling merchants. Even cities were beginning to grow up in several places in the British Isles and on the continent—hundreds of small but slowly growing settlements. The cities grew as centers for specialized production and for trade. Some of the adventuresome people were breaking loose from the feudal manors and were going to the towns or traveling with the merchants. Some went to work on ships as trade between the port cities expanded. More and more people were breaking their feudal ties.

COUNTRIES WERE EMERGING

As the Middle Ages wore on, nation-states (countries, or kingdoms) were growing, becoming more powerful. Most of the feudal manors had been under the jurisdiction of some king all along, but these kingdoms existed in name only. Also, the Byzantine Empire of the Eastern Mediterranean and the Holy Roman Empire of Western Europe had claimed jurisdiction over large areas for many centuries. But so far as the day-to-day matters of living were concerned, these "empires" usually had little or no influence.

In the later centuries of the medieval period, some of the kings began to develop the power to maintain law and protect the people throughout their kingdoms. Travel became safer so trade became easier. Cities could more easily flourish and grow. Business could be conducted more regularly, more dependably, more safely.

EXPLORATION AND WORLD TRADE

As the nation-states became stronger and travel increased and cities grew, there were more fairs, more traveling merchants, more shipping and trade. Markets were developing here and there. There were many voyages of exploration. Gold and silver were becoming more plentiful and more widely used as money. These new developments were providing more opportunities for people to escape their feudal bonds, and more and more of them did.

ENCLOSURES OF COMMON LAND

While some of the people were trying to sneak away from the feudal manors, others were being pushed off the land. Traditionally, much of the land (especially in Britain) had been available for common use. This common land was important to many serfs for their subsistence. But as the population expanded, more land was enclosed—the land was fenced in by the lords; the common users were fenced off.

The enclosures didn't make the common users happy. Some fences were torn down from time to time, but the enclosures continued. The common land was becoming private property, with fences and "no trespassing" signs. Remember what it was like in the "Old West" when the homesteaders came and started fencing in the open range? That's the kind of thing that was happening from time to time and from place to place in late medieval Europe.

The enclosure movement began as far back as the twelfth century and continued (sometimes rapidly, sometimes slowly) for more than seven centuries—through the nineteenth century. As the enclosure movement proceeded, those who had previously used the common lands were forced to move elsewhere. Many of them moved to the towns to seek jobs or some other means of staying alive.

THE INCREASING USE OF MONEY

With the land enclosures pushing on some of the people and the attractions of the growing towns pulling on others, the towns grew. Trade and money became a part of everyday life for more and more people.

Gold and silver had served as money far back into history. But even in the years when England and the other Western European countries were emerging from feudalism, there were many people who had never seen a gold coin. Then, as feudalism continued to erode, more aspects of life began to be related to money. More people began to produce things *for sale*. The market forces of demand, supply, and prices were beginning to direct more of the economic choices of the society.

What we are watching is the slow crumbling of the rigid structure of feudalism and the gradually increasing role of market forces in directing the economic life of society. But the ethics of medieval times didn't approve of letting market forces run things. So what happened? Soon that problem got itself worked out, too. Here's how.

THE PROTESTANT ETHIC

Remember what St. Thomas Aquinas, the Christian philosopher, had said about not being acquisitive, not producing and trading for profit, about "just price," and about not charging interest (usury) and all that? How can the market forces direct the economic choices unless people are trying to *acquire*, to get ahead by producing something that other people want to buy? The market forces can't work unless people are producing and working to earn more money!

That "don't acquire" philosophy of the Church was really a drag. But then it happened that the opposite philosophy burst forth. The Protestant Reformation occurred just in time to justify the emerging market forces. The one person most responsible for this new philosophy was John Calvin. The philosophy was, of course, *Calvinism.* You can find some of the philosophy of Calvinism buried deep in the teachings of most of the Protestant churches.

According to the medieval Catholic Church, anyone who would produce and trade for the purpose of personal enrichment would be doing wrong. But now, suddenly, in the mid-1500s John Calvin offers the world a new economic philosophy—the Protestant Ethic: Work hard. Stay busy. Be thrifty. Save. "The Idle Mind is the Devil's Workshop." Produce a lot and get wealthy. You will produce a lot for yourself, and for your society, too. That will show the world that you are a godly person! (That was quite a switch!)

As Calvin and his followers were spreading the word, the Spanish explorers were over in Mexico and Central and South America relieving the local inhabitants of their gold and silver and bringing it back to Europe—just in case more money might be needed. Somehow the pieces were beginning to fit together.

See what's happening? It's beginning to seem that the market forces of demand and supply and prices are going to get a chance to have their day after all!

THE CUMULATIVE EFFECT OF THE EROSIVE FORCES

The many changes—these erosive forces you have been reading about—were chipping away at the frozen structure of feudal society for more than five centuries. Surely, for a long time it wasn't clear to anyone that anything very different was going on. But the worms were in the woodwork. It was just a matter of time.

As the centuries passed, the forces for change began speeding up. By the time of John Calvin and the Spanish Conquistadores, irreparable damage to the old social order had already been done. Many cities had emerged as centers of economic life, with money and trade, and each with its own set of customs and rules—its own ways of doing things.

Life in the emerging cities was distinctly different from the traditional ways of feudal society. City dwellers couldn't be farmers! They had to depend on production and trade for their living.

The slow, steady growth of these urban producing and trading centers resulted in the development of "the city" as a new form of socio-political-economic unit—a new kind of little political and economic system. Each city had its own developing customs and traditions. But the newly developing "traditional ways" of the cities were designed *to accept and respond to market forces.* Then, as trade expanded, the cities were ready to play an ever-increasing role in the economic life of the society.

THE PACE OF CHANGE SPEEDS UP

In the sixteenth century the pace of change in the Western World was beginning to speed up a little. But in Asia the traditional ways of life continued. No cumulative chain reactions of economic progress were touched off in India, China, or Japan. The peoples of Asia, just as those of Africa and the Americas, were unwittingly waiting to fall under the domination of the progressing, progress-hungry, profit-seeking Westerners.

At first the economic progress of the Western World was slow. Even after America had been discovered, it would be yet another three centuries before the forces of the market process—supply and demand and prices—would really thrust aside the restrictive, rigid forces of tradition and claim control over most of the economic choices of society. Three hundred years still had to pass before the world would be ready for the Industrial Revolution.

During this three-hundred-year interlude between the discovery of America and the beginning of the Industrial Revolution, the world was unknowingly preparing itself. Money was becoming more important. The expanding nation-states were trying to increase their national power. They exercised tight controls over economic activities and trade. The economic policies and philosophies which dominated this transitional period are called *mercantilism*. That's what you will be reading about in the next chapter.

REVIEW QUESTIONS

1. Briefly describe the socio-economic-political arrangements of feudalism. Is feudalism an economic system? Explain.

2. How were the economic choices made in feudalism? Was tradition, command, or the market process more important? Explain.

3. List several factors that helped to bring about the death of feudalism. Is there any single factor which could be called most influential in bringing an end to feudalism? Explain.

4. What role did the enclosures of common land play in bringing an end to feudalistic society? Explain.

5. What role did the Crusades play in bringing an end to feudalism? Explain.

6. Briefly explain the economic philosophy of John Calvin—the Protestant Ethic. Compare this philosophy to the "economic morality" discussed in the previous chapter.

5 MERCANTILISM, TO THE INDUSTRIAL REVOLUTION

🔑 KEY TERMS

- mercantilism
- the mercantilist view of gold
- corn laws
- the Industrial Revolution
- capitalist industrialists
- Friedrich Engels
- Karl Marx
- *Communist Manifesto*
- Adam Smith
- *Wealth of Nations*
- "Father of Modern Economics"

The basic idea of mercantilism (MER'cantilism) was that the government should direct the economy so as to gain more national wealth and power. More national wealth and power was usually thought of as "more gold and silver." Many of the production and distribution choices were made by the political process—by the king and the nobility. The government would (a) stimulate the output of goods which could be exported in exchange for gold, and (b) limit domestic consumption, both of exportable goods and of imported goods. (The people must not be allowed to overeat, or to own many things. Only kings and queens and other nobles should do that!)

Every king knew that if he had enough gold he could hire enough soldiers, buy enough armaments, and build enough ships to be the most powerful king in the world. Then he could send out many explorers and privateers and get back even more gold. Gold was seen as the key to the nation's wealth and power. The economic condition of the average person was not a matter of much concern to those who were making the economic choices for the society under mercantilism.

MERCANTILISM IMPOSED STRICT ECONOMIC CONTROLS

In a word, then, mercantilism was a closely controlled economy, aimed at maximizing exports so as to maximize the inflow of gold. Imports of raw materials were good because these would go into more manufactured goods for export. It was good to import cotton, make shirts and skirts, then export the shirts and skirts to trade for more cotton—and for gold. But imports of consumer goods "for the people to enjoy" (like wheat, to eat) were discouraged. Exporting industries were favored in various ways. Imports were restricted.

THE IMPORTANCE OF GOLD

Does gold make a nation wealthy? Or powerful? If we're thinking in medieval terms, it does. In the days of the feudal kingdoms, gold was power because with gold you could buy those things necessary to be powerful. But when things are exported in exchange for gold, the people have to make do with less. Obviously. So, from the point of view of the rulers and wealthy merchants of the nation, the nation with the greatest inflow of gold would be gaining the most wealth and power. But in terms of the welfare of the people, the greater the gold inflow, the less "wealthy" the nation would be—the fewer things (food, clothing, etc.) would be available for the people.

COMPETITIVE NATIONAL SELF-ENRICHMENT

What was happening? The emerging nations were grabbing at the new opportunities and trying to use them to play the old "national power" game, by the old medieval, feudal rules. The very conditions which were bringing the end to feudalism offered the opportunity for the emerging nations to engage in "competitive mercantilism."

But mercantilism was based on the idea of every nation getting rich and powerful at the expense of every other nation. The ultimate objective was national wealth and power—not of the *people* (of course not!) but of the few who were running things. And wealth and power were judged by the old medieval, feudal criteria: gold, and military might.

EMPIRE-BUILDING

Under mercantilism, each nation should establish colonies to provide guaranteed sources of raw materials. With these raw materials the nations should produce things, then sell the things back to the colonies and to anyone else who will buy and pay with gold. It might be an overstatement to say that the American Revolution came as a result of the mercantilist policies of England during the 1700s. But certainly British mercantilism was an aggravating factor.

When we look back, mercantilism may not seem to make much sense. But if you can picture the tenor of the times, you can understand it. It was partly medieval, partly "modern world." And as with so many things, once the competition began, once *everyone else* was a mercantilist, no one could afford to be anything else.

MERCANTILISM CONTINUED FOR ABOUT THREE CENTURIES

Various forms and shades of mercantilism persisted for about three centuries. We still hear mercantilist utterings from time to time, even today. And what about all that gold, first dug out of the ground and refined, then traded to the government for dollars, then reburied in the ground at Fort Knox? We still do strange things. (More on that later.)

For almost three centuries—from soon after the discovery of America to the time of the American Revolution—mercantilism was the name of the game. The British, the French, Dutch, Spaniards, Portuguese, Italians, and some others all tried to do whatever they could to increase the "wealth of the nation"—the nation's gold. The rulers and merchants of each nation worked together, playing their own little game, trying to enrich themselves, their nation—both at the expense of all the other nations, and at the expense of their own common people and their colonists as well.

This idea, "There's only so much wealth around, so more for me means less for you," was still accepted as a basic truth. The world was not yet ready to accept the idea that there might be economic growth, with a growing amount of total wealth for everybody.

MERCANTILIST IDEAS STILL INFLUENCE THE MODERN WORLD

It is easy to look back at mercantilism and criticize this hangover of medieval psychology. But we can forgive them. Even today we can see several medieval hangovers still alive in the modern world.

Powerful nation-states still wage medieval wars (using modern weapons) and everyone knows that *everyone* will lose. No one can win in such a conflict!

Yet wars persist. Nations keep building weapons. And so long as military power is the name of the game, no nation seems to have any choice but to play it that way. This is one of the sad realities of our moment in history. But we are in the midst of an explosion, remember? We should expect to find fragments and chunks from the pre-explosion period hurtling with us through time. And so we do.

A THREE-HUNDRED-YEAR TRANSITION

All the time mercantilism was controlling things, trying to hold down consumption, control trade, limit imports, and all that, the conditions for the market economy to emerge—or rather *explode*—were getting set. During this three hundred years of mercantilism—of exploration, colonization, urbaniza-tion, the increasing use of money, and the emergence of prices as economic incentives—all this time the conditions were being laid for the real explosion.

Quietly, almost without notice and certainly without plan, came the Industrial Revolution. As a small fire in the low grass begins creeping and nobody notices until suddenly it reaches the tall brush and then the trees and then the forest and all is out of control—like that came the Industrial Revolu-tion.

THE INDUSTRIAL REVOLUTION

The Industrial Revolution destroyed the traditional ways of doing things. It destroyed the traditional ways of making the economic choices. It blasted away the previous way of life and brought a new one which was for some much better, for others much worse. But for everybody it was different. We, today, are still in the midst of the explosion which was touched off by the Industrial Revolution. We are hurtling along at a dizzying pace—and the pace seems to be picking up all the time. No wonder things are confused these days!

ECONOMIC GROWTH SPEEDS UP

The Industrial Revolution gave the capitalist industrialists the opportuni-ty to hire the displaced peasants. There were many workers looking for jobs. Wages were low. The new machine production was much more efficient than the hand-tool production of the craftsman. Output per worker was higher; businesses made big profits. With the high profits, the capitalist industrialists bought more machinery. They built more factories, produced more goods, and made even more profits, built even more factories. On and on went the process of industrialization. Faster and faster and faster.

The early thrust of the Industrial Revolution was in England, in the textile industry. From there it spread to other places and to other industries. You've heard all the names of the famous inventors and their famous gadgets—from John Kay and his "flying shuttle" (about 1750) to Hargreaves' "spinning jenny" (about 1770) and to Eli Whitney's "cotton gin" (about 1790). By 1800 the output per person had increased greatly in the textile industry. Much more cloth was being made, and the demand for cotton and wool was expanding rapidly. The increased demand and the higher prices made cotton-growing and sheep-raising very profitable.

In the United States, Southern plantation owners got rich, bought more slaves, cleared more land, planted more cotton, and got richer. In England the landlords speeded up their enclosures of land, forced the peasants off, turned the lands into grazing pastures for sheep—and got rich. The peasants went to the cities where jobs in the textile mills were available. More and more of the pieces were fitting together. Labor and land and capital were responding to demand. The automatic market forces of the "price mechanism" were beginning to direct and control society's scarce resources.

MARKET FORCES BEGIN TO DIRECT PRODUCTION

With the breakdown of the *traditional* uses for resources—land, labor, and capital—the owners of these "factors of production" began to sell their factors to the highest bidders. For example, before the enclosures, land was just land, available for common use. After the enclosure of a piece of land, that land became a person's private property. The owner would use the land the way it would bring the biggest return. Once the land became enclosed private property, it became a "responsive factor of production," ready to do the bidding of the forces of the market—of changing demand, and prices.

In the case of labor, as long as tradition establishes each person's occupation and station in life, that person is not available to "sell labor" in response to the market's demands. But after a person gets pushed off the land, with no money and no source of food, that person's labor suddenly becomes very responsive to the market forces of demand, and prices.

When you're free and on your own you look for a job anywhere you can get a price (wage or salary) for your labor. Market forces begin to direct your labor. This transition wasn't always pleasant for the person involved. But for the productivity of the economic system, and the growth which was about to happen—growth which would bring freedom from want to so many people in future generations—the long-run benefit of the transition was undeniable.

Back in history, whenever the traditional society was to be induced to do things differently—to get people to produce more things and consume less, or to move from one kind of activity to another—the political process (government command) usually was required to bring about the change. But here, as the Industrial Revolution is getting going, we see *market forces* directing more and more people and things. Desire for reward is replacing fear of punishment as the motive force driving and directing the energies of people.

THE ECONOMIC CHOICES WERE SHIFTING

When all this begins to occur, there are major shifts in both the production and distribution choices in the society. And notice this: The political process does not need to be involved at all! In fact, quite the opposite. The unleashed forces of the market are exercising their great power, wresting the economic choice-making functions both from the traditional heritages of the society and from the political control of the kings and nobles. The "natural process of the market" is moving the factors of production (land, labor, capital) into different uses, causing the factors to respond to *prices*, which reflect the *market demands* of the society. And production is expanding in a way that never happened before in the history of the world!

MARKET FORCES GENERATE ECONOMIC GROWTH

Capitalist industrialists were making big profits. With their profits they bought more machines, built more factories, and caused more and better kinds of capital goods to be produced. More factors of production flowed into making more capital. More and better factories and machines were built. This was the process of economic growth in action. This is what was happening rapidly during the industrial revolution.

This process of rapid growth was going on in the late 1700s and throughout the 1800s and on into the present century. This is the process which built the industrial base for the economically advanced nations. It's because of this economic growth process that most of us in the advanced nations are enjoying so much freedom of choice, so much leisure time, such easy working conditions, and so many products and services—warm houses, fast cars, medical attention, and all that.

WORLD SOCIO-ECONOMIC UPHEAVAL IN THE 1800S

The big thrust of industrial growth in the world didn't really get going until the early 1800s. By that time steel had been developed and the bugs had been worked out of the steam engine. Now better machinery could be built and driven by steam power. Then came the steamboat, the railroads, and the telegraph. By the mid 1800s, not just Great Britain, but all of Europe and the United States were undergoing the violently disruptive impact of rapid industrialization.

During the 1800s, centuries of social tradition were ripped apart. This was the period which rang the death knell on a way of life. It marked the beginning of another way of life—one of continual, explosive change. It was during this time that in the United States, in a few short decades, "the West was won." And it was during this time that in Europe, Friedrich Engels helped a bitter and impoverished Karl Marx as they wrote the *Communist Manifesto* calling for and predicting the end of capitalism. You'll be reading more about that later.

It isn't much of an overstatement to say that during the 1800s the entire society of the industrializing part of the world, restructured itself—physically, geographically, socially, and economically. Population was growing rapidly. People were moving toward industrial centers—toward the coal and iron deposits—and along the expanding railroads, to the seaports, the transportation and trade centers—and to the United States and Canada. Some poor people got very rich. But most of them just moved somewhere else, got jobs, worked hard, and stayed poor.

Most working people in most places were living under miserable conditions. Were they miserable? Who can say? Perhaps they accepted their fate in the sameway that most of the people of the world always have had to accept their fate. Hunger has been the "natural condition" of most of the people in the world, much of the time. In the 150-year period of rapid socio-economic turmoil between 1750 and 1900, many people looked very miserable. Their meager possessions, their lack of opportunity to get ahead, the many hours they had to work just to keep going—these conditions certainly didn't give them much time or cause to be happy.

TRADITIONAL PATTERNS WERE STRIPPED AWAY

What was happening? Suddenly people were no longer being cared for by the traditional social processes. A person no longer had a "niche" in society as in feudal times. The "social security" of traditional society was gone. Everything was changing. It was a new ball game.

Suddenly people were living in a world in which they had no choice but to take care of themselves. Each person received an income (a "distributive share" of the output) on the basis of what "factors of production" that person owned, and could "sell in the market." People (most people) who did not have any land or capital, had to sell labor. So that's just what they did. As Bob Dylan would say, "the times they were a-changin'." The Industrial Revolution was in progress and the market process—the price mechanism—was taking control of society's economic choices. People and things were being shifted. Yesterday was suddenly thrust into tomorrow.

Who likes to see the former peasants working in the sweat shops from before sunrise until after sunset? And their children too! While the rich factory owners are making millions, building new factories up and down the valley and living off the fat of the land? Nobody. What a miserable, unjust solution to society's economic problem!

To be sure, the peasant is glad to have the job because it's a way of staying alive. But an economic arrangement which distributes so much of the output (income) to the factory owners and so little to the workers? This is capitalism? Yes, this was the capitalism of these disruptive days of the nineteenth-century Industrial Revolution. The market forces of demand and supply and prices were being unleashed. The *market process* was exerting its influence. Overthrowing tradition. Sidestepping command. A new, powerful, explosive force was being set loose in the world.

RAPID ECONOMIC PROGRESS WAS BEING MADE

Anyone who wasn't too concerned about the poverty of the people could see that progress was afoot. More product was being made. More factories being built. More people hired. More output per worker. But still, poverty among the masses. Everywhere.

The enclosures continued to spread. More and more people were forced off the common land. They drifted into the cities to seek jobs. Miserable though the jobs were, and miserably low the wages—still, it was a way to survive. In England, the "corn laws" (mercantilist tariffs to limit the import of all kinds of grain) forced high prices for grain and flour and bread and for most other kinds of food eaten by the common people. The high prices limited consumption—so the common people didn't get very much to eat.

People worked for low wages and had to pay high prices for food. But profits were being made. The landowners were doing very well. The capitalist entrepreneurs were making high profits and investing in more factories and better machinery and equipment. They were doing just fine. And as a result of all this, the productivity and output of the economy was growing by leaps and bounds.

THE POPULATION EXPLOSION

Population was expanding rapidly. After all the thousands of centuries that people have been on earth, and then over the many centuries from the cradles of civilization to the days of the ancient Greeks and Romans, to the Roman Empire and on into the Middle Ages—up to the time of the first of the Crusades (about 1100 A.D.) the population of the world was still only about *300 million people.* By the time Columbus discovered America (only four centuries later) the population of the world had *increased by about 50 percent*—to about *450 million.* Then from 1492 until the time the United States became a nation (only *three centuries later*) the world's population *doubled*—to about *900 million.* Can you see what's happening? It's a population explosion!

But the figures for world population don't really show the seriousness of the true picture. What was going on in Europe? In the places where all this new activity was underway?

During the 1700s—only *one century*—Europe's population *doubled.* And look at this: During the 1800s, England's population expanded from about nine million to thirty-five million—a *fourfold increase!* By 1900 the world's population stood at 1.5 billion. It was destined to double again (to *3 billion*) by 1960, and to *double again* (to *6 billion*) before the end of the twentieth century. From 1.5 billion to more than 6 billion in less than 100 years? That's right!

Now do you wonder why the world suddenly finds that it has a pollution problem? A problem of ecological imbalance? More on this later.

During the 1700s and 1800s, the rapidly expanding population compounded the human tragedy of poverty—but it supplied labor to support the rapid industrial growth, and markets for the industrial output. There is no question that growth was rapid. Was all this economic growth—this increased industrialization and increased output—the result of the mercantilists' economic controls? Or was some other force at work?

THE CHALLENGE TO MERCANTILISM

During the 1700s the mercantilist philosophy of "restrict local consumption, export more goods, get more gold, and make the nation wealthy" was much in evidence. But as the industrial revolution exploded on the scene the voices of others began to be heard—the voices of *the new industrialists.*

Many of the industrialists wanted to be free of the government restrictions and regulations of mercantilism. The new industrialists saw the advantages of selling wherever they had the opportunity to sell at the highest price, and of buying inputs or whatever else they wanted from wherever they could find them available at the lowest price—in England, France, Germany, the United States, or wherever.

The industrialists and the mercantilists did not agree. And the humanists who were concerned about the poverty of most of the factory workers in the rapidly expanding cities were not happy with the situation, either. What was going on? Why were conditions as they were? Why was there so much disruption and poverty? What was it all leading to? What should the government be doing? What should anybody be doing? What had gone wrong with the world?

THE RATE OF CHANGE BECOMES EXPLOSIVE

During the industrial revolution, the rate of change in the developing world was becoming explosive. But no one could know that. Things just looked confused. Not enough cumulative change could be seen to be able to tell what was happening. To many people it must have looked like chaos. Certainly they never could have dreamed of what really was going on.

It wasn't easy to see order or purpose in all that misery and turmoil! Maybe it takes until about now—until the end of the 20th century—for us to be able to look back and see what really was beginning to happen. We can't see where it's all going, even yet. Only time will reveal the answer to that question.

Today we can look back over the broad sweep of history and see the cumulative effect of hundreds of years of little, erosive changes—changes which like worms in the woodwork were eating away at the old, stable, traditional social structure and preparing the world for violent change. We can see how the rate of change started speeding up—leading into, supporting, and then being whisked along by the rapid-fire series of new inventions and innovations.

The growing factories and machines, the socio-economic disruption, all this turmoil—this is the period we call the Industrial Revolution. It was really the blast-off on this trip that now we all are taking—this trip of explosive change, hurtling us through time, heading at breakneck speed into an unknown future.

How did it look in the late 1700s to the people who were trying to figure out what was going on? There was a lot of human suffering. People disagreed about what was happening. But there was no question that *new things were going on.*

Various philosophers, scholars, industrialists, commercial dealers, and others were trying to figure out what was going on—many were trying to explain and evaluate the situation. Some were suggesting ways to try to improve things. Mercantilism had both its proponents and its critics as far back as the 1500s. But during the late 1700s the critics of the government's economic controls of mercantilism were becoming more insistent and more effective.

BEHOLD! THE MARKET PROCESS TAKES OVER

You and I can look back and understand some of what was happening. We can see that the market forces were exerting their influences more and more over the economic choices of the society.

The great supply of labor was holding down the wage rate, providing markets for products and keeping profits high. The high profits were providing great stimulation—both the money and the incentive—for building capital. So economic growth was proceeding rapidly. But it wasn't easy to look at the rapidly expanding population and all the suffering and confusion and make any long-run sense out of what was happening.

ADAM SMITH OFFERS AN EXPLANATION

How could they know that the market process—the free market forces of supply and demand—were taking over, automatically directing the economy? They couldn't. Then, in 1776, a new book appeared. It explained the whole thing—all about the automatic operation of the market process, and how it works for the ultimate good of everybody.

The book was written by a professor, a Scotsman with an unlikely name: Adam Smith. Professor Adam Smith was not the first to talk about "free market forces" and how they work. But he was the first to pull it all together. He explained the whole process in his big economics book, titled: *An Inquiry into the Nature and Causes of the Wealth of Nations* (usually referred to as *Wealth of Nations*). That's what Adam Smith did. For that he is called "the father of modern economics."

Adam Smith gave the philosophers and the other thinking people of the world a new way to look at what was going on. He gave them a new explanation of what it all meant, where it was all going, and how. Soon you'll be reading about what Adam Smith had to say. But that discussion, and the discussion of who else said what—the economic ideas of Malthus, Ricardo, Mill, Marshall, Owen, Marx, and others who were trying to make sense out of what was going on in the world—that must wait for the next chapters.

THE WORLD "TURNED UPSIDE DOWN"

For now, take a few minutes to think about this broad sweep of history leading up to the Industrial Revolution. Then take a few more minutes and try to picture the turmoil the world had gotten itself into. Explosive, cumulative, accelerating economic change, like a tidal wave, was sweeping away the stable social structures of the past and leaving in its wake masses of people struggling for new ways to survive.

As the people struggled to survive they followed the pull of the powerful forces of the market—forces which were grasping control, taking over, beginning to direct the economic choices of society. The answers to the basic production and distribution questions were being made in a new and different, totally unfamiliar way.

REVIEW QUESTIONS

1. Briefly explain the basic idea of mercantilism. Was mercantilism a command- or tradition- or market-process-oriented economic philosophy?

2. Discuss the importance of gold in mercantilist philosophy. Explain how this philosophy led to empire-building, and how it affected the welfare of the general population.

3. Explain how the Industrial Revolution drastically changed society's methods for solving the three basic economic questions. How did this change affect the distribution of wealth in the economy?

4. Briefly explain how the Industrial Revolution destroyed the traditional uses for resources, and encouraged land, labor, and capital to respond to market forces. Who profited and who was hurt as these changes took place?

5. Describe the "population explosion."

PART THREE

THE EMERGENCE OF NEW ECONOMIC CONDITIONS, IDEAS, AND THEORIES—THE INDUSTRIAL REVOLUTION (1750s–1850s)

The classical economists tried to explain the world and the utopian socialists tried to change it.

6

THE PHYSIOCRATS, ADAM SMITH, AND JEREMY BENTHAM

KEY TERMS

- Physiocrats
- Francois Quesnay and *Tableau Economique*
- Adam Smith and *Wealth of Nations*
- laissez-faire
- classical economics
- Thomas Jefferson and the *Declaration of Independence*

- nineteenth-century liberalism
- natural laws of economic behavior
- trade and specialization
- Jeremy Bentham and *Principles of Morals and Legislation*
- total social welfare
- Bentham's Felicific Calculus

It was the late 1700s. Hard times were everywhere. What a miserable world! Hungry, cold, sick people. Split up families. Very tedious work. Very long hours. Very low pay. No wonder people were trying to understand the economics of all this. What was going on? Wasn't there some better way? Couldn't something be done? Some new government policies or programs perhaps? Surely life on earth could be made into something better than this! But how? The answers were not easy to find.

THE INCREASING CHALLENGE TO MERCANTILISM

One thing was dawning on an increasing number of people: Mercantilism did not seem to be the answer. During the Middle Ages and on back into ancient times, the philosophers, religious writers, and concerned citizens of each day and age were commenting on (frequently criticizing) the economic issues and policies of the day. As you might expect, the critical commenting continued throughout the three-hundred-year period of mercantilism. As time went on, mercantilism came more and more under attack.

During the 1700s the mercantilist philosophy suffered some serious blows. The most devastating came from the perceptive Scotsman, Professor Adam Smith. But during the mid-1700s (a few decades before Smith's *Wealth of Nations*) some French philosophers were developing a new explanation of what was going on. Before getting into Smith's *Wealth of Nations* you need to know a little bit about these French philosophers—the ones called the "Physiocrats" (FIZZYocrats).

THE PHYSIOCRATS

The Physiocrats said that it would be better if the government would just leave people alone. They concentrated on *physical production* and emphasized the economic importance of *agriculture.* Only agricultural production created "new things out of nowhere." Manufacturing and trade were "sterile" activities. Such activities only moved or changed things. Nothing was really "created."

It was their idea that when people produce from the soil, nature and people are working together. This partnership was necessary to produce more physical output—that is, more *real wealth* for the nation. They said that mercantilist controls interfered with this process. The term "laissez-faire" comes from the French Physio crats. The term means that the government should let people alone to make their own economic way—to do whatever they want with their time, energy, resources, capital, and with whatever else they have to work with.

THE "TABLEAU ECONOMIQUE"

The French Physiocrats called attention to some of the fallacies of mercantilism. Francois Quesnay (frawn-SWA kay-NAY), a leading Physiocrat, developed the concept that economic activity follows a kind of circular flow. His *Tableau Economique* shows that the people of the society produce, then consume some and save some, then produce again. Using what they have saved, they can produce more. Around and around goes the production-consumption circle. Each time, some is saved. The economy grows. This was Quesnay's explanation of *how the nation gains its wealth.*

The Physiocrats attacked the mercantilists by offering a new, different explanation of both the *form* and *source* of the nation's wealth. To the Physiocrats, the nation's wealth was the *physical output* produced from the soil. Government controls only interfered with the wealth-producing process, so the Physiocrats called for a policy of laissez-faire.

To the mercantilists, wealth was the *gold* acquired by selling things. Government controls were called for, to force the people to produce the "right" products and not to consume too much, and to force trade to flow in the "right" directions.

THE NATURE AND CAUSES OF "WEALTH"

The Physiocrats and the mercantilists disagreed about both (a) the *nature* of a nation's wealth and (b) the *causes* of a nation's wealth. Perhaps now you can understand why Adam Smith chose for his book the title: *An Inquiry into the Nature and Causes of the Wealth of Nations.* You know by now that Smith's book is going to say that the mercantilist concept of the *nature* of wealthy is wrong, and that the mercantilist explanation of what *causes* a nation to be wealthy is wrong. You probably also know that Smith is going to explain the automatic operation of the market process—how the forces of free markets (demand, supply, prices)—work to bring about the wealthiest nation.

Smith's book explains *how* a nation will become wealthiest if it will follow a laissez-faire policy and just let the automatic market process take care of things. That was the real purpose of his book—to make that point. He made the point very well. So well, in fact, that his book had quite an impact on the world and on all future ideas about economics.

ADAM SMITH AND THE WEALTH OF NATIONS

Adam Smith's historic book was published in the historic year 1776. It offered some comprehensive and plausible answers to the question: "What's going on in this confused, miserable world?" His answers were good. Much of what he said is as true today as it was then.

Adam Smith's book contained a lot of economics. It talked about the advantages of specialization and trade. It talked about savings and investment and economic growth. It explained how the market process automatically gets the "right" things to be produced, how it automatically moves the factors of production to the "right" places to do the "right" things, and how it automatically arranges for the "right" amount of the output to be shared by each person. Truly, *Wealth of Nations* was, and is, an outstanding economics book.

LAISSEZ-FAIRE AND COMPETITION

Wealth of Nations explained how the trader, industrialist, landowner, worker, or anyone else, in trying to get ahead, would automatically be tricked (by the free market forces) into serving the best interests of the society—by conserving resources, and by producing the right numbers of the right kinds of goods.

It worked like this: People who used their energies and resources to make what the society *wanted most,* would get paid a lot. The businesses which would produce a much-wanted, highly-valued product—while being careful to conserve society's scarce resources—would be doing a great service for society. For this they would be rewarded with big profits. Everyone in the society would have a strong incentive to be productive, so everyone would work hard producing the most valued things. The total product would be great. The nation's wealth would grow more and more. A neat, automatic system!

Wealth of Nations explained how everything would come out best if the government followed a policy of laissez-faire—that is, if it just kept its hands off and did not interfere with what people were producing or consuming, or with prices, or with anything about the operation of the automatic market process.

The book emphasized the essential role of competition, to protect the society against monopolistic sellers or buyers, or groups of sellers or buyers. It explained that "laissez-faire" would *not* mean economic chaos, because the natural market forces would keep the economy in control and moving in desirable directions. And it explained even more.

Yes, there is much good economics in Smith's book. Also, there is much anti-mercantilism—much argument for individual freedom and against government interference and controls. While Thomas Jefferson in the *Declaration of Independence* and other philosophers in other writings were offering the world justification for *political freedom,* Adam Smith was offering the world justification for *economic freedom.*

NINETEENTH-CENTURY LIBERALISM

The *Declaration of Independence* (also, as you know, written in 1776) and the *Wealth of Nations* both reflected their times—the emergence of "nineteenth-century liberalism"—the idea of freedom of the individual, the "inalienable rights" of every person. The United States, a new nation created in the midst of this newly emerging philosophy, still carries a deep commitment to democracy, and to laissez-faire. You can see it in the U.S. political system and economic system. This anti-government philosophy was really strong at the time the United States Constitution was written. Perhaps this helps to explain why the U.S. government for so many years showed such great reluctance to take *any action* to influence conditions in the economy. Even today, many Americans stand strong against almost any kind of government involvement in the economy.

CLASSICAL ECONOMICS, AND SMITH'S "INVISIBLE HAND"

Adam Smith's book marks the beginning of "classical economics." It tells the world that *laissez-faire can work.* It explains the market process. It says that if the government leaves the people free to make their own economic choices, people who seek to follow their own best interests will be guided "as though by an invisible hand" to do the things which are best for the whole society.

In *Wealth of Nations*, Adam Smith explains how self-interest will drive individuals—as though guided by "an invisible hand"—to do those things which others want them to do. He explains how people will be financially rewarded for the good things they do for society. He explains how the market process will generate savings and investment and bring economic growth, more output, and more good things for everybody. He explains how a nation which follows laissez-faire will automatically become more wealthy, more powerful, more productive—how the people will enjoy higher standards of living if *market forces* are in control than they would if the *government* tried to control things.

SMITH WAS OPTIMISTIC ABOUT THE FUTURE OUTCOME

Adam Smith thus explained the misery and hardship of England and the Western World in terms which seemed to make it all worthwhile in the long run. He was optimistic. He explained how businesses, making profits, would reinvest in more capital to try to make even more profits. The result: more growth, greater production, and (eventually) higher wages and better conditions for the common people.

Adam Smith's work was greatly appreciated by the capitalist industrialists during the hectic days of the Industrial Revolution. *Wealth of Nations* gave them a way to justify their self-serving activities and a respectable explanation for their great wealth and profits. The wealthy business leaders could explain that as they were being selfish in seeking profit, they were really working for the good of society. Adam Smith had told them so!

NATURAL LAWS OF ECONOMIC BEHAVIOR

Adam Smith explained a kind of "natural law of economic behavior." If the government followed any policy other than laissez-faire, it would thwart this natural law. The government would keep the economy from working properly. How stupid that would be! Talk about an effective argument against the government controls of mercantilism! With the natural laws of economic behavior controlling things, it made sense to permit individuals to be free to make their own economic choices.

Adam Smith didn't invent the natural laws of the free market. The market process was already there, busily at work. Tradition had already given way to the new order of things. There was a new kind of control over the economic choices—a new kind of influence directing economic life. Smith just showed it to people. He gave them a way to look at and recognize it—a way to understand and explain what was going on. He gave the world the first systematic explanation of how the market process works—of how all individuals, working for their own greatest benefit, will automatically bring the greatest benefit to all of society.

His thesis was that the nation will be most wealthy and the people will "fare best" if they are left free to follow their own selfish interests. He emphasized the need for free markets, for competition, and for the factors of production to move freely in response to market prices—for each person to produce whatever will bring the most income, or profit.

DIVISION OF LABOR, SPECIALIZATION, TRADE

Smith emphasized the essential role that trade plays in bringing about the most productive, most efficient uses of the society's resources. He explained the importance of specialization, of division of labor. A jack-of-all trades can't be as productive as one who specializes. But it's obvious that a person who is going to specialize, must be able to trade the output produced—to sell it and get some other things in return. Smith emphasized the indisputable fact that specialization requires trade—that only with *trade* can people specialize.

THE FUNCTIONS OF GOVERNMENT

Smith said the functions of government should be closely restricted. Since the natural laws of the market process could direct things so well, the government could only hurt things by interfering. People left alone would generate their maximum income (and wealth, well-being, and all that), so that in total, the nation's wealth and well-being would be maximized. Interference by the government could only reduce the nation's wealth and cut down on the economic well-being of the people.

Smith said the government should maintain law and order, protect the rights of private property, regulate the monetary system, and undertake the few necessary public projects—building harbors and highways and such things. But the government should *not* use the resources of the society for things the people would not want to spend their own money to pay for. The government should stay out of it and let the natural forces of the market direct and control the society's productive activities and resources.

ADAM SMITH'S IMPACT ON ECONOMIC THINKING

Adam Smith's book was a great book at the time it was written. It is still a great book. It explained what was going on. To the business leaders of the day, Smith gave a justification for selfish profit-seeking. To the poor he gave a promise of a better life through economic growth: Profits would be reinvested; more capital would be built; eventually there would be more income and a better life for everyone.

Smith showed how all the painful and seemingly heartless conditions could be justified by this larger picture—by long-run benefits for everybody. He showed how all this misery was really leading to something good in the future—something good in which all people would share. He explained that there was some *purpose,* and some *ultimate relief* for all the hunger and misery in the world. Looked at from Smith's point of view, perhaps the miserable conditions of the early years of the industrial revolution weren't quite as hard to take.

Smith's explanation of the natural laws of economics—of how free market forces can control the economy and direct things into desirable directions—were destined to live on to the present time, and almost certainly, far beyond. But his optimistic conclusion about the outcome—about the *ultimate relief* for all the hunger and misery—about the long-run betterment of the economic welfare of the masses—this idea was soon to be challenged. By whom? By the next two great classical economists: The Reverend Thomas Robert Malthus and the self-made millionaire David Ricardo. But before we get into the ideas of Malthus and Ricardo, there's someone else who needs to be mentioned: Jeremy Bentham.

JEREMY BENTHAM

In the very same year the *Declaration of Independence* and the *Wealth of Nations* appeared, young Jeremy Bentham also published his first book. But it wasn't until thirteen years later (in 1789) that his major work, *Principles of Morals and Legislation,* appeared. Bentham's book was not a book on political economy. It was not on the question of the wealth of the nation, but on "the welfare of the society"—how to measure it and how to achieve it.

Bentham's book was a very different kind of economics book—but it was an economics book, just the same. It talked about how the wealth (the good things of the society) *might be shared* among the people for the greatest *total welfare*—for the "greatest good" the society could achieve.

BENTHAM'S "PLEASURE MEASURE"

Bentham's "Felicific Calculus" (his "pleasure-measure") was based on the idea that the greatest total welfare of the society would result from the greatest *sum total* of the welfare of all the individuals. If I might *lose* some "welfare"—and thereby you might *gain more* "welfare" than I lost, then there would be a net gain for the society. Get the idea? It's the idea of "the greatest good for the greatest number."

What's so important about Bentham's contribution to classical economics? Just this: He explained the motives of the individual—the driving force which directs each individual's activities and behavior. Bentham said that each person is essentially a self-serving unit—that all individuals are powered by the desire to do things which serve their own best interest—the desire to seek pleasant experiences and to avoid or escape from painful ones.

BENTHAM ANALYZED THE "MOTIVE FORCE"

Remember how Adam Smith explained how the market system worked? All people would act to serve their own best interests, yet each would be guided "as though by an invisible hand" to serve the best interests of the society. The only way people could get more of what they wanted would be by doing or making something somebody else wanted. Now can you see how Bentham's ideas fit in?

Smith talked about *how* individual self-interest is automatically directed toward improving the welfare of the society. Bentham *dug into* the self-interest question; he analyzed and offered new insights into the motive force—the "engine" which powered Smith's economic machine. He did that, and he did much more than that.

Bentham tried to explain human behavior and the things which influence the welfare of mankind in society. Some of his ideas can be found deeply imbedded in all of today's social sciences. Certainly his ideas influenced the next classical economists we'll be talking about—men who were greatly concerned about the record-breaking, historically unprecedented rate of population increase during the late 1700s and early 1800s. What men? Malthus, Ricardo, and John Stuart Mill. You'll be reading about them in the next chapter.

REVIEW QUESTIONS

1. Compare and contrast the philosophy of mercantilism with that of the Physiocrats. According to these philosophies, what is wealth? And how does a nation acquire wealth? And what would Adam Smith have to say about that?

2. Explain how, according to Adam Smith's *Wealth of Nations*, laissez faire and competition would automatically solve society's three basic economic questions.

3. What are the "natural laws of economic behavior" which Smith outlines in *Wealth of Nations?* Do we see these "natural laws" at work today? Explain.

4. According to the classical economics of Adam Smith, what is the role of (1) government and (2) trade in the economy?

5. Explain what contributions Jeremy Bentham made to the development of classical economics. How do Bentham's ideas compare to those of Adam Smith?

MALTHUS, RICARDO, AND JOHN STUART MILL

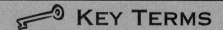

KEY TERMS

- Thomas R. Malthus and *Essay on Population*
- Malthusian Law of Population
- David Ricardo
- the Iron Law of Wages
- Ricardo's theory of differential rent
- marginal land
- Jean Baptiste Say
- Say's Law of Markets
- James Mill
- John Stuart Mill
- positive economics
- normative economics

Thomas Malthus was only ten years old when *Wealth of Nations* was published. David Ricardo was only four. Obviously neither of them was very impressed with Adam Smith at the time! But as they grew up and observed the chaotic, miserable world in turmoil around them, they began to study, and to think. Then each in his own time decided that he had something to say. And each said it—to each other, and to the world.

MALTHUS AND RICARDO WORKED WITH "NATURAL LAWS"

Essentially both Malthus and Ricardo agreed with the natural laws of economics as presented in Smith's *Wealth of Nations*. They agreed that there was a *natural order* in economic affairs and that the government should follow a policy of laissez-faire to let the natural laws operate freely. Both Malthus and Ricardo published books called *Principles of Political Economy*, both at about the same time (around 1820), not quite half a century after *Wealth of Nations* was published.

Both Malthus and Ricardo carried forward and added to what we call *classical economics.* Both writers helped to further explain the process of the market—howthe free market forces can control and direct the economy. But both disagreed with Smith about the optimistic ultimate outcome of laissez-faire economics. Both said that *population expansion* would prevent the improvement of mankind's economic welfare.

Malthus said that for the poor, hard times were here to stay. He said that population would expand so rapidly that people always would be going hungry. The gains from increasing food production would be eaten up by the expanding population.

THE MALTHUSIAN LAW OF POPULATION

The population of Europe had more than doubled in the 1700s. In the 1790s Malthus wrote his *Essay on Population.* He said there was a tendency for the population to expand *more rapidly* than the food supply could expand. Therefore, most people's food consumption always would be held down to bare subsistence. Malthus admitted that people might voluntarily limit their reproductive urges and dodge this unpleasant outcome, but he didn't expect that to happen.

This idea expressed by Malthus—that population expansion would keep the people poor and hungry—is called the *Malthusian Law of Population.* It made a lot of sense at that time. It makes a lot of sense now.

In most of the less-developed nations of the world today, population growth is the greatest single obstacle to economic development and improved standards of living for the people. Whenever gains are made in production or in living conditions, population seems to expand and wipe out the gains.

Malthus dealt with more than just the population issue. He had more than that to say about economics. But he will always be best remembered for calling the attention of the world's thinkers to the population problem—a problem which today is much more serious than it was then—a problem which some people now consider so serious as to ultimately threaten the continued existence of mankind on earth.

RICARDO'S THEORETICAL MODEL OF THE "PURE MARKET SYSTEM"

Ricardo was a brilliant economic theorist. He developed a theoretical model to show the intricate way in which the market process directs and controls an economy of "laissez-faire and competition."

Ricardo emphasized the importance of the growth of capital, through savings and investment. He could see that widespread poverty was contributing to growth. But, like Malthus, he was pessimistic about the future welfare of most of the people.

THE IRON LAW OF WAGES

Like Malthus, Ricardo agreed that the population would continue to expand and force wages to stay very low—at or near (sometimes below) the level of bare subsistence. Like Malthus, Ricardo agreed that if wages were *less* than subsistence, the population and the labor force would get smaller. How would that happen?

People would die—more children would die of malnutrition and old or sick people would not survive as long. Young people would delay marriage and/or have fewer children. The population would shrink. So the work force would shrink.

With a smaller work force there would be a shortage of workers. The shortage of workers would cause businesses to overbid each other—to offer higher wages to try to hold on to their workers. Wages would be pushed upward to the subsistence level.

If wages ever got *above* the subsistence level, population would expand. People would marry earlier and have larger families. More children would be healthier and would survive and become workers. There would be more workers around than the businesses wanted to hire. The surplus workers would be trying to get jobs, underbidding each other. Workers would accept lower wages in order to get jobs, or to hold on to their jobs. Wages would be pushed down to subsistence again. Economic misery would be perpetuated.

This bare subsistence theory of wages is sometimes called "the iron law of wages." No wonder economics in the early 1800s was called "the dismal science"!

HIGH FOOD COSTS FORCE UP WAGES

Here are more of the results of Ricardo's model: Since wages must hover around the subsistence level, the higher the subsistence cost of living, the higher wages must be. If grain and other foods are cheap, the cost of subsistence will be low; the wages the manufacturer will have to pay will be low. The manufacturer's profits will be high. But suppose the cost of living is high. Then the subsistence level of wages will be high. The manufacturer's profits will be low.

With high living costs and therefore high wages and low profits, manufacturers will not have much money to invest in new capital. Economic growth will be stunted. Can you see why Ricardo fought against the high import tariffs on grain (the corn laws)? The corn laws increased the cost of living and therefore kept wages up. The higher wages reduced industry's profits and stunted economic growth! (Leave it to a sharp thinker like Ricardo to figure out something like that!)

THE PROFIT SQUEEZE

Ricardo's analysis went much further. He went on to show that as the population expands, the cost of living will increase. As there are more and more people eating up the food supplies, more land areas will have to be cultivated. But the new land areas will be less and less fertile. Intelligent farmers will cultivate the best land first. No one will cultivate any *more* land (the poorer land) unless the price of grain goes high enough to pay the cost of growing the grain on the poorer land. Obviously! And it costs more (obviously) to grow grain on poor land. So the subsistence cost of living must go up. Then wages must go up. This squeezes profits and slows economic growth.

RICARDO'S THEORY OF RENT

Something else happens, too. When the price of grain goes high enough to justify cultivating the *very poor* land, think of the high profits the owners will be making on the *very best* land! If you own a lot of good land and you have been making a pretty good rent from your wheat-growing tenants, think how much rent they will pay you so they can keep using your good land after the price of wheat goes up! This was Ricardo's "differential rent" theory.

Ricardo talked about the "marginal" land on which the farmer would just make enough to break even. This land could command no "rent." But any land which is more fertile than the marginal land would bring its owner a "surplus"—a *rent*. So as population expands, you see what is going to happen. Poorer and poorer lands will have to be cultivated. But higher prices will have to be paid for grain in order to get this to happen. Now, as the grain prices go up, the people who own the *fertile* land (and who were doing okay already) will find that they are beginning to make a lot more money.

THE LANDOWNERS RECEIVE SURPLUS INCOME

You can see that as the grain prices rise more and more, landowners will receive larger and larger *surplus incomes* from their fertile lands. This will put the landowners on easy street. The more the population expands, the more of the poorer lands must be farmed. So the higher must go the price of grain (and the cost of food, and the wages of labor), and the bigger will be the surplus incomes (rents) of the landlords. Can you see that rent is "price-determined" (determined by the demand for and the price of grain)? Sure. Oh to be a landlord!

What does Ricardo's model predict for the manufacturers—the ones who are making profits and investing in more and better capital and bringing about economic growth—adding more and more to the wealth of the nation? For them the prediction is not so good. As wages go up to pay for the high cost of food, profits are squeezed. As profits shrink, the boom slows down and stops. The industrial expansion gets choked off.

According to Ricardo, the economic deck was stacked in favor of the landowner and against everyone else. Ricardo concluded that by the very nature of the marketsystem—by the natural laws which guided it—the landowners were bound to be big winners over the long run. The workers would be receiving just enough to live on, the capitalist-industrialists would be struggling to survive, and the wealthy landowners would be getting richer and richer as the rents for the land went higher and higher. (After Ricardo made his fortune in stocks, he invested in good land. He must have really believed in the real-world relevance of his theoretical model!)

THE LONG-RUN IMPACT OF MALTHUS AND RICARDO

As history would have it, many of the predictions of both Malthus and Ricardo didn't come true exactly as they had expected. Both were making assumptions about the *permanence* of the world as they saw it in their lifetimes. They didn't allow—they *couldn't have* allowed—for the explosive rate of change which at that time was already well underway.

As it turned out, population in the advanced countries has not expanded exactly as expected. Wages have risen *far* above subsistence. And technology and productivity in both agriculture and manufacturing have gone forward so much more rapidly than Malthus, Ricardo, or anyone else could have expected. It shows something about the perils of predicting. It was perilous then. It's just as perilous—maybe even more perilous—now.

Both Malthus and Ricardo made important contributions to the development of our present understanding of economics. The Malthusian Law of Population focused early on a problem which today is very real and very serious. Hunger in the poor nations and pollution in the cities are only two of the many present-day manifestations of rapid population expansion.

Ricardo's theoretical model identified and explained in detail many of the economic forces which previously had been understood only in general terms. His model helped us to see some of the "economic laws" at work in the world. Ricardo is considered by many to be the greatest economist of his time. Some call him the greatest economist *of all time.* He was that good. His theoretical model of how the pure market process would work has had a profound influence on economic thought and policy, from Ricardo's day to the present. And certainly Ricardo's influence on economic thought isn't all used up yet. It will go on, far into the future.

OTHER CLASSICAL ECONOMISTS

During the time of Malthus and Ricardo many others were thinking and writing about economic matters—about "political economy." Jean (pronounced Zhon) Baptiste Say and James Mill were both about the same age as Malthus and Ricardo. J. B. Say was nine in 1776 when *Wealth of Nations* appeared. James Mill was three. Both these men published "Political Economy" books in the early 1800s. Both wrote in the classical tradition of Smith, Malthus, and Ricardo, explaining how the market process works—explaining the intricate workings of the market system. And there were several others—before, at the time of, and after Smith, Malthus, and Ricardo. But we just don't have time to talk about them all.

Say is best known for his "Law of Markets"—the idea that *supply* creates its own *demand.* The more a producer takes to the market (supply), the more he can get in trade (buy) and take home with him (demand). Say's law explains an important "natural balancing tendency" in the way markets operate. As with other economic theories, Say's law doesn't always work out exactly right in the real world. But the tendency is there, and sometimes it's helpful to know about it.

James Mill is not best known for his contributions to economics, but for his contributions in history and political theory. But probably he is even better known as the father and teacher of a truly unique, great philosopher and economist of the nineteenth century—John Stuart Mill.

JOHN STUART MILL

John Stuart Mill was born in 1806. He was not yet fifteen years old when his father and his father's friends, Malthus and Ricardo, were coming out with their political economy books. But even at fifteen, he was ready for them. Very ready.

Ever since he had been about old enough to talk, John Stuart Mill had been studying under the demanding tutelage of his father. It is said that he was reading classical Greek at the age of three. (I don't know how well.) By the time he was thirteen he had finished his studies of Aristotle and Plato and the other philosophers who wrote in Greek and Latin. He had read profusely in English history and in other areas, had mastered calculus, had written history books and, among other things, was then studying the writings of Smith, Malthus, and Ricardo. All by the age of thirteen, would you believe!

Although he was writing on economics and various other subjects from the time of his teens, it was not until 1848 (when he was 42) that his *Principles of Political Economy* was published. This book became the leading text on economics for several decades. Much of John Stuart Mill's *Principles* was orthodox classical economics. It integrated much of what had been done by the various writers from Adam Smith on. It further clarified Ricardo's theoretical model of the pure market system. But it wasn't all orthodox. It challenged classical economics—specifically, the Ricardian model—on a very basic, fundamental point—on "the laws of distribution."

MILL CHALLENGED RICARDO'S MODEL

The Ricardian model described an economic system in which the pure market process was allowed virtually complete control over everything. People owning productive factors would produce. Those who produced could have something to consume. The iron law of wages kept the worker's share low. Increasing rents kept the landlord's share high and rising. All this happened as the result of natural market forces. To tamper with the results would be to interfere with the system. And that would only make matters worse. The poor people would stay poor, and that was that. John Stuart Mill challenged this conclusion.

CAN THE SOCIETY REDISTRIBUTE INCOME?

Mill's point was this: It isn't necessary to let the natural market forces decide how much each person is going to get to eat. It is possible for the *society* to decide whether or not it wants some of its people to starve, while others (the land-owners) are filthy rich and getting richer. He pointed out that the laws and customs of the society (that is, the political process and the social process—not just the market process) can have a lot to say about how the output is distributed.

At least to an extent, it's obvious that Mill was right on this point. In all modern societies the market forces are modified to take something away from the productive people and give a share to the nonproductive ones. But, of course, we have no way of knowing how much these "income redistributions" may have stunted growth, and contributed to low wages, high unemployment, and other undesirable effects. Economists wonder about things like that, but there's no sure way to find the answers to "what might have been."

POSITIVE ECONOMICS AND NORMATIVE ECONOMICS

Mill sort of straddled the line between what we call "positive economics" and "normative economics."

POSITIVE ECONOMICS

Positive economics deals with the "laws" of economic behavior—that is, with general statements of fact: "If you don't *pay* a person to work for you, then that person will not work for you." "If you offer a lot more money for corn than wheat, then people will grow and sell you more corn than wheat." "If the fried chicken price doubles and the hamburger price goes down, people will buy less of the high-priced fried chicken and more of the low-priced hamburgers." These are statements of positive economics.

Positive economics doesn't say it's good or bad—it just tries to tell "what would happen if . . ." It just tries to "tell it like it is."

NORMATIVE ECONOMICS

Normative economics gets into questions of how things *ought to be*—of how things ought to be changed—how to make things better. Normative economics is what John Stuart Mill was talking about when he suggested that the people of the society could distribute and share products and resources among themselves in any way they chose—in any way they thought best.

Mill addressed some of these normative issues—the "value" issues—the issues of good or bad, right or wrong, better or worse, and of how to make the economic choices *better* for society. He sort of "straddled the positive-normative fence." Perhaps that was the best thing for him to do—or perhaps not. Who knows? Certainly many (perhaps most) economists are doing it today.

SHOULD ECONOMISTS DEAL WITH "NORMATIVE" ISSUES?

What do you think? Should economists get involved in the issues of "what's best"? Or only "what is"? The "scientific tools of economic analysis" are tools of positive economics—of finding out and explaining "what is," and "what would happen if."

When the economist gets into questions about how much income a family of four *should* have, and how high wages of unskilled workers *should* be, the scientific tools of economic analysis don't help at all. Still, economists can talk about such things as guaranteed annual incomes and minimum wages, and be at least one step ahead. At least the economist can work up a pretty good answer to the question: "What would happen if the government decided to set up this program or that program?" or "What kind of program might we set up to achieve the normative objectives?" Unless you know some positive economics, you don't know what's going to happen when the government (or somebody) starts making normative changes in the economic system.

Economists are no better than anyone else at deciding what objectives we'd *like* to achieve. No worse, mind you. But no better. But economists are (or at least should be) better at working out feasible ways (and throwing out infeasible ways) of getting to the objectives. Still, there are many economists who prefer to bypass these issues entirely and spend their energies finding out more about the interrelationships among the variables in Ricardo-type models.

Which is the proper role for the economist? That question has been at issue for quite some time. It isn't likely to be solved anytime soon.

 REVIEW QUESTIONS

1. Compare and contrast the theories on population of David Ricardo and Thomas Malthus. Can you find any current real-world examples of either of these theories?

2. What does Ricardo's theoretical model predict for: (1) workers? (2) capitalist-industrialist manufacturers? (3) land-owners? Explain how Ricardo arrives at these predictions.

3. Using Ricardo's economic model, trace the effects throughout the economy of an increase in wages above the subsistence level (effects on population, profits, cost of living, etc.).

4. State and then explain "Say's Law of Markets." Give an example of how Say's Law works in the economy today. Can you also give examples of when Say's Law does not hold true?

5. Define and explain the difference between positive and normative economics. Of the classical economists discussed in the text, which dealt with positive economic issues? Which with normative issues? Did any of them deal with both? Explain.

6. In Chapters 6 and 7, you have been reading about the classical economists. What are the basic themes and ideas which tie together the writings of these economists? That is, what *is* classical economics? Explain and discuss.

8 THE UTOPIAN SOCIALISTS

There were several philosophers about John Stuart Mill's time (and some before and some after) who didn't straddle the fence any more than Ricardo did. They were clearly on the *other* side of the fence—the normative side. We call these philosophers the "utopian socialists."

THE UTOPIAN SOCIALISTS WERE NOT CLASSICAL ECONOMISTS

Most of the utopian socialists really didn't know much about the natural laws of positive economics. But they saw that the world looked like a miserable place for most people. They saw many rich and powerful people—industrialists, entrepreneurs—being very cruel to a lot of poor and hungry people. Men and women—and children too.

The utopian socialists responded in various ways. But most of their responses were not very realistic. The problem? They didn't understand some of the real-world limitations imposed by the natural laws of positive economics.

Most of the utopian socialists weren't bothered by the restricting influences of the laws of positive economics. But it's a fact of life that the economic laws which do hold true in the real world *are real*. Anyone who goes along trying to change things and ignoring these laws is inviting failure. Several of the utopian socialists did that.

THERE WERE SEVERAL "UTOPIAN SOCIALISTS"

There were several different, unique writers who can be grouped under the broad heading "utopian socialists." Who were they? What were their similarities? Their unifying characteristics?

All of them were people who looked at the world, didn't like what they saw, and set about the task of trying to change it. Each had a different idea, a different approach. But generally, all were interesting and dedicated, but not too realistic people who were trying to reorganize the society to get rid of some of the harshness and cruelty—to build more love, friendship, sharing, and mutual assistance into people's daily lives. They worked for reforms to improve the conditions of the common people. This chapter gives the highlights of the ideas of three of them.

SAINT-SIMON AND FOURIER

In France there were two utopian socialists who were contemporaries of Malthus and Ricardo: Count Saint-Simon (pronounced SOHn-see-MOHn) and Charles Fourier (Foo-ree-A). Saint-Simon, an aristocrat himself, attacked as unjust the high incomes of the unproductive aristocrats. He founded a small religious sect—a sort of industrial religion.

Fourier worked for the reorganization of people into communes, called "Phalanxes." Small groups of people would live in a big hotel—or those who preferred could live in a cluster of houses—and all would work for the good of the group.

Both of these French socialists had followers; people really did attend the Saint-Simonian churches, and Fourierist Phalanxes were actually set up in several places. Would you believe there were some forty of them in the United States in the early to mid-1800s? You may have heard of the Brook Farm community in Massachusetts (mid-1800s). Nathaniel Hawthorne joined it for awhile. Brook Farm was one of these Fourierist "utopian" communities. Two other well-known ones were the North American Phalanx at Red Bank, New Jersey, and the Wisconsin Phalanx.

THE UTOPIAN SOCIALISTS WORKED FOR SOCIAL CHANGE

We really don't need to go into much detail about the utopian socialists. The important thing is to be aware that while the classical economists were accepting certain things as given and trying to understand and explain what was going on, the utopian socialists were *refusing to accept* the givens. They didn't ask why, or where it was all going. They jumped right in and tried to change things. Each one approached the task in his own unique way.

One of these utopian socialists stands out, because he did accomplish some things. Not all that he wanted to accomplish—not by a long shot—but he did accomplish some things. The man was Robert Owen.

ROBERT OWEN

The Englishman Robert Owen was one of the most interesting and versatile of the utopian socialists. Owen was in the same age group as the several classical economists we have been talking about. Owen, Malthus, Ricardo, Say, James Mill, Saint-Simon, and Fourier were all approaching or in their 30s at the beginning of the 1800s. They were all observing the same real-world conditions, but they certainly were interpreting them differently! Owen set out to improve the world.

OWEN WAS A SUCCESSFUL MILL-OPERATOR

Robert Owen started out as a poor boy and worked his way up in the textile industry. Eventually he owned and made a fortune operating a textile mill in Scotland. His mill and the local town were operated on policies which were, at that time, unbelievably humane. He was trying to prove that people would respond favorably to a benevolent environment. The profits of his mill seemed to prove his point; but no one else rushed to follow his example.

OWEN'S "VILLAGES OF COOPERATION"

Like Fourier, Owen suggested that society be reorganized. He suggested that people set up "villages of cooperation." To prove that these villages would work, he sold his factory in Scotland, came to the United States, bought some land, and (in 1826) established a utopian community in Indiana.

Owen's new community was named New Harmony. Too bad it didn't live up to its name. Owen placed much trust in the people who came to join. As it turned out, it appears that there was too much trust and too little planning. In less than two years the community had fallen apart.

OWEN HAD A LASTING IMPACT

After the failure of New Harmony, Owen became a leader in the co-op and trade union movements in England. He never ceased to work, to write, and to press political leaders, to try to achieve reforms to help the common people. He worked hard at the task of improving the world, and he generated a sizeable following. His writings inspired several cooperative communities; he had a lasting impact on the labor and co-op movements in Britain. He is credited with coining the word "socialism."

THE EFFECTS OF THE UTOPIAN SOCIALISTS

Both the utopian socialists and the classical economists were looking at and thinking about all the hardship and misery in the world around them. Some of the classical economists (Adam Smith and others) explained that all this hardship was *necessary* to serve the long run good of the society. Other classical economists said it was *inevitable*—that any attempt to ease the hardship and misery of the poor would only bring more suffering. The natural laws of economics said so. There could be no escape from these natural economic laws!

But the utopian socialists refused to believe this. They would not accept and give in to the natural laws of economics. Really, most of them didn't even study these laws. They were too busy trying to change things—trying to improve the economic conditions of the common people.

The writings of the utopian socialists generally carried none of the precise and scientific analysis which is found in the writings of the classical economists. The utopian socialists weren't theoretical analysts. They were impatient activists. All of them had their followers, and all of them had some influence on the lives of some people.

THERE WERE MANY UTOPIAN COMMUNITIES

In the United States alone, more than 150 utopian communities were established, inspired by the philosophies and teachings of the utopian socialists. Most of the communities didn't last long—probably because they refused to recognize some basic laws of economics and some basic facts about the nature of human beings. But a few of the communities still exist (in modified form) even today.

The utopian socialists didn't help us much to understand the sweep of economic evolution, or to understand the natural economic forces at work in the world. But the lives of some people were influenced—perhaps improved. Some of the ideas and dreams of the utopians are still living, influencing the lives of some people, even today. These utopians cared a lot. And they fought hard. It's pleasant to think that some lasting good may have come from it all.

ENTER: THE COMMUNIST REVOLUTIONARIES!

Now it's time to move on and take a look at a very different "breed of cat"—people who were not nearly so mild and gentle, so optimistic and dreamy as the utopian socialists. These were angry, bitter, coldly logical people who were ready for the violent overthrow of the social, political, and economic systems which were permitting such hardships and misery to exist. Who? The communist revolutionaries. You'll be reading about them in the next chapter.

REVIEW QUESTIONS

1. Compare the ideas and philosophies of the classical economists with those of the utopian socialists. What are the major differences? Do you think the utopian socialists were economists? Explain.

2. Which of the three basic economic questions were the utopian socialists most concerned with? Why were their attempts to redirect the solutions to these questions so often unsuccessful?

3. John Stuart Mill was a classical economist, yet some of his ideas were similar to those of the utopian socialists who were not classical economists. Explain.

4. What basic philosophical flaw brought the failure of so many utopian socialists' theories and communities?

CHAPTER 9

PART FOUR

RAPID CHANGES IN THEORY AND IN SOCIETY—THE EVOLUTION BECOMES EXPLOSIVE (1850s–1920s)

Marx attacks capitalism, monopoly power grows, and Marshall helps to rebuild economics. Enter: neoclassical economics and supply and demand curves.

KARL MARX, AND DAS KAPITAL

In 1848 the kind and gentle philosopher John Stuart Mill published his *Principles of Political Economy.* He raised a question about the Ricardian model and its natural economic laws of distribution. Remember? Well, in that same year there appeared a much different, most outspoken pamphlet which mounted a major attack on the market system.

THE COMMUNIST MANIFESTO (1848)

The pamphlet was *The Manifesto of the Communist Party.* Its principal author was a man you have already heard of: Karl Marx. In the *Communist Manifesto,* Marx and his colleague Friedrich Engels called for revolution—for the workers to violently overthrow the governments in Europe, and take over the factories from the capitalists.

EUROPEAN CRISIS CONDITIONS

Marx and Engels were looking at Europe in the mid-1800s. Conditions were bad. Very bad. There was hunger. Starvation. Popular revolts against the governments of several European countries seemed very likely. People were rioting in several cities—Paris, Brussels, Berlin, Prague, Vienna, and elsewhere. In France, King Louis Philippe was forced to resign. It was in this turmoil that Marx and Engels called for the workers of the world to unite, to forcibly overthrow their governments and to take over the factories from the capitalists.

At that moment in history it looked very much like this Marxian revolution might really happen! But somehow things held together and ultimately began getting better for most people. You need to know about this remarkable man who has had such a profound impact on the lives of all of us—this brilliant, angry "classical economist-revolutionary"—Karl Marx.

THE LIFE AND WORK OF MARX

Marx was in radical protest against "the system" throughout most of his life. He was born in Germany in 1818. That was when John Stuart Mill was twelve years old and the *Principles* books of both Malthus and Ricardo were about ready to appear. Before Marx was twenty-five years old he was already in trouble.

Marx had studied philosophy (and had become an atheist). He went into journalism, began writing radical articles and got himself expelled from the German city of Cologne. Then he went to Paris, developed an association with socialists and other radicals, wrote more radical things and wound up getting kicked out of Paris. Then he went to Belgium. But after the *Communist Manifesto* appeared in 1848 (when Marx was thirty) he was exiled and went to England where he spent the remainder (the last thirty-five years) of his life.

MARX LIVED IN POVERTY

During most of his life Marx was very poor—frequently hungry—often angry. During his thirty-five years in England (until his death in 1883) he studied the writings of the classical economists, the socialists, and other philosophers. And he thought, and wrote. In 1867, almost twenty years after the *Communist Manifesto,* he completed and published the first part, or "book" of *Das Kapital* (in English, *Capital*). The second part was not published until almost twenty years later—in 1885, two years after Marx's death. The third part did not appear until nine years later, in 1894. Parts two and three were published by Marx's long-time friend, colleague, and supporter, Friedrich Engels.

MARX STUDIED RICARDO, FOR A PURPOSE

During his years of study and thought (and poverty) in England, Marx became one of the great economists of the last century—and, really, of all time. But he was a revolutionary and an angry man long before he was a great economist. Marx studied the classical economists (especially Ricardo) long and hard, for a purpose. He was building a case to support his conviction—a conviction he had already stated (most forcefully!) in the *Communist Manifesto*.

Marx learned and then used the precise concepts, the "natural economic laws," of the Ricardian "market system" model to show that the economic system described by the model contained within itself "the seeds of its own destruction." Marx used the Ricardian model to prove that his (Marx's) already-stated convictions really were supported by natural economic laws— that the outcome was predictable. *Inevitable.*

It shouldn't surprise you that different people can look at the same real-world conditions and use the same economic concepts and principles and yet arrive at very different conclusions about the ultimate outcome. Think back. Smith, Malthus, Ricardo, other classical economists all more or less agreed about the basic concepts—the "natural laws" of economics. They all agreed about laissez-faire and competition, and about the responsiveness of the factors of production to the demands of the society. Yet each came to a somewhat different conclusion about the future.

To Smith, everyone was going to share in the economic growth. To Malthus, the industrialists would do fine but the people would be poor. To Ricardo the landowners would ultimately be the really fat cats and their high surplus incomes (rents) would choke off economic growth. What Marx did (in his *pure economic* writings) really was not so different from this. Smith, Malthus, and Ricardo all observed the same "natural forces" at work. But each came to a different (and, as history would have it, wrong) conclusion about the ultimate outcome. And so did Marx.

MARX WAS A CLASSICAL ECONOMIST

Marx "the economist" was really a classical economist, dealing with positive economics—even more than, for example, John Stuart Mill. Mill challenged some of the "natural economic laws." Marx worked within them, and with them. Marx understood and used the principles of classical economics to support his conclusion about the ultimate collapse of the market-directed system—the collapse of the system which he had the honor of naming "capitalism." What did he say in his big economics book?

Marx's Economics Book: Das Kapital

Das Kapital (Dahs Kah-pee-TAL) is a most remarkable book. Just as *Wealth of Nations* at times shows us the thoughts and feelings of Smith the economist, and at other times Smith the antimercantilist; so *Das Kapital* reflects the several faces of its author. We see Marx the visionary, the revolutionist, the rejected philosopher, the hungry, angry, sometimes bitter man. But we also see Marx the meticulous, precise economist—the one who set out to build the airtight case showing the inevitable collapse and oblivion of this "most dastardly" economic system—capitalism.

Revolution Was Inevitable

In *Das Kapital*, Marx undertakes economic analysis with the precision of Ricardo. He uses the Ricardian laws to build his system and to explain the "inevitable sequence" of economic change—change that, to Marx, was predetermined within narrow limits by economic laws—by the natural economic forces at work in the society.

The Marxian theoretical system shows how the economic forces will lead to *inevitable revolution*—to the overthrow of capitalism. The careful, logical, precise explanation of how capitalism will lead itself to its own destruction is presented in detail in *Das Kapital*. The essence of the argument isn't difficult to understand. Here are some of the highlights.

Surplus Value

Marx agreed with Malthus and Ricardo about the iron law of wages—that wages will stay at about the subsistence level. But, said Marx, workers doing a long day's work can produce more than enough for their subsistence. That is, workers produce more "product value" than they receive in wages.

Workers may work a fourteen-hour day (not particularly unusual in the mid-1800s) but they may produce enough "product value" to cover their wages in only eight hours. Everything they produce after that (the six extra hours' worth of output) is *surplus value*. The "surplus value" goes to the capitalist. The capitalist *exploits labor* by keeping this surplus—when the surplus really belongs to the workers who produced it. (So said Marx.)

CAPITALIST EXPLOITATION OF LABOR

Marx said that the capitalist gets profits from exploiting labor—from forcing workers to work longer than they should work to earn their subsistence wages. Next, the capitalist invests this profit (surplus value) in more capital—factories, machines, equipment. Then, with all the new capital equipment, the expanding businesses need more labor. So they try to hire more people. This increases the demand for labor and pushes up the wage rate. So what do the capitalists do? They buy even more capital to replace some of the high-wage workers. With more labor-saving capital, the capitalists can get by with less labor.

Ah, but the trap! To Marx, surplus value comes *only* from labor, and surplus value is the *only* source of profit for the industrialist. So, in the Marxian model, as the number of *workers* declines, *surplus value* falls. So profit falls. When profit falls, capitalists will try to cut costs by introducing *even more* labor-saving equipment. But in the Marxian model this only makes matters worse. Obviously. The more the capitalists try to fight the fall in profits, the worse things get. So what's the answer?

ONLY A FEW CAPITALISTS WILL SURVIVE

Eventually times will get very bad. Depression. Some businesses will go broke. When they do, other businesses will buy up their capital for almost nothing. According to Marx, there will be one crisis after another until a very few, very large and powerful businesses are in control of all the capital. They will own just about all of the means of production.

The wealthy people who own these businesses will have great monopoly power over all the others in the society. Also, they will have gained control of the government so they can make sure that the government will protect their *private property* rights—their rights to own and control their monopolistic businesses and to keep their monopoly profits for themselves.

Almost all of the people will be poor, hungry, wretched. The only way for this bad scene to be improved will be for the poor people—the "proletariat"—to overthrow the government. Then they can (and will) take back "their" capital from the "bourgeoisie" (BOOR-zhwa-ZEE)—the wealthy monopolists.

The capital was built out of the surplus value "stolen" from the workers (the proletarians) in the first place. It's rightfully theirs. So they take it back. Thus endeth capitalism. So says Marx.

A BEAUTIFUL SOCIETY WILL EMERGE

What happens after the overthrow of capitalism? Marx doesn't have much to say about that. At first things will be a little rough. The capitalist-types must be eliminated. But after that, things are going to be much better.

Ultimately a beautiful society will emerge. It will be built on the high productivity of the "reclaimed capital." All will share in the output, and without the selfish greed of the capitalists there will be enough for all of the people to have all they want of everything. A beautiful world, right? Some communist "true believers" are still waiting for it to happen just as Marx predicted. How utterly ridiculous. If Marx himself were alive today he would laugh (or be distressed) that anyone could be so out-of-touch with reality.

Instead of continuing down the harsh and bitter road which Marx expected, capitalism has been continually tempered more and more to soften the harshness—to lessen the socially unacceptable conditions of "raw capitalism." And some progress has been made in limiting the monopoly power and controlling the market behavior of big firms. Certainly Marx never could have foreseen the extent of social justice that now exists in the world's "mixed economies of modified capitalism"!

Marx blamed the misery of the times on the capitalist system—not on the effects of a rapidly industrializing society caught in the early years of disruptive, explosive change.

Marx was looking at the same world that the other classical economists were looking at. But because Marx looked at it in a different way he saw different things. The theories, ideas, concepts, and other preconceptions a person has when he or she looks at something, often *determine* what that person will see. This was as true of Marx (and of the other classical economists and of the Utopian Socialists) as it is of you and me.

THE LASTING IMPACT OF MARX

Marx really gave the economists some things to think about. He made some contributions to our understanding of how the market system functions. But, of course, his predictions did not come true.

Did Marx have an impact on economics? On the world? You know the answer to that. It would be difficult to find anyone who has had more impact. He inspired and gave a rationale, a justification, for the revolutions in the

Soviet Union, China, Cuba, and elsewhere. His writings have been carried forward by several neo-Marxist philosophers and revolutionaries—Lenin and others in the Soviet Union, Mao Tse-tung and others in China, Castro and others in Cuba, and others who can be found in most nations throughout the world.

It was Marx who first gave these people a logical position—a way to justify revolting and taking over the private property of the capitalists—and of eliminating the capitalists in the process. There is no question that Marx has left an indelible imprint on the world.

 REVIEW QUESTIONS

1. Explain why Karl Marx is included among the classical economists, even though the Marxian system concludes that capitalism will lead to its own destruction.

2. Compare (in general) the Marxian theoretical system to the theories of Smith, Malthus, and Ricardo. How are they similar? How different? Offer some explanations as to why and how each philosopher examined the same economic scenario, yet arrived at different conclusions.

3. Explain how, in the Marxian system, the capitalist exploitation of labor leads to the demise of the capitalist industrialists, and to capitalism itself.

4. List the stages in the Marxian model which lead to the revolutionary overthrow of capitalism. Are there any basic flaws in the model? Explain.

10 MONOPOLY POWER AND THE NEW U.S. ANTITRUST LAWS

During the late 1800s and early 1900s, two kinds of problems were emerging. One was the problem of increasing monopoly power. The other was the problem of recurrent financial panics and depressions. According to the theories of the market system, neither of these was supposed to happen. But both of them *were* happening.

EXPLOSIVE CHANGE AND GROWING MONOPOLY POWER

During the decades when Marx was studying and writing, the rate of economic change seemed to become more and more explosive and more violent—rapidly expanding production of coal, oil, and steel; rapidly expanding use of steam power, railroads, and ships; the growth of industrial centers—

truly phenomenal! And trade within and between nations was growing rapidly. The rate of change surpassed anything the world had ever known.

While the industrializing nations were growing explosively, some businesses were doing the same thing. They were developing and using new technology, becom-ing more efficient, making big profits—and building more capital to make even more profits.

THE CONCENTRATION OF ECONOMIC POWER

By the end of the 1800s the names of such Americans as John D. Rockefeller, Andrew Carnegie, and J. P. Morgan were household words. These were some of the powerful industrial and financial giants who were building mammoth business organizations, with monopoly positions in oil, steel, railroads, and other industries. Some people were becoming concerned about all this bigness—all this concentration of economic power in the hands of a few individuals and families.

Throughout the 1800s in the United States, England, and Western Europe, wages remained low. Profits were often very high. The rate of industrial invention, innovation, and growth was phenomenal. Output continually expanded. Some of the increased output consisted of consumer goods for the rapidly growing population. But much of the output was made up of new industrial machinery, basic materials, steel rails, new factories, and so on— the essential inputs for economic growth.

INCREASING CONCERN ABOUT GROWING MONOPOLIES

By the late 1800s, many people began to be concerned about the rapid growth and mammoth size of some of the industrial corporations. More than a hundred years had passed since Adam Smith's *Wealth of Nations* had appeared, and more than half a century had elapsed since Ricardo developed his theoretical model of the pure market system. The laissez-faire idea was strongly embedded in the philosophy of the Western World. Still, people were beginning to worry about the growing power of big businesses.

It was well known that for laissez-faire to work, effective competition was required. Only competition prevents big businesses from exploiting their workers, the consumers, the resource suppliers, the landowners, and everyone else. The writings of Marx helped to emphasize the need for concern about big business—about industrial monopolies. Various groups began to call for limitations on the monopoly powers of businesses.

THE ANTITRUST LAWS

In 1887 the United States Congress passed the Interstate Commerce Act, regulating the railroads. The Act established the Interstate Commerce Commission to set rail rates and to see to it that the railroads provided adequate service to their customers. This was a start. Three years later the basic antitrust law of the United States was passed—the Sherman Antitrust Act.

THE SHERMAN ANTITRUST ACT (1890)

The Sherman Act made it illegal for businesses to put their assets into a "trust," or to otherwise pool their assets to eliminate competition among themselves. This Act made it illegal for businesses to reduce competition either (a) by getting together with their competitors, or (b) by destroying their competitors. Businesses were using both these tactics to gain monopoly power to restrict supply (that is, restrain trade) and push up and hold up prices.

The phrase "restraint of trade," which means businesses stop selling in competition with each other, was used in the Sherman Antitrust Act because there had to be some constitutional justification for the federal government to pass laws regulating businesses. The U.S. Constitution does not give this specific power to the federal government. But the Congress found the constitutional justification they needed in Article I, Section 8. This section grants to the federal government the specific power to regulate interstate commerce (interstate trade). So the Congress just made it illegal for businesses to combine or conspire to restrain interstate trade. That made the Sherman Act constitutional.

SUPREME COURT CASES AGAINST STANDARD OIL AND AMERICAN TOBACCO

The Sherman Antitrust Act was not noted for its success. In the 1890s and on up to the beginning of World War I, big businesses in the United States (as throughout Britain and Western Europe) continued to combine and expand. In 1911, two big monopolies in the United States—Rockefeller's Standard Oil Company and the Duke brothers' American Tobacco Company—were broken into smaller units by order of the Supreme Court. But other big businesses continued to grow.

THE CLAYTON AND FTC ACTS (1914)

In 1914, the U.S. Congress passed two more antitrust laws—the Clayton Act and the Federal Trade Commission (FTC) Act—to try to further restrict the powers of businesses to get together to eliminate competition and/or to deceive their customers or engage in other "unfair" or anti-competitive activities.

HOW BAD IS THE MONOPOLY PROBLEM?

Neither the Sherman Act nor the Clayton Act nor the FTC Act was really effective in maintaining a high level of competition in American industry. In most of the other countries of the Western World, even less action was taken to curb the growing monopoly power of the industrial giants. There is no question that considerable monopoly power existed, and still exists, in the United States and throughout the industrialized world. How bad is this? How much does it interfere with the proper working of the market process? No one really knows.

Everyone knows that without some kind of effective competition, laissez-faire is a license to steal. On the other hand, everyone knows that we aren't going to have so many sellers and buyers in every market that no one has *any* monopoly power at all! Of course not.

In today's world, purely competitive markets with hundreds of small producer-sellers of everything, are completely out of the question. Arguments about whether or not a real-world economy made up entirely of such markets would result in efficiency or inefficiency, stability or instability, growth or stagnation, or whatever—are just no help at all in getting the answers to the questions: "How bad is the monopoly problem today?" and "What should be done?"

THE BASIC DILEMMA OF "BIGNESS"

The monopoly issue presents the policymakers with a dilemma: We want all the advantages of bigness: stability, financial security for workers and for local communities, social responsibility, outstanding management, research and development and innovation—all that and more. But at the same time we don't want to let anyone escape from "effective competition." We don't want anyone to get a license to steal. We would like to have our cake and eat it too—to have the *efficiency* advantages of bigness, and the *competitive* advantages of smallness at the same time. But of course we can't.

Many economists say that for the most part some kind of effective competition does exist in the modern world of "mixed socio-capitalism." Various explanations have been offered as to how this effective competition works. Other economists (and noneconomists, too) charge that big businesses have *too much* power and that they should be either (a) broken up into smaller, more competitive units, or (b) more closely regulated by the government, or (c) taken over by the government. It is not likely that these conflicting views are going to be resolved soon. (You'll be reading more about the present-day monopoly question in Part VIII.)

REVIEW QUESTIONS

1. Describe the economic scenario of the late 1800s and early 1900s in the United States, England, and Western Europe. How did this scenario compare with Marxian predictions?

2. Discuss the effects of concentrated economic power (monopoly power) on the laissez-faire system. What are the major disadvantages of "corporate bigness"? The advantages?

3. Explain the provisions and purpose of the Sherman Act. Was the Act (1) legal? (2) necessary? (3) successful? Discuss.

4. Consider the "second round" of antitrust legislation (the Clayton and FTC Acts) of 1914. Was this legislation necessary? And was it successful in preventing monopoly power from interfering with the workings of the laissez-faire system? Discuss.

5. Explain the "basic dilemma" of bigness.

11

ALFRED MARSHALL, NEOCLASSICAL ECONOMICS, GENERAL EQUILIBRIUM THEORY, AND SOME DISSENTERS

KEY TERMS

- international gold standard
- Alfred Marshall
- neoclassical economics
- German historical school
- Austrian marginalist school
- Leon Walras

- partial equilibrium analysis
- general equilibrium analysis
- Henry George and *Progress and Poverty*
- Thorstein Veblen and *The Theory of the Leisure Class*
- conspicuous consumption

Judged by almost any measure you can choose, the "developed" world of 1900 was truly a different world from that of 1800. Never before in history had there been anything like it. In one short century (less, really) the total number of human beings in the developed countries more than doubled. In the most rapidly growing places the population expansion was as high as tenfold or more. The techniques of production were almost completely different. The total outputs of industrial and agricultural products were many times as great. The rate of change had become explosive!

THE EARLY 1900S: HEYDAY OF CAPITALISM

Some economists like to say that it was during the first decade or so of our century—during the period from 1900 to about the beginning of World War I—that old-style Western capitalism reached its peak of glory. Outputs had expanded greatly. Businesses had very few restrictions and paid very little taxes. Economic growth was rapid.

The trading nations were on "the international gold standard." This meant that international trade could move easily. Since all the countries used gold as their basic money, anyone could use gold (if necessary) to buy things from foreigners. World trade was carried on with very little restriction. The trading nations were prospering. The industrial and commercial enterprises were profiting and growing. All of the trading nations were enjoying economic expansion, and all of them seemed to be benefitting.

World War I brought an end to all this. It marked the end of an era. Many people have tried to bring back the old era. Some are still trying. But it has never and will never work that way again. You, with your awareness of the explosive change which has been (and is now) going on in our world, could have guessed that. Measured by the extent of change, the years before World War I (in historical time) were many centuries ago! If some people want to be nostalgic about it, okay. But bring it back? No chance.

It's natural to want things to settle down and stabilize someplace. When so many things are changing so fast all the time, we get confused—it's hard to know what's going on. But that seems to be the nature of our moment in history. And if that's the way it is, best we recognize it and somehow learn to live with it.

The Problem of Depressions

Throughout the late 1800s and the early 1900s, a series of financial panics and depressions occurred. Periods of depression have been noted as far back as the 1700s. Malthus recognized the possibility that "general gluts" (overproduction) might sometimes present a problem.

Ricardo and others considered depression conditions to be temporary, short-run, and automatically self-correcting. Nothing to worry about. If there was a surplus of anything—labor, or products—the price of whatever was in surplus soon would go down. Then, at the lower prices, the surpluses would be bought up, and presto! No more surpluses! It was as simple as that. Depression just wasn't a matter of much concern to the classical economists.

So during the late 1800s and early 1900s while the problems of monopoly power and repeated depressions were bombarding the world, what were the economists doing? Addressing themselves to these issues? Generally, no. Economists continued to argue with each other and to refine their models of how the pure market process works. It was not to be until the 1930s that major breakthroughs were made by the economics profession in the analysis and understanding of these two problems—the problem of depression and the problem of monopoly power.

ALFRED MARSHALL AND NEOCLASSICAL ECONOMICS

During the time the last parts of *Das Kapital* were appearing (the late 1800s) the neoclassical school of economics was adding its modifications and refinements to the Ricardian model. Also, a number of schools of economic thought were developing. Each one was aiming off more or less in its own direction.

DISILLUSIONMENT WITH ECONOMICS IN THE LATE 1800s

During the late 1800s there was a good bit of confusion and some disillusionment about economics. Economists were busy disagreeing among themselves, and the theories of economics didn't seem to be much good in explaining the urgent problems of the real world.

Three major schools of thought arose: the German historical school, the Austrian marginalist school, and the neoclassical school. It was an Englishman of the neoclassical school—the Cambridge University economics professor Alfred Marshall—who "rebuilt" economics. By drawing on the works of the classical economists and integrating the marginal concept from his contemporaries of the Austrian school, Marshall pulled it all back together again.

THE CLASSICAL "ECONOMIC LAWS" DIDN'T SEEM TO HOLD TRUE

Neoclassical economics pushed aside andPIshor modified several of the natural economic laws of the classical economists. Something had to be done about the idea of the inescapable inevitability of the laws—of the Malthusian Law of Population, of the iron law of wages, of the labor theory of value (Marx's law that value comes only from labor), and several others.

In the industrializing world of the *earlier* 1800s these "laws" had seemed to fit real life, to be perpetual, immutable. But in the industrialized and rapidly changing world of the *late* 1800s, anyone could see that these laws simply weren't holding true. No wonder the esteem of economics (and economists) was slipping!

It was becoming obvious that some of the basic ideas and concepts of economics needed changing. And the *marginal concept* needed to be brought in. The neoclassical economists took care of these problems for us. But that isn't all they did. They sharpened the theoretical model of the pure market system. And they used the model to show how free people and free markets (laissez-faire and perfect competition) would bring maximum welfare for the whole society. Alfred Marshall made a major contribution to this "reconstruction of economics."

ALFRED MARSHALL'S PRINCIPLES OF ECONOMICS

Marshall's *Principles of Economics*—"the new Bible," the complete integration, synthesis, and explanation of neoclassical economics—came out in 1890, the same year the U.S. Congress passed the Sherman Antitrust Act. Marshall's *Principles* was the latest word on neoclassical economics. It explains the workings of a laissez-faire, competitive market system. It shows very precisely and in detail how the total welfare of the society would be maximized in a "theoretical model economic system" of laissez-faire and perfect competition—that is, in a model economy directed entirely by the market process and the price mechanism, in the absence of any government regulations, or monopoly power.

Marshall's *Principles* explained—and used supply and demand graphs to show precisely—how the market process directs the economy in response to the wishes of the society. Marshall's *Principles* lets you actually *see* (graphically) how the price mechanism directs the resources of the society into the best places—how it gets all the resources to do the things the people of the society most want to be done.

Marshall's *Principles* went through eight editions. It was *the* economics book throughout the world for some thirty years. It was widely used up to and beyond the time of Marshall's death, in 1924. It is still a good book to study, to see how the theoretical model of the pure market system works—how it brings maximum welfare to the people of a society.

In the following chapter you'll be learning about the neoclassical model—about how supply and demand and the price mechanism work together to direct the economy. But first, here's a little more about what was happening in Alfred Marshall's time.

MARSHALL HAD MANY CONTEMPORARIES

There were many other neoclassical economists, and many challengers, in the late 1800s and early 1900s. In England, France, Germany, Austria, Italy,

Scandinavia, and other countries, there were scholars, teachers, business executives, politicians, and others, all working to develop new economic ideas and to influence economic thinking. Some made important contributions to our understanding of economic theory—of the cause-and-effect interrelationships at work in an economic system.

LEON WALRAS AND GENERAL EQUILIBRIUM THEORY

One person during this period who made a very important contribution to economic thought was Leon Walras (val-RAHs). You probably don't know it, but *neoclassical* economic theory rests on what we call "*partial* equilibrium analysis."

NEOCLASSICAL ECONOMICS IS BASED ON PARTIAL EQUILIBRIUM ANALYSIS

"Partial equilibrium analysis" means we assume that "everything else stays the same." Then we try to see what would happen if there was too much corn and not enough tomatoes. You know what would happen. The price of corn would go down and the price of tomatoes would go up. People would start eating less and growing more tomatoes, and eating more and growing less corn. Pretty soon the problem would be solved. This is partial equilibrium analysis.

Partial equilibrium analysis doesn't tell us anything about what happens to the price of Iowa corn land, the demand for tomato pickers, the number of pickup trucks running from Ames to Waterloo, the demand for steel to make farm tractors, or any of the other hundreds of things which, in fact, will *not* "stay the same." Suppose there was some kind of theoretical system which could take into account all these simultaneous changes and show how it all works out. That would be a "*general* equilibrium analysis." Now can you guess what Walras did? Of course. He developed a *general equilibrium analysis*.

WALRAS DEVELOPED GENERAL EQUILIBRIUM ANALYSIS

Walras built a theoretical model which tied the whole economic system together. It shows how any change in one thing will cause changes in other things and how all these changes will work themselves out throughout the entire system. And after all the changes have worked themselves out, the economy will be in a new general equilibrium.

His model was a system of mathematical equations representing the total economic system. Each equation represented one part of the economy, and all the equations were tied in with each other so that any change in one caused changes in all the others.

Walras' system enabled economists to see the total picture. He showed that the theoretical model of a pure market economy really does all fit together, that it really is a self-contained, "mutually determined system"—that everything really does work out right. For this, Walras deserves to be listed among the greatest economists of all time. Modern-day econometric models of the entire economy can trace their beginnings to Walras.

SOME DISSENTING VIEWS

While mainstream classical and neoclassical economics was being developed, not all writers on economics were following in the mainstream. You already know about the dissenting utopian socialists of the late 1700s and the 1800s. In addition there were several important dissenters in the late 1800s and early 1900s. Two of these were important enough to be discussed here: Henry George, and Thorstein Veblen.

HENRY GEORGE AND THE SINGLE TAX

In the late 1800s Henry George wrote his very popular book *Progress and Poverty*. The one point of his book was that the economic system should not permit lucky landowners to get wealthy just because they happened to own some land in a good place—like Manhattan Island or some other place where a city is going to grow up, or where a railroad is going to come through, or where oil is going to be discovered, or where something else lucky is going to happen. He said these landowners do nothing to deserve their wealth. Their wealth is unplanned, unnecessary, and *undeserved*—a rip-off.

Henry George suggested that the money landowners get from this kind of undeserved good luck should be taxed away. This land tax should be the "single tax"—the only tax necessary. The land tax revenues would be great enough so that no other taxes would need to be levied. Henry George had an interesting thesis and a large number of followers. He gave all of us something to think about. And in fact, even today there is a "Georgian Society" promoting the theories and recommendations of Henry George.

Thorstein Veblen and Conspicuous Consumption

Thorstein Veblen was an unusual and interesting person and a brilliant and challenging economist. He was a professor at the University of Chicago in 1899 when he wrote his very popular book *The Theory of the Leisure Class.* Veblen criticized the whole approach of materialistic society—the "keeping up with the Joneses" hangup which he saw in American life.

One of Veblen's best known phrases is "conspicuous consumption." It's the idea that people buy and use up things unnecessarily, just to show off. Veblen thought that conspicuous consumption was inherent in the market system, and that it results in a great waste of resources.

In the early 1900s, Veblen wrote several more books. All of them carried forward his initial thesis—that the market economy as it works in the real world is aimed off in the wrong direction. It's wasteful, and too much influenced by rich people with vested interests. He predicted continuing, rapid technological and sociological changes and readjustments in the society. His impact on economics and on economists was (and is) great. Many of today's economic policies and programs—for consumer protection, income redistribution, and others—have deep roots somewhere in Veblen's theories and philosophy.

Capitalism Was Thriving and Growing

To be sure, capitalism had its dissenters. There were many in addition to Henry George and Thorstein Veblen. The neo-Marxists continued to be active, to be sure! The Bolshevik (communist) Revolution occurred in Russia in 1917. But for the most part the Western World at that time was little touched by the dissenters.

The Social Ethic Supports Capitalism

Capitalism was strong, productive, growing, and clearly justified by its religious and social ethics. By now, most of society had come to accept the Protestant Ethic: "God helps those who help themselves." "The idle mind is the Devil's workshop." "*Work* for the Night is Coming." Among the successful and affluent members of the society, it was widely believed that people who are poor *should be* poor. They are poor because that's what they deserve. They haven't worked hard enough—haven't been productive enough—to deserve anything better.

You can tell a person's worth by what he or she owns. Poverty is a sign of worthlessness. Poor people are not much good. But rich people are honorable and respectable. A wealthy person is good and worthy and should be looked up to. Such were the generally accepted values of the capitalism of the 1920s.

I'm sure you know that such value judgments still exist today. The economic philosophies and theories of "capitalism" have contributed to the acceptance of value judgments such as these—such ideas as the relationship between the "value" of something and its price, and the idea of the "productivity principle of distribution" (those who produce a lot should earn a lot and those who don't, shouldn't).

THE NEOCLASSICAL MODEL: EVERYTHING AUTOMATICALLY WORKS OUT BEST!

Alfred Marshall's *Principles of Economics* book was published in 1890. Ever since, the neoclassical model has been providing strong support for *laissez faire* and capitalism. The model shows very precisely how the "free market economic system" works. And it shows how the market system automatically brings the highest possible levels of economic welfare to the society. The purpose of the next chapter is to explain the basics of how the system works. It would be well worth your while to take your time and learn that chapter well.

 REVIEW QUESTIONS ────────────────────────

1. Compare neoclassical and classical economic philosophy. What are the similarities and differences? What are the advantages of neoclassical over classical theory? Explain.

2. Define neoclassical economics, and discuss the contributions of Alfred Marshall to neoclassical theory.

3. What is partial equilibrium analysis? What is general equilibrium analysis? Who first developed general equilibrium analysis? Why is it a major contribution to modern economic theory?

4. What is "conspicuous consumption"? Explain its role according to Thorstein Veblen's writings. Did Veblen's theories have any influence on modern economics? Explain.

5. Compare the "single tax" concept and landowner philosophy of Henry George with Ricardo's ideas concerning landowners.

12
THE NEOCLASSICAL MODEL: HOW SUPPLY, DEMAND, AND PRICES DIRECT THE MARKET SYSTEM

🔑 KEY TERMS

- supply curve
- demand curve
- market price
- law of demand
- equilibrium market price
- equilibrium quantity
- shortage
- surplus
- short-run profit
- short-run loss
- normal price
- surplus (excess) profits
- long-run equilibrium
- normal profit
- powerful price mechanism
- Alfred Marshall
- Adam Smith's "invisible hand" doctrine

The neoclassical model is of much more importance than just "historical interest." Although it was presented in Marshall's *Principles* book over 100 years ago (1890), it still forms the "solid-rock foundation" of much of modern economic theory. In fact, it is the *key* to understanding how a free market economy functions. So it would be well worth your time and effort to learn it well. That's what you'll be doing in this chapter.

For an overview understanding of neoclassical economics you need only to know (1) how supply and demand work to set prices, and then (2) how prices work to direct and control the economic system. But first, you may need a quick review of some principles you read about back in the beginning of this book.

THE BASIC CHOICES

What kinds of "directions and controls" must a society's economic system have? Somehow, three basic kinds of choices must be made. It must somehow be decided:

1. Which kinds of products will be produced (and how much of each);
2. Which resources (natural, capital, and human—and how much of each) will be used to produce each of the chosen products; and
3. How much of the total output will each individual be able to claim—that is, how much income will each person get?

THE SUPPLY AND DEMAND CURVES

Can supply and demand and prices (the powerful price mechanism) cause these choices to be made automatically—through the market process? You already know the answer: Yes! Adam Smith and other classical economists explained how it works *in general.* Alfred Marshall used supply and demand curves (and other mathematical tools) to explain how it works *specifically.* That's what you'll be learning about in the sections coming up.

THE MARKET SUPPLY CURVE

A market supply curve is a line in a graph which illustrates this basic principle:

> *As the market price of something goes up higher and higher (and if you'll wait awhile), more and more of that something will be offered for sale in that market.*

And conversely:

> *If the price goes lower and lower, after awhile less and less will be offered for sale. If the price goes low enough, none at all will be offered for sale.*

Figure 12-1 shows a supply curve and a supply schedule that illustrate this principle. Take a look at that figure and you'll see that there's a *positive relationship* between prices and quantities offered for sale—the higher the price, the greater the quantity offered.

THE MARKET DEMAND CURVE

A demand curve is very much like a supply curve. What's the difference? You could guess:

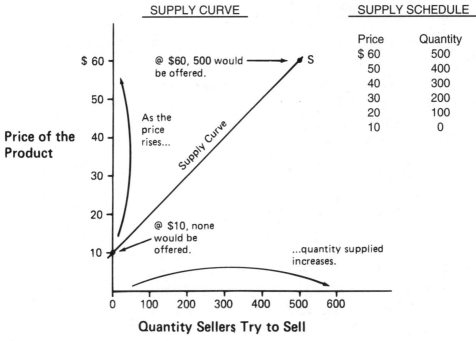

FIGURE 12-1. Market Supply: The Higher the Price, the More Would Be Supplied

OF SPECIAL INTEREST . . . ⎯⎯⎯⎯⎯⎯⎯⎯⎯⎯⎯

THE MARKET SUPPLY OF A PRODUCT MEANS HOW MUCH (HOW MANY UNITS) OF THAT PRODUCT WOULD BE OFFERED FOR SALE AT EACH ONE OF THE VARIOUS DIFFERENT PRICES WHICH MIGHT EXIST FOR THAT PRODUCT IN THE MARKET. YOU CAN SEE THAT THE MARKET SUPPLY OF A PRODUCT CONSISTS, NOT OF ONE QUANTITY, BUT OF A WHOLE SERIES OF QUANTITIES, WHERE EACH QUANTITY CORRESPONDS TO A SPECIFIC MARKET PRICE. THE HIGHER THE MARKET PRICE, THE GREATER WILL BE THE QUANTITY OFFERED FOR SALE. THE MARKET SUPPLY OF A PRODUCT CAN BE ILLUSTRATED EITHER BY A CURVE IN A GRAPH, OR BY A TABLE (SCHEDULE) SHOWING THE VARIOUS MARKET PRICES WHICH MIGHT EXIST AND, FOR EACH PRICE, THE CORRESPONDING QUANTITY WHICH WOULD BE OFFERED FOR SALE.

The supply curve shows how much the sellers would want to sell (and would be trying to sell) at each of the many different prices which might exist in the market. The demand curve shows the same idea from the other side—the buyers' side—of the market.

The market demand curve shows how much the buyers would want to buy (and would be trying to buy) at each of the many different prices which might exist in the market. The demand curve illustrates this basic principle:

As the market price of something goes down lower and lower (and if you'll wait awhile), buyers will be trying to buy more and more of that lower-priced something.
Also:

As the price goes higher and higher, after awhile less and less of it will be bought. If the price goes high enough, perhaps none of it will be bought.

This principle—the lower the price, the more people will be trying to buy, and vice versa—is what economists call "the law of demand." Figure 12-2 shows a demand curve and a demand schedule that illustrate this principle.

The demand curve shows that there is a *negative relationship* between prices and the quantities buyers would be trying to buy—the lower the price,

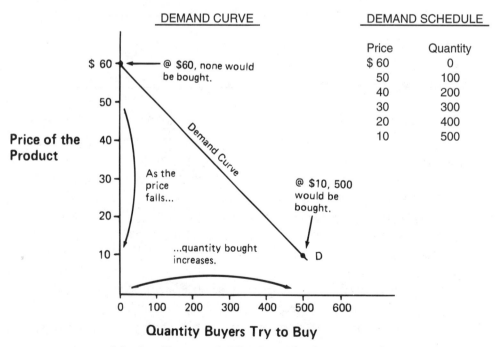

FIGURE 12-2. Market Demand: The Lower the Price, the More Would Be Bought

the greater the quantity demanded. But you already know that. How? Because *the law of demand* says so!

OF SPECIAL INTEREST . . .

THE MARKET DEMAND FOR A PRODUCT MEANS HOW MUCH (HOW MANY UNITS) OF THAT PRODUCT THE BUYERS WOULD BE TRYING TO BUY AT EACH ONE OF THE VARIOUS DIFFERENT PRICES WHICH MIGHT EXIST FOR THAT PRODUCT IN THE MARKET. THE MARKET DEMAND FOR A PRODUCT CONSISTS, NOT OF ONE QUANTITY, BUT OF A WHOLE SERIES OF QUANTITIES, WHERE EACH QUANTITY CORRESPONDS TO A SPECIFIC MARKET PRICE. THE LOWER THE MARKET PRICE, THE GREATER WILL BE THE QUANTITY THE BUYERS WILL BE TRYING TO BUY. THE MARKET DEMAND FOR A PRODUCT CAN BE ILLUSTRATED EITHER BY A CURVE IN A GRAPH OR BY A TABLE (A SCHEDULE) SHOWING THE VARIOUS MARKET PRICES WHICH MIGHT EXIST AND, FOR EACH PRICE, THE CORRESPONDING QUANTITY WHICH WOULD BE DEMANDED.

HOW SUPPLY AND DEMAND DETERMINE PRICES

Think about the two previous graphs. Suppose the price for this product happened to be $10. People would be out there trying to buy 500 units (per month, or week, or day—per hour, maybe—the graph doesn't say). And how much would the sellers be trying to sell? None!

The point is obvious. Neither the supply curve nor the demand curve, standing alone, can tell you how much the sellers will be selling—or how much the buyers will be buying. Sellers can't sell without buyers! And buyers can't buy without sellers. Of course not.

So what to do? That's easy. Just look at the supply curve and the demand curve on the same graph. Then you can see that there's a price—*only one price*—where the quantity the buyers are trying to buy is exactly equal to the quantity the sellers are trying to sell. This price is called the "equilibrium market price."

HOW THE EQUILIBRIUM MARKET PRICE OCCURS AUTO-MATICALLY

1. At any price *lower* than equilibrium, buyers will be trying to buy more than the sellers will be offering for sale. There will be shortages of that product in the market. Disappointed buyers who can't find the product begin offering to pay more. They bid the price up to equilibrium.
2. At any price higher than equilibrium, sellers will be trying to sell more than the buyers want to buy. There will be surpluses of that product in the market. Disappointed suppliers who can't sell their products begin cutting their prices. This price cutting continues until the price moves down to equilibrium.

THE SUPPLY AND DEMAND CURVES

Figure 12-3 shows a supply curve, a demand curve, and the equilibrium market price—the only price which will bring this market into balance.

As you look at Figure 12-3 you can see that the equilibrium market price is the only stable price in this market. At no other price would the quantity offered for sale be in balance with the quantity demanded.

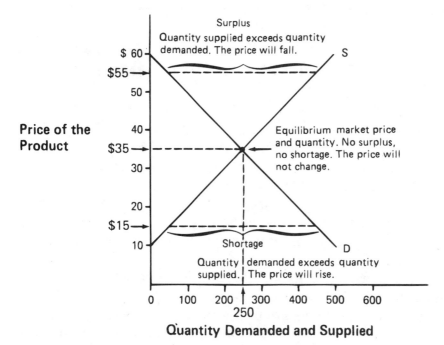

FIGURE 12-3. Supply, Demand, and Equilibrium Market Price

Figure 12-3 shows that $35 is the equilibrium market price. The equilibrium quantity is 250 units. That's how much the sellers want to sell at a price of $35, and that's how much the buyers want to buy at that price.

At a price of $35, the market is in balance. But at any lower price there would be shortages—too much demanded for the available supply. At any higher price there would be surpluses—too much supplied for the available demand.

HOW THE SOCIETY'S DEMANDS AUTOMATICALLY DIRECT THE ECONOMY

Remember when Adam Smith (in 1776) spoke out in favor of *laissez faire?* He said that people who are left free to produce whatever they wish will be automatically directed "as though by an invisible hand" to produce the things most wanted (most valued) by the society.

Now that you understand the basics of supply and demand and equilibrium market price, you are ready to see how Alfred Marshall and the neoclassical economists explained more precisely exactly what Adam Smith was saying. Here's a simple example.

Suppose the economy is operating freely and everything is in balance and running smoothly. Then suppose a lot of people decide they like corn bread a lot more than they like wheat bread. So the demand for corn increases and the demand for wheat decreases.

THE CORN MARKET: DEMAND INCREASES, THE PRICE GOES UP, AND MORE IS SUPPLIED

The higher demand for corn creates a shortage of corn. The disappointed corn buyers begin paying more. The price of corn goes up to a higher "equilibrium market price."

Figure 12-4 shows exactly what all this looks like on a supply and demand graph. Study that figure for a few minutes and learn it well because there's more to come.

In Figure 12-4 you can see that the initial equilibrium price was $35. Buyers were buying (and sellers were selling) 250 units. After the increase in demand, buyers were trying to buy 450 units. But only 250 units were available. Big shortage!

The buyers bid up the price to the new equilibrium market price of $45. The higher price causes sellers to be willing to offer more (up from 250 to 350

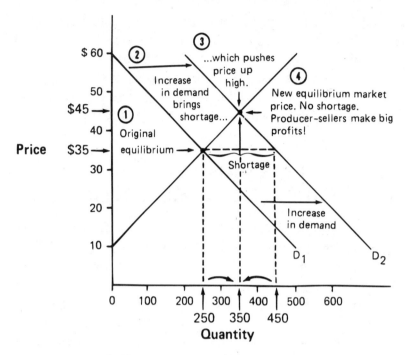

FIGURE 12-4. The Corn Market: Demand Increases, Shortages Develop, and the Price Goes Up

units) and causes buyers to be willing to buy less (down from 450 to 350 units). The market is again in balance, and corn sellers are producing and selling more corn to meet the wishes of the society. As though directed by an invisible hand? Yes.

THE WHEAT MARKET: DEMAND DECREASES, THE PRICE GOES DOWN, AND LESS IS SUPPLIED

Meanwhile, what has been happening in the wheat market? Just the opposite. Look at Figure 12-5, and you'll see.

Figure 12-5 shows what happened when the demand for wheat decreased. At the initial price of $35, buyers cut back their purchases from 250 units to only 50 units. This left a surplus of 200 units in the market. Disappointed sellers who couldn't sell their wheat began cutting prices. The market price of wheat went down to a lower equilibrium market price—down from $35 to $25.

The lower price ($25) caused the surplus of wheat to disappear. Why? Because two things happened: (1) sellers weren't willing to offer as much for

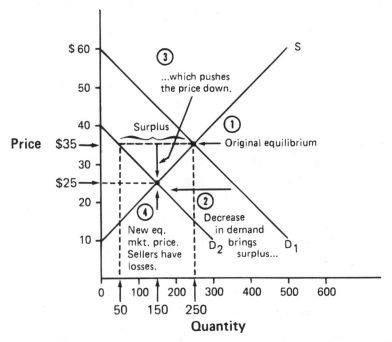

FIGURE 12-5. The Wheat Market: Demand Decreases, Surpluses Develop, and the Price Goes Down

sale at thelower price (the quantity offered for sale went down from 250 to 150 units), and (2) buyers were willing to buy more at the lower price (the quantity demanded went up from 50 to 150 units).

The market is again in balance. The equilibrium market price is now lower (down from $35 to $25). The wheat-sellers are producing and selling less wheat. They are responding to the changed wishes (choices) of the society. As though directed by an invisible hand? Yes.

SHORT-RUN PROFITS AND LOSSES BRING LONG-RUN ADJUSTMENTS

In the above examples, who would you rather be? A corn producer? Or a wheat producer? That's easy. Corn, of course!

Back before the demand for corn increased and the demand for wheat decreased, everything was in balance. Remember? So that means that the $35 equilibrium market price (for both wheat and corn) was the "normal" price— that is, it was just high enough to cover all costs of production including a "normal profit" for the producer-sellers.

But then the price of corn went up to $45. So the corn producers are making big profits! And the price of wheat went down to $25. Big losses for the wheat producers? Right.

HIGHLY PROFITABLE INDUSTRIES EXPAND, WHILE THE LOSERS CONTRACT

It doesn't take a genius to figure out what's going to happen next. The wheat producers are going to start shifting out of wheat production as soon as they can and into something else—maybe into corn production. And everybody who can (wheat producers, dairy farmers, sunflower growers, and lots of others) will start producing corn to try to get some of those big profits!

Will there be a big shift of natural, capital, and human resources into corn production? And out of wheat production? As though directed by an invisible hand? Right again.

THE ADJUSTMENT CONTINUES UNTIL SURPLUS PROFITS AND LOSSES ARE ELIMINATED

How long will this resource shifting (out of wheat and into corn) continue? Until the excess profits in corn and the losses in wheat are eliminated.

The supply of corn will keep increasing until the price comes down to where no more surplus profits are being made by the corn producers. The supply of wheatwill keep decreasing until the price goes up to where no more losses are being suffered by the wheat producers.

LONG-RUN EQUILIBRIUM

Eventually the corn price will move back down to "normal," where only "normal profits" (no excess profits) are being made by the corn producers. And the wheat price will move back up to "normal." When that happens, both the corn industry and the wheat industry will be in *long-run equilibrium.*

When normal profits are being made in both industries there are no longer any special incentives for producers either to enter or to leave either industry. Both industries are profitable enough to hold on to their present producers, but not profitable enough to attract new producers.

SUPPLY CURVES CAN SHIFT IN THE LONG RUN

Now it's time for you to see how this long-run adjustment looks on supply and demand graphs. First, Figure 12-6 shows how it works for an expanding industry (the corn example). After that (in Figure 12-7), you'll see how it works for a declining industry (the wheat example).

Any short-run price which is above normal (i.e., which brings excess profits) will attract more producers and eventually will create surpluses which will push the price down to normal. Take a look at Figure 12-6 on the next page and that's exactly what you'll see. Do that now, then come back here and read on.

In Figure 12-6, first the demand increased from D_1 to D_2. That created shortages and pushed the price up from the normal price of $35 to the highly profitable price of $45. That's what you saw back in Figure 12-4.

The $45 price is the new "market equilibrium" price for corn. It's also called a "short-run" equilibrium price because it can't remain that high in the long run.

EFFECTS OF A LONG-RUN INCREASE IN SUPPLY

The supply increase from S_1 to S_2 and the price drop from $45 to $35 (as shown in Figure 12-6) doesn't really happen all at once. What's really supposed to happen is this: As soon as the price goes up to $45, lots of producers

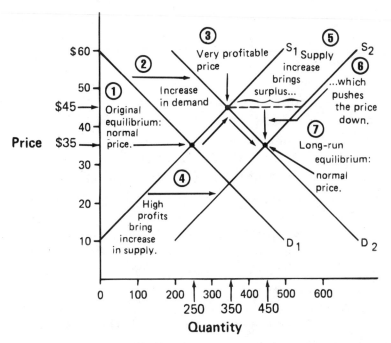

FIGURE 12-6. The Corn Market: Supply Increases, Pushes the Price Down to "Normal," and Reestablishes "Long-Run Equilibrium"

want to get into the corn business. They want to get in on the big profits as quickly as they can.

Maybe some sellers start importing corn from Canada or Mexico or some other place. So the supply of corn begins to increase very soon. The curve starts shifting to the right and the increased supply begins to push the price down.

THE PRICE MOVES DOWN.   This process continues as more suppliers find ways to supply more corn to the market. As the supply increases more and more, the price moves down more and more. Then when the supply reaches S_2, the price is down to $35. That's the normal price—the long-run equilibrium price—so the adjustment process is complete.

THE QUANTITY IS GREATER.   Figure 12-6 shows this final "long-run equilibrium" position. Look at the intersection of D_2 and S_2. The price is $35 and the quantity bought and sold is 450 units. The normal price is the same as before: $35. But the quantity has increased from 350 units to 450 units. Did that happen in response to the wishes of the society? Automatically? As though directed by an invisible hand? Yes.

Notice that after the shifts to curves D_2 and S_2, curves D_1 and S_1 are of only historical interest. They don't really exist in this market anymore. Curves D_2 and S_2 are the ones which now illustrate the demand and supply conditions in this market.

EFFECTS OF A LONG-RUN DECREASE IN SUPPLY

What about the wheat market, where the price is below normal? You probably already know that in the long run the supply curve for wheat will shift to the left and push the price up. That's right. And that's exactly what you see in Figure 12-7. Take a minute to study that figure now.

In Figure 12-7, first the demand decreased from D_1 to D_2. That created surpluses and pushed the market price from the normal price of $35 down to $25. The producer-sellers were losing money, so they started getting out of the industry. Nobody likes to lose money!

As the producers shift out of wheat production, the supply of wheat in the market begins to decrease. The supply curve begins to shift to the left. Each time the supply decreases (the curve shifts leftward toward S_2), shortages appear in the market and the price goes up.

This process continues until the supply has shifted all the way to S_2 in the graph, where the normal price of $35 has been reestablished. The wheat market and the wheat industry are now in long-run equilibrium.

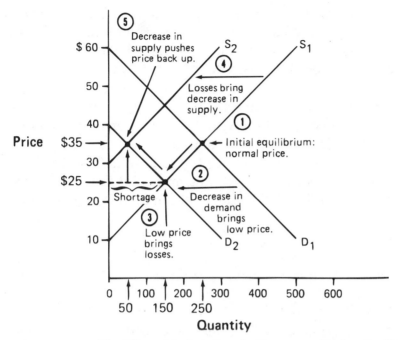

FIGURE 12-7. The Wheat Market: Supply Decreases, Pushes the Price Up to "Normal," and Reestablishes "Long-run Equilibrium"

The graph shows that only 50 units of wheat will now be bought (and sold) in the market. But notice this: That's all the society wants to buy at the normal price of $35! The society is getting exactly as much wheat as it's willing to pay for—i.e., to pay for at the normal price, which is just high enough to cover the full cost of production (including normal profits but no excess profits for the producers).

OVERVIEW OF THE NEOCLASSICAL "SUPPLY, DEMAND, AND PRICE" MODEL

When everything is in long-run equilibrium in the neoclassical "pure market" model, then all of the society's resources are being used in the most desired ways. The desired quantities of all products are being produced. The most resource-conserving production techniques are being used as producers try to minimize their costs and maximize their profits. And each person's income reflects that person's productivity—the value of that person's contribution to society's total output.

Does the neoclassical model describe the U.S. economic system? Or any other real-world economic system? No. Not exactly. In the model there are several "assumed conditions" which don't exactly fit the real world.

But the neoclassical model certainly does describe forces which do work and which are very powerful in every modern market system—forces such as, for example, the operation of the powerful price mechanism. You'll be reading more about this issue in connection with the Keynesian (KAYN'sian)-monetarist debate, coming up later. But that's enough theory for now.

Now it's time to go back to the real world of the 1920s and 30s—to prosperity and depression—to see what was happening and what the economists were saying about it. That's what you'll be reading about in the chapters coming up.

 REVIEW QUESTIONS

1. What is the meaning of "normal price"? Explain what processes guarantee the existence of "normal price," in long-run equilibrium.

2. Draw a supply curve. What does this curve tell you? Explain the basic principle this curve illustrates. Why does it slope as it does?

3. Draw a demand curve. What does this curve tell you? Explain how it illustrates the "law of demand." Why does it slope as it does?

4. Explain, and illustrate graphically how the equilibrium market price and quantity are determined. What happens if demand increases? If demand decreases? Explain exactly what happens when demand changes to make the equilibrium price and quantity change.

5. Draw a supply and demand curve on a graph. Label the *curves* D_1 and S_1. Show an equilibrium price of $5 and a quantity of 100 units. Then answer the following questions:
   A. How can you be sure that $5 is the equilibrium price?

B. Suppose a price of $6 existed. What would be the situation in the market? What would happen to overcome this situation?

C. Suppose a price of $4 existed. What would be the market situation? How would this situation be corrected?

6. Now draw a new demand curve to the right of D_1 on your graph. Label it D_2. Show the new market equilibrium price and label it E_2. Then answer the following questions:

A. What caused the price to go to E_2? Explain.

B. Is E_2 a short-run or long-run equilibrium price?

C. In the long run, supply will change. Draw in the new supply curve. Label it S_2, and explain how and why supply changed and what happened after that.

7. Explain how the exercises you just performed in questions 5 and 6 illustrate, in the neoclassical model, the idea of "the invisible hand."

PART FIVE

THE GREAT DEPRESSION AND KEY-NESIAN (KAYN'SIAN) ECONOMICS (1930s–1940s)

Neoclassical economics didn't seem to explain the depression, so some new ideas and theories were developed.

13 THE GREAT DEPRESSION

In the United States in the 1920s there was rapid economic expansion. The conditions of most of the people seemed to be improving, and (with the exception of some problems in agriculture) economic harmony and a happy life for most people seemed to have arrived. Of course, nothing was said about the "invisible members" of the society. But it is only in more recent years that people seem to have taken much notice of the minority people—the very poor, the dispossessed, the under-privileged, the discriminated against, or the incapable and unsupported ones.

PROSPERITY, THEN DEPRESSION

By the late 1920s the American economy was heralded as being on a "high plateau." People talked about how difficult it would be to think of anything better. The economies of Britain and all of Western Europe had largely overcome the destructive effects of World War I. It seemed for a moment that economic conditions in the world were going to be all right again—that the golden age of the early 1900s was about to remanifest itself. But as you know, this was not our destiny. Instead, the whole economic structure was about to fall apart. A sudden, powerful, bewildering change was coming. The American—and world—economy was about to move into the Great Depression of the 1930s.

CONDITIONS IN THE 1920S

When the year 1929 began, everybody was sure that the booming American economy was in great shape. Then in October of 1929, the bubble burst. The decade of the 1920s had been one of growth, prosperity, good times, high employment, happy days for most people. The total real value of the nation's output (value of goods and services produced) had increased from about $73 billion in 1920, to more than $100 billion in 1929—a total increase of more than forty percent.

Population was expanding, of course. More people were sharing this larger output. But even so, output *per person* increased by about 25 percent over this decade. When Herbert Hoover accepted the nomination of the Republican Party in 1928 he said: "We shall soon with the help of God be in sight of the day when poverty will be banished from this nation." But as you very well know, after he was elected President things didn't turn out that way.

THE STOCK MARKET "BOOM AND BUST" OF THE 1920S

Throughout the decade of the '20s, while employment and output were increasing, prices of stocks on the stock markets were going up faster and faster. Throughout the first half of the decade, stock prices increased only moderately. Then the speedup began. A person holding an average group of stocks in 1925 would have seen the value of those stocks increase by about 50 percent before the end of 1926—a 50 percent increase in about one year. And the same thing happened again in 1927.

Ten thousand dollars invested in "an average group" of stocks in 1925 would be worth about $20,000 before the end of 1927. Before another year had passed, that $20,000 would just about double again—to about $40,000 before the end of 1928. And by August of 1929? Would you believe it doubled again? And more? That's right. A $10,000 investment in stocks in 1925 would very likely have reached a value of $100,000 before the crash came in October 1929.

Here's another thing: A person could have bought that $10,000 worth of stocks for as little as *10 percent down*. So for an actual cash investment of $1,000 in 1925, the "average person" would have wound up with $100,000 in 1929. Is it any wonder that a lot of people were "playing the stock market"?

THE STOCK MARKET COLLAPSE

By 1929 the ever-growing demand for stocks had pushed stock prices up far beyond the *real* values of the assets which the stocks represented. Many people knew they were holding overvalued stocks. But as long as stock prices kept on going up, why sell? Then, in the fall of 1929, some investors began to sell, to get their cash. This selling pushed down stock prices and caused others to lose confidence. There was more and more selling until finally, on October 29, the market collapsed. Everyone was trying to sell but no one was buying.

ECONOMIC CONDITIONS GOT WORSE AND WORSE

For the next three years stock prices kept falling. Suppose a person had owned $100,000 in General Electric stocks in 1929. By 1932 those stocks would be worth about $3,000. As stock prices fell month after month, businesses all over the country were failing. Unemployment was increasing. More and more banks were failing. Economic collapse continued to visit one company after another, one place after another, one family after another. There seemed to be no end to the downtrend.

THE ECONOMY GOES INTO DEPRESSION

Probably you've already heard a lot about the Great Depression. What a confusing, bewildering time of social, economic, and political turmoil that was!

Each year it seemed that conditions were so bad they couldn't get worse. But the next year *was* worse. Some people were actually starving in the cities. Food—grain, potatoes, livestock—was going to waste on the farms. Crops were rotting in the fields. Sometimes food prices were so low in the cities that it didn't even pay to ship the goods to market. Farmers couldn't get enough for the potatoes they shipped to pay the freight bill!

People in the cities were hungry, all right. But they didn't have any money. They couldn't buy the potatoes which were already there in the city, getting old in the grocers' storerooms. The economic system just wasn't working.

During this period many people in the United States joined the Communist Party. Veterans of World War I marched on Washington demanding that the government do something to help. The people didn't understand what was going on, but they knew they were hungry. Surely *any kind* of economic system must be better than this! An economic system that lets people starve while goods go to waste is obviously not doing a very good job. A person doesn't have to study economics to figure that out!

THE MARKET SYSTEM WASN'T WORKING

The market system is supposed to work by getting people to produce things for other people. That's the way people get the things they want—by producing things "for the market." It's all supposed to work out neatly. But during the depression the markets weren't working. So the system wasn't working.

The people in the cities were wondering how they could get some potatoes to feed their families. The farmers were wondering how they could sell their potatoes so they could get some money to pay their debts and keep going. But the city people had no jobs and no money so they couldn't buy, so the farmers couldn't sell. When nobody's buying, then nobody's selling. The market system just isn't working.

The potatoes rotted in the fields. The city families went hungry. What had gone wrong with the world? What was causing all these bad times? What could be done to get the system working again? Nobody seemed to know.

NO ONE KNEW WHAT WAS HAPPENING, OR WHAT TO DO

The nation's leaders asked their economist-advisors what was happening, and why—and when things would start getting better. But the economists didn't know. This was a new situation. Neither the classical nor the neoclassical nor any of the other theories of economics were of much help in explaining how such serious and prolonged depressed conditions could exist—or what (if anything) might be done.

It was easy to see that the model of the pure market system didn't help much to explain what was going on. This was some kind of new problem—a brand new ball game—a game the economists hadn't learned to play.

THE SERIOUS ECONOMIC CONDITIONS OF 1933

The U.S. economy and the economies of the other free nations of the world kept getting worse and worse throughout the early 1930s. Then in

1933 things leveled off at a very low level. There was serious depression—U.S. and worldwide. There were some improvements over the next five or six years, but not much. The recovery of the U.S. economy was painfully slow.

In 1933 the total output of the U.S. economy was only about one-half the size of the 1929 output. Much of the nation's productive capacity was idle. About one-half of the nation's banks failed and the depositors lost their money. More than 25 percent of the people who wanted to work couldn't find jobs. So they (and their families) had no incomes.

SERIOUS POVERTY WAS EVERYWHERE

The families of most farmers and fishermen were living in serious poverty. Some of the lucky ones who had jobs were getting paid *less than* (would you believe?) $10 a month. Sure, $10 then would buy a lot more than $10 now—maybe as much as 10 times as much! But how would you like to try to support a family today on $100 a month? In many parts of the country a wage of $20 a month was considered very good. People were begging for jobs—for *any* way to make money, at *any* wage.

Between 1929 and 1933, some 85,000 businesses failed. One bank out of every five went out of business. Some *nine million people* lost their savings as the banks collapsed. On March 4, 1933, the U.S. government ordered all the banks in the country to close—that was to keep *all* the banks from failing under the increased assault of panic-stricken people withdrawing their deposits, demanding cash.

Things really were miserable. There were millions of hungry, desperate people. It's no wonder that some committed suicide—and that many joined the Communist Party. And it's no wonder that some committed crimes just to be sent to jail—where they could get shelter and food. I don't suppose freedom or liberty has very great appeal to one who is freezing or starving to death. Many Americans found that out in the 1930s.

THE DEPRESSION WENT ON FOR MANY YEARS

It's hard to believe how long this Great Depression lasted. It never got any worse than it was in March 1933, but as the years passed it didn't get much better. The government was trying out all kinds of programs. But the economy just didn't seem to respond very much.

Things got somewhat better in '35 and '36, but then in '37 and '38 there was another sharp drop. Unemployment all this time had been more than

15 percent of the labor force. In 1938 it was up to almost 20 percent. Also, in 1938 big surpluses began piling up on the farms again. Farm prices fell again.

GOVERNMENT MILITARY SPENDING FINALLY OVERCAME THE DEPRESSION

It wasn't until 1939, when the government began to increase spending for military production, that total recovery began. By 1944 there was virtually no unemployment. The value of the nation's output was double that of 1929. Half the total output was being produced in response to the huge military spending program of the government. The government alone spent as much in 1944 as *total spending in the economy* had been in 1929 (about $100 billion).

See what happened when the government began its unlimited spending for World War II? How quickly the economic system began running full speed again! No more depression. No more unemployment. No more idle factories or unused surpluses of farm products or labor or anything else. A miraculous recovery! This experience taught us one thing: If the government is willing to spend enough money to employ enough people and buy enough output, it certainly can overcome a depression.

Did the government wait for World War II before it tried to do anything about the depression? Of course not. Lots of things were tried. Some seemed to help. Some didn't. What was the government doing? And what new ideas were economists coming up with during this long, miserable, bewildering decade of the 1930s? That's what you'll be reading about in the chapters coming up.

But first, here's an interesting question.

What did neoclassical economics have to say about the depression? How did it explain what was happening and why? And what did it say should be done?

NEOCLASSICAL ECONOMICS COULDN'T EXPLAIN THE DEPRESSION

Neoclassical economics didn't help much to explain what was happening during the 1930s. Economists, politicians, business and finance experts *all* were trying to figure out and explain this new real-world happening: prolonged, persistent depression. To get at it, things had to be looked at in a new and different way.

For more than 100 years there have been times of boom and slump—some times when employment was high and wages were rising, prosperity was in the air; then other times when people found it hard to get jobs, incomes were low, and businesses had trouble surviving. These recurrent periods of prosperity and depression—these ups and downs of business—had been recognized as "normal cycles" in business activity. For a long time economists had been talking about and explaining these *business cycles.*

BUSINESS CYCLES WERE NATURAL AND SELF-CORRECTING

Neoclassical economics explained these recurrent depression periods as a necessary part of the system. There were several different theories, but all of them explained how a depression was a short-term, self-correcting condition—how depression conditions soon would move on into a period of recovery and then prosperity. But what about the 1930s? The U.S. economy (and the economies of most of the modern world) went into a devastating economic slump that just kept going on, year after year. What about that?

Neoclassical economics had no way to explain an entire *decade* of continuous depression. And without the massive government spending required by World War II, when might it have ended? And how? Neoclassical economics really didn't offer any good answers to these questions.

NEOCLASSICAL ECONOMICS DESCRIBES "THE MARKET SYSTEM AT WORK"

There must be a thousand different ways of looking at the world. And how you look at it determines what you will see. The classical and neoclassical economists looked at it as "a market system at work." They saw people buying things and they saw businesses producing the things people were buying. They saw the demand of the people controlling the uses of the society's resources. They saw everybody seeking more—workers seeking higher wages, landowners trying to get better rents, owners of money and capital trying to maximize their incomes, and businesses working for maximum profits. They saw all these "owners of the factors of production" seeking more for themselves and thereby automatically responding to the demands of the society.

The business was supposed to make profits, then invest the profits and bring more economic growth. Competition was supposed to keep each business, each worker, each landowner, and everyone else doing the most productive, most valuable things for the economy. Competition was to keep everyone in line. That's the way Adam Smith and the other classical economists, and Alfred Marshall and the other neoclassical economists looked at the world.

Even the theories of Marx and the other radical critics of the laissez-faire market system were aimed in the wrong direction to help to explain the persistent, prolonged depression. Generally, *all* economists were concerned with the *inter-workings of the parts* of the economic system. How do the pieces fit together? How are society's choices made—about what to produce, which inputs and techniques of production to use, and how much "distributive share" each person will get? These were the kinds of questions economists were prepared to answer. The microeconomic questions? The questions of price theory? Yes.

THE DEPRESSION QUESTION WASN'T CONSIDERED RELEVANT

To the classical and neoclassical economists, these "production" and "distribution" questions seemed to be the relevant issues, since neoclassical economics explains how depression will take care of itself automatically. But the 1930s presented the world with some new kinds of questions. And on these new questions the old ways of looking at the economy didn't help very much.

With surplus farm commodities, prices were supposed to fall so that people would buy up the surpluses. With surplus workers, wages were supposed to fall so that more workers would be hired. With surplus industrial output, prices of products were supposed to fall until people would buy them all. With surplus savings, interest rates were supposed to go down until investors would borrow all the savings, and invest.

SURPLUSES SHOULD BE ELIMINATED BY FALLING PRICES

All of the surpluses of everything—food, workers, products, loanable funds—were supposed to be automatically cleared away by falling prices. But that didn't happen. The surpluses persisted. The economy slowed down more and more. Hungry people couldn't get the surplus food. People experienced "starvation in the midst of plenty."

The goods weren't moving across the market. Why not? The otherwise very useful concepts of classical and neoclassical economics simply couldn't answer this question. The neoclassical explanation of "how the system works" is just great—so long as the system is working. But when the system *breaks down* that's something else! And sure enough, the system had broken down.

Neoclassical economics has excellent explanations of why the market system must work—why it will not break down. So when the system did break down, neoclassical theory was not in a position to help very much. According to neoclassical theory it couldn't happen. The automatic price adjustments would not let it happen—at least not for very long. But it *did* happen.

WHAT WAS DONE TO TRY TO OVERCOME THE DEPRESSION?

So as the months and years went by, what was done to try to overcome this serious economic malady?—to try to bring an end to this socially destructive period of starvation in the midst of plenty?

And who (if anyone) was trying to explain what was wrong?—and what could be done to remedy the situation?

That's what you'll be reading about in the two chapters coming up on (1) the "New Deal," and (2) Keynesian economics.

REVIEW QUESTIONS ───────────────────

1. Describe the "boom and bust" cycle of the stock market in the 1920s. What events led to the crash? Explain.

2. Briefly describe the economic scenario during the worst years of the Great Depression.

3. What finally brought an end to the Great Depression? Explain.

4. Explain how neoclassical economics deals with business cycles. Why couldn't neoclassical theory explain, or offer solutions to, the Great Depression?

5. What are the major questions addressed by neoclassical economics? Are these mostly micro- or macroeconomic questions? Explain.

14

THE "NEW DEAL": BASIC CHANGES IN THE ECONOMIC SYSTEM

With things so bad and getting worse following the stock market crash in October 1929, many voices clamored for government action. The clamor came from businesses large and small, from state and local governments, from welfare agencies and private charities, from religious organizations, from groups of irate citizens, from just about everybody. The veterans of World War I marched on Washington demanding relief. But no one seemed to know what to do.

When Franklin D. Roosevelt was inaugurated on March 3, 1933, he promised to do something. He promised a "New Deal." He promised *action*. A real flurry of action is what he delivered. When he was all through, the American economic system was a *different* economic system than it had been before. A *better* system? Perhaps. Some people disagree on this. But everyone agrees that it was different.

WHAT WAS ROOSEVELT'S "NEW DEAL"?

What was meant by the "New Deal"? You can answer that question in many different ways. One way would be to list the fifteen or so major pieces of legislation which were pushed through Congress during the first 100 days after Roosevelt took office, and to describe the impact of these important federal acts on how the American economic system functions.

Another way to answer the question "What was the New Deal?" is to say that it was an idea, a concept, a vision of major change in the American economic system—a change away from the philosophies and policies of laissez-faire. The idea was that we were going to "reshuffle the cards and deal them out again"—to give the people with "bad hands" a chance to do better—that is, a "new deal."

This New Deal means that we will give the farmers some help, and some economic power to protect themselves from economic adversity. We will let workers join unions and bargain with (and if they wish, strike against) their employers. We will establish a social security program so that the welfare of each individual will be (to some extent) a responsibility shared by all members of the society.

The New Deal tried to do something specific, something direct to help those who were in difficulty—and that included farmers, workers, businesses, young people, old people, city people, country people: just about everyone. The government started programs to employ people, and to buy up the surplus food and give it to hungry people.

INCREASING THE ECONOMIC ROLE OF GOVERNMENT

Ideas about the proper role of government were changing fast. The New Deal idea was that wages and farm prices need to be kept high enough to support people adequately; that people have a right to live in decent housing—and that the government has a responsibility to *do something* to bring about these results.

The New Deal also included the ideas that the banks and stock markets and other financial institutions should be watched over and regulated by the government to be sure the interests of the people are protected; and that the government should watch over and regulate employment practices—should prohibit child labor, should set limits on the length of the work week, and should require that higher wages be paid for overtime work. And there were many other changes to the economic system—all away from laissez-faire toward more influence and control by government in the economy.

A NEW PHILOSOPHY: CHALLENGE TO LAISSEZ-FAIRE

Perhaps we could summarize the philosophy of the New Deal this way:

> *It is the responsibility of the government to be concerned about the operation of the economic system, and about the material welfare of the people. The government has a responsibility to keep the system running properly, to oversee all of the activities within the economic system which might adversely affect the lives and conditions of the people of the society, and to see to it that everyone has an opportunity to share in the high level of well-being which this "modern economic system" can produce.*
>
> *Even those people who are unproductive—because of health or age or unemployment or some other misfortune—should still get a share of the output. The government should take some income from the productive people and give it to the unproductive ones.*

What a basic change this New Deal was! The American economic system *before* the New Deal was quite a different system from the American economic system *after* the New Deal. *Quite* a different system! It's no wonder that many people—especially those who had been enjoying most of the benefits of the pre-New Deal system—were strongly opposed to President Franklin D. Roosevelt's New Deal.

But in 1933 and the years following, almost everyone was feeling the squeeze of the depression. Most of the people were disillusioned, confused, bewildered. The depression had been dragging on, getting worse and worse each year. People who in 1929 would have considered the New Deal subversive and un-American (or maybe even a Communist take-over!), in 1933 were ready to try anything. By then it seemed obvious to most people that sitting around waiting for the natural forces of the laissez-faire market system to solve the problem just wasn't the answer.

The real world wasn't behaving the way the neoclassical model said it should. The model just didn't fit the reality of the 1930s. So what happened? What *always* happens when the theoretical explanations don't offer workable solutions to the real world's economic problems? Pragmatism takes over. That's what happened.

THE NEW DEAL LEGISLATION AND PROGRAMS

It has been said that when Roosevelt took office he mounted his horse and galloped off in several directions at once. And really, that's sort of what he did. So many programs, each aimed at overcoming some visible problem, and some of the programs inconsistent and conflicting with each other—but there was no question that something was being done. *Action* was being taken.

A UNIQUE PERIOD IN AMERICAN HISTORY

The depression years of the Roosevelt administration are a truly unique period in American history. The things which happened during these few years brought major changes both in economics and in politics. The greatest changes were in the rapidly increasing functions of government in the economic system.

Many vital pieces of legislation were passed during the 1930s. It would be easy for you to spend an entire semester or an entire year studying the effects of the New Deal legislation on the economic system. Several books have been written about the changes wrought during these few hectic years. I hope that some day you will have the opportunity to study the interesting things that were going on then. But this book is not the place for that.

The purpose here is only to give you a quick overview of the kinds of changes which were made by the New Deal legislation and programs. Many of the programs were temporary. But many initiated permanent changes in the nature of the American economic system and in the role of government in the economy.

President Roosevelt had to do several things *immediately*. He had to get the banks open again, and make the people confident that they would *remain* open. He had to somehow get some emergency funds to the state and local governments throughout the nation, almost all of which were in bad financial shape. And he had to get some food (or some money) into the hands of the unemployed and hungry people. All three of these objectives were worked on immediately.

The most difficult objective was getting money into the hands of people— getting them employed. The government started creating new money and undertaking all kinds of programs, including local conservation projects of all kinds and, later, public works projects. What to build? Build anything any- body can think of that seems to need to be built! Even if it didn't really need to be built, maybe it was better to build it than to leave the people unemployed.

THE NATIONAL INDUSTRIAL RECOVERY ACT (NIRA), 1933, AND THE NRA

After the banks were reopened and the state and local governments were provided some emergency funds and the first steps were made toward over- coming starvation and unemployment, then attention was turned to the task of industrial recovery. The National Industrial Recovery Act was passed. It included "something for everybody."

[The Act provided for minimum prices and production limits in agriculture; it permitted labor to unionize and bargain with employers; and it permitted the business firms in each industry to get together and work out a "code of fair competition," which, in effect, gave them monopoly power over outputs, marketing territories, prices, and other things.

Truly, the National Industrial Recovery Act (NIRA) was one of the most far-reaching pieces of legislation ever passed by the U.S. Congress. It was a radical departure from the concept of competition—in the agricultural markets, in the industrial-product markets, and in the labor markets. The NIRA was based on the idea that if everybody had enough *market power*, they could keep their prices up, thus keep their incomes up, thus keep their spending up, and thus assure prosperity in the economy.

The Act also established a public works program which provided for the construction of highways, dams, housing, post offices, other public buildings, water and sewer systems—any kind of public works project anyone could think of.

The NIRA, and the National Recovery Administration (NRA) which it created, lasted only about two years. In 1935 the Act was held unconstitutional by the Supreme Court. But soon, new acts were passed reestablishing and expanding many of the provisions of the NIRA. Agricultural markets were again placed under government control, and the monopoly powers of labor (to unionize and bargain and strike) were reaffirmed and strengthened. So it's true that although the NIRA was held unconstitutional in 1935, many of the changes initiated in that Act were reestablished by new legislation and still live on today.

SOCIAL WELFARE LEGISLATION

During the early days of the Roosevelt administration, emergency funds were provided to the state and local governments to bail out the welfare programs in the state and local areas. People needed relief, but the local governments didn't have much money for relief programs. Even with the federal grants the welfare programs couldn't meet the needs. Soon it was clear that the people wanted the government to take a stronger, more continuing role in providing for economic welfare.

THE SOCIAL SECURITY ACT. In 1935, the Social Security Act was passed. This Act set up the old age and survivor's insurance program which has continued and been expanded repeatedly to the present time. This is a program of income redistribution: income from the wage earners (through social security taxes) and from the public (through taxes on businesses, which are ultimately paid by the public through higher product prices) is redistributed to people who are retired or disabled or sick or dependent survivors of wage earners. This is the OASDHI program (Old Age, Survivors, Disability, and Health Insurance Program—also more recently called the "Retirement, Survivors, and Disability Insurance and Medicare Program") which now redistributes billions of dollars of income every year.

THE FAIR LABOR STANDARDS ACT. In 1938 the Fair Labor Standards Act was passed. It established minimum wages, set the forty-hour workweek, and established various other "fair labor standards." This Act has also been continued and expanded to the present time.

THE EMPLOYMENT ACT OF 1946

One of the important pieces of New Deal legislation—legislation committing the government to an increased and continuing responsibility for the welfare of the people and for the functioning of the economy—was not passed until after the depression was over—not until the year after the sudden death of President Roosevelt in 1945.

As World War II came to an end, many people were aware that massive government spending for the war had brought an end to the great depression. So now that the war was over, what was going to happen? Many people expected another depression. It was in this atmosphere that Congress passed the *Employment Act of 1946.*

This 1946 Act did not spell out any program. It simply stated that it is the continuing responsibility of the federal government to see to it that the economy will keep operating fast enough so that people can get jobs and incomes—so that employment and production and output will be maintained. If the economic system doesn't appear to want to run at the right speed on its own power, the government is responsible for doing something to keep it running at the right speed. This Act set up the Council of Economic Advisers to keep the administration in touch with conditions in the economy, and to advise the President whenever action should be taken.

THE LONG-RANGE IMPACT OF THE NEW DEAL

It would hardly be correct to say that following the years of the depression and World War II, laissez-faire was dead in the American economy. But certainly in many ways laissez-faire had been significantly reduced. The influence of the political process on economic choices had been greatly expanded. Most of the changes that were made were more "pragmatic," trial-and-error changes than changes directed by either theory or philosophy.

But what were the economists doing all this time? If the economic theories couldn't help to explain what was going on and couldn't provide any guidelines as to what the government might do, then what were the economists doing?

You remember that back in the late 1800s economists weren't held in high esteem by laymen and policymakers because their "economic laws" didn't seem to be working in the real world. That's what happened again in the 1930s, when the accepted economic theories didn't seem to help to understand what was going on. But some economists were working on new explanations—trying to develop new ways of looking at and explaining what was going on in the world.

The economist who made the greatest contribution—the one who has had the greatest impact on economic thinking in this century (perhaps in any century) was John Maynard Keynes (KAYns). It's time now to talk about the evolution of economic ideas during the 1930s—especially about the new ideas introduced by this brilliant and outspoken Englishman, Lord John Maynard Keynes. You'll be reading about who he was and what he did in the next chapter.

REVIEW QUESTIONS

1. What was Roosevelt's New Deal? Explain the New Deal philosophy about the economic role of the government.

2. Explain how and why the New Deal was a major departure from neoclassical economics and *laissez faire*.

3. Explain the purposes and provisions of the National Industrial Recovery Act. How did the Act treat the concepts of competition and market power?

4. Discuss briefly the long-range impact of the New Deal on the American economic system.

5. What were the major pieces of New Deal legislation designed to do? Briefly discuss their purposes and provisions and their impact, both short- and long-run.

15 THE ECONOMICS OF JOHN MAYNARD KEYNES (KAYNS)

> 🔑 **KEY TERMS**
>
> - John Maynard Keynes
> - macroeconomics
> - *The General Theory of Employment, Interest, and Money* (1936)
> - *Treatise on Money* (1930)
> - *Economic Consequences of the Peace* (1919)
> - Bretton Woods
> - Special Drawing Rights (SDRs)
>
> - Keynesian economics
> - the spending and income equation
> - the income multiplier
> - the Keynesian savings gap
> - the Keynesian prescription for preventing depressions
> - monetary policy
> - fiscal policy

During the depression of the 1930s the neoclassical economists were unable to explain what was happening—or what might be done to remedy the situation.

Explanations of how the market functions when it is operating properly are not very helpful in understanding what's wrong when the market breaks down. Perhaps a "non-properly-functioning" economic system needed to be conceptualized differently—to be looked at in a different way.

NEEDED: A NEW WAY OF LOOKING AT THE ECONOMY

Think back. Every era in history which has created a new set of conditions and problems has seen philosophers and activists arise to try to explain things and/or to change them—Adam Smith and Malthus and Ricardo and

Saint Simon and Fourier and Robert Owen and Karl Marx and so many oth-ers—all arose more or less as products of their times. Each of them took on and tried to explain and/or change the real conditions of their day.

In the 1930s we needed a new way of looking at the total economy. We needed to better understand what keeps it running—and what makes it speed up or slow down. We needed to understand what is now called "macroeconomics." John Maynard Keynes gave us the new approach—the new principles and theories.

KEYNES' BOOK OFFERS A NEW GENERAL THEORY (1936)

John Maynard Keynes gave the world a new way of explaining the depression problem. His book *The General Theory of Employment, Interest, and Money* (1936)* explains how it is possible for the economy to go into a persist-ent depression. And it explains what governments can do to overcome depression.

Keynes offered *positive* suggestions. He didn't suggest (as neoclassical economists did) that we suffer along and wait for the "natural economic laws" to work things out. The Keynesian *General Theory* recommended increased government spending. And it explained why.

The first chapter of *The General Theory* consisted of a single paragraph in which Keynes slapped the economics profession in the face. Even now, more than 60 years later, some economists are still smarting from the blow. What did Keynes say? Only that neoclassical economics didn't fit the real world of the 1930s—that neoclassical economics was "misleading and disastrous" if we tried to use it in the 1930s to guide public policy. Nothing timid about Keynes!

The economics profession scurried around trying to defend its position. But as time went on, more and more people came to accept "Keynesian eco-nomics" as an essential addition to our understanding of how the market sys-tem works in the real world.

It was not that Keynesian economics invalidated neoclassical economics. Of course not. The most basic, most essential principles of economics are described and explained in neoclassical economics. But Keynes said that there are times when that model—that way of looking at the world—is more

---

*John Maynard Keynes, *The General Theory of Employment, Interest, and Money* (New York: Harcourt, Brace and World, 1936).

misleading than helpful—that sometimes the real world doesn't behave the way the model *assumes* it will behave. When that happens, the neoclassical model may lead its followers off in exactly the *wrong* direction. Keynes said that's what was happening in the 1930s.

KEYNES GAVE US MACROECONOMICS

What Keynes did was comparable, in a way, to what Adam Smith had done about 160 years earlier. Keynes looked at the real world and gave us a new way of looking at what was happening.

Many economists have shown much greater brilliance in dealing with models than in dealing with real-world issues and problems. But Keynes saw and understood the real world. And more than that. He had the unique ability to understand the real-world forces which influence and control the level of economic activity—the speed at which the economy runs.

Keynes explained the forces which control the speed of the economy. He built a theory explaining the depression—a theory which was aimed *directly* at the problem, and which offered avenues of *positive action* for dealing with it. Keynes gave us much of what we now call "macroeconomics."

KEYNES' EARLIER WRITINGS

Keynes was about fifty years old when *The General Theory* appeared in 1936. But much earlier, before he reached thirty-five, he had indicated his ability to see and understand the economic realities of the world. In 1919 he wrote a book called the *Economic Consequences of the Peace.* In this book he explained why the World War I peace agreement was unworkable. The book was straight from the shoulder; it named names, and it left no doubt that Keynes thought the whole agreement proceeding was an exercise in stupidity. He said that the agreement would break down, and he predicted serious economic disruptions as a result. The book cost him some friends. But as it turned out, he was right.

During the 1920s, Keynes was the editor of the *Economic Journal* (one of Britain's most honored economic publications). He continued to write articles criticizing the government. In the mid-1920s he attacked Britain's decision to return to the gold standard. He predicted that this move would be harmful to the nation and that it would fail. But no one seemed to be listening. Again, as it turned out, he was right.

In 1930, Keynes published his two-volume *Treatise on Money.* This *Treatise* explained many of the concepts which later were integrated into his *General*

Theory in 1936. But in 1930, no one was ready for a "new look" in economics. Everyone expected the depression to be short. Soon everything would be rolling along again. Keynes disagreed. He saw some serious fundamental problems. Some of these are explained in his *Treatise on Money.* But at that time no one was listening very well.

As the years passed and the depression deepened, Keynes continued to give advice to government leaders. He wrote an open letter to President Roosevelt (published in the *New York Times* in 1933) and he served as occasional adviser to Roosevelt in the 1930s. In 1936 *The General Theory* was published. But it would not be until several years later that most of the economic theory expressed in that book would become integrated into the thinking of most economists.

KEYNES AT BRETTON WOODS

From the time *The General Theory* appeared in 1936 until his death ten years later, Keynes continued to play an active role as an adviser to governments on national and international policy. One of his last major involvements was in the Bretton Woods conference (at Bretton Woods, New Hampshire) in 1945. There the postwar system of international exchange was worked out.

At Bretton Woods, Keynes suggested that some alternative to gold should be used in international finance. He suggested using some kind of "paper credits" instead of gold. But at that time the idea of using paper credits was just too far out. He predicted that the time would come when the world would have no choice but to move to some such system. Almost twenty-five years later the major nations agreed that it was essential to establish paper credits as an alternative to gold in balancing international financial accounts. A system of "special drawing rights" (SDRs) was initiated in the late 1960s. These SDRs are deposits in the international monetary fund held by all of the major trading nations, and are used for balancing international payments between nations.

John Maynard Keynes was one of the great economists. Most of the economic concepts and principles we now call "macroeconomics" have their roots in Keynes' *General Theory of Employment, Interest, and Money.* His ideas have had a very real influence on the lives of all of us. No economic discussion, no prescription for attacking an economic problem, no economic policy has been quite the same since. Even those who have consistently opposed "the Keynesian way" of looking at the world have been unable to ignore Keynesian economics.

KEYNESIAN ECONOMICS

What is Keynesian economics? It's a different way of looking at the world. It looks *directly* at the questions: What determines the *speed* of the economy? What determines *how much* (in total) will be produced? What determines whether or not all the labor, capital, land (the factors of production) will be employed as fully as their owners (and the society) want them to be employed?

THE MARKET SYSTEM WAS "FLOODED OUT"

During the depression it was obvious that the total (aggregate) supply of goodsin the market was greater than the total (aggregate) demand for these goods. In other words, *total spending for output* was not great enough to buy up all of the output. So businesses slowed down or stopped production.

Unemployment went from bad to worse. Many businesses collapsed. When businesses collapsed, workers lost their jobs so they couldn't buy things.

Many farmers couldn't sell their products. So they couldn't buy tractors, gasoline, or fertilizer. The tractor, gasoline, and fertilizer companies had to cut back. Banks couldn't collect on their loans so many of them failed.

The moving finger of economic ruin touched more and more units in the economy—more households, industries, firms. Things just kept getting worse. Why? And what could be done? These are the questions that Keynesian economics came forward to try to answer.

KEYNES FOCUSED ON THE "SPENDING SECTORS"

Keynes focused *directly* on the problem: not enough total spending. It's obvious that if the people and businesses and governments are spending enough to buy up all of the output of the economy, then the economy will keep producing: Full speed ahead! And it's just as obvious that when the total amount that the people and businesses and governments are buying *decreases*, then total output and employment will slow down. If businesses can't sell enough to keep all their workers busy, then they will lay off some workers. Keynes focused on this obvious fact.

Keynes analyzed total spending. He took it apart and looked at *who* was doing the spending, and why. Essentially, he split the "spending stream" into two sectors—spending for consumer goods, and spending for capital goods. Then he tried to get at the *motives* underlying each kind of spending—to try to see what underlies, what determines how much *each sector* of the spending stream will spend. The Keynesian idea: If we can understand the *causes* of spending increases or decreases by each sector, then maybe we can understand why the economy speeds up and slows down. And maybe we can induce total spending to adjust to the desired level.

The Keynesian Spending and Income Equation

The basic Keynesian spending and income equation says that consumer spending (C) plus investment spending (I) equals total spending for output (and therefore total income) in the economy. The equation is:

$$C + I = Y$$

where Y is the symbol for national income.

Suppose consumers are saving more (spending less). Then unless investors are spending more, national income will go down. What can be done?

Keynes said the government can follow easy money policies and cut taxes and perhaps stimulate increases in either C or I (or both). Or the government can increase its own spending and add that much more spending into the income stream. Then the equation becomes:

$$C + I + G = Y$$

where G is the symbol for government spending.

The Income Multiplier

Keynesian economics says that when the government increases its spending (G), this generates more income for people. As people receive more income, they, in turn, spend more. This generates more income for others who, in turn, spend more. This is the Keynesian "income multiplier" concept.

The multiplier can also be triggered by easy money and lower interest rates, which will stimulate increases in both investment spending (I) and consumer spending (C), or the government could stimulate the economy by lowering taxes and leaving both consumers and investors with more money to spend.

Keynesian economics says that in times of depression the government can and should use all of these "monetary and fiscal policies" to try to trigger the income multiplier and get the economy back on the road to recovery. And Keynesian economics offers much more—more detailed breakdowns and analyses of the spending-income flow in the economy, and many more policy recommendations. But you've already seen enough to understand the basics of the Keynesian approach.

So you can see that Keynesian economics is the economics of understanding *why* each sector of the spending stream (essentially consumers and businesses) spend as much as they do, and what makes their spending change. Also, Keynesian economics tries to explain how adjustments in the money markets and in government spending and taxes (and other things) can influence the total spending flow and thereby influence the speed at which the economy will run.

THE KEYNESIAN "SAVINGS GAP"

There was another important principle in Keynesian economics which challenged one of the basic conclusions of neoclassical economics—the conclusion that the forces of the market system would automatically maintain full employment in the economy. According to the neoclassical economists, *price adjustments,* if permitted to occur without interference, would move the economy to full employment. The prices (or wages) of any "surplus" (unemployed) resources (labor, or other inputs) would go down until it became profitable for businesses to employ them. These price adjustments would continue until full employment was achieved.

Keynes challenged this neoclassical conclusion by introducing the idea of the *savings gap.* The idea is that as the economy grows and prospers, most people enjoy rising incomes. As this happens they tend to save more—to spend a smaller proportion of their incomes on consumer goods. As people save more, this amounts to a withdrawal—a drain from the "spending flow" (the "income stream") of the economy.

When a person earns $100 in a week, that means that person has been responsible for adding at least $100 worth of output into the economic system. But suppose that person only buys $80 worth of the output. That leaves $20 worth of output still in the market, unbought (unless someone else buys it).

INVESTMENT CAN OFFSET SAVINGS

Suppose businesses decide that they want to increase their investment spending. Perhaps they will buy up all of the unbought (surplus) output left in the economy by the savers. If so, the total or "aggregate" demand in the economy will be great enough to buy up all of the output and there will be no surplus (unbought) products left in the market. When that happens, it means that *investment injections* in the economy are great enough to offset the *savings withdrawals*. When investment spending equals savings, there is no problem of excess supply (or insufficient demand) in the nation's markets.

THE "SAVINGS GAP" TENDS TO GET LARGER

As the economy keeps growing and people's incomes keep rising, the percentage of their incomes which they withdraw from the spending stream (by saving) increases. This causes a larger "savings gap" which must be made up by more investment spending. If businesses don't decide to increase their investment spending enough to offset this growing "savings gap" then all of the output will not be bought. Surpluses will develop in the economy. When businesses can't sell all of their products they cut back production and lay off workers. So there will be increasing unemployment.

Unemployed people don't spend as much money. So as unemployment increases, total spending decreases even more. This causes businesses to cut back production even more and results in even more unemployment. So the economy winds up with a recession. Maybe depression.

According to Keynesian analysis, the unemployed workers *might* be willing to try to get jobs at lower wages and thereby increase their chances of getting rehired. But in the "real modern world" (as contrasted with the "model world" of neoclassical economic theory) Keynes did not expect wage and price adjustments to solve the problem. Wage and price adjustments did not seem to be doing much to overcome the depression in the 1930s when Keynes was writing.

WHAT CAN BE DONE ABOUT THE "SAVINGS GAP"?

If we accept the Keynesian theory of the "savings gap," what can be done? Keynes prescribed monetary policy (easing money and lowering interest rates to try to stimulate more investment and consumer spending) and government fiscal policy (adjusting taxes and government spending) to offset the savings gap.

The government should ease money and should cut taxes and leave people more money to spend. Also, when necessary the government should increase its own spending (with newly created money) to offset the deficiency of investment spending. It should buy up the surplus products, employ the unemployed workers, and get the economy moving again.

In short, the Keynesian idea was this: "If private investment is not great enough to offset the savings gap, then money should be eased and interest rates lowered to stimulate more investment. If that doesn't work, then government spending should be increased and/or taxes should be cut enough to make up the difference. Then full employment and full production in the economy can be maintained."

You can see how different the Keynesian prescription was from the "hands-off" recommendations of the neoclassical economists. You can see that each approach looks at the world in quite a different way than the other.

THE PRAGMATIC KEYNESIAN PRESCRIPTION

See the great importance of Keynesian (and neo-Keynesian, or post-Keynesian) economics? It tells us how to prevent and how to overcome depressions! How? By doing things to *keep total spending high*—high enough to keep the economy prosperous.

Once we focus on the *spending flow,* then the most *direct* government policy to overcome depression becomes obvious: Spend more money. Do things to get businesses and consumers to spend more money. In a nutshell, this was the Keynesian prescription.

Much of what was done during Roosevelt's New Deal went along (more or less) with the Keynesian prescription—not because the actions were theoretically inspired, but because they were pragmatic. They seemed to be aimed in the right direction. When people are unemployed in every little town in the country, it's quite obvious that if the government will create enough money and spend it to hire all the unemployed people to build new post offices and other things, unemployment will be overcome.

See how obvious and pragmatic the Keynesian prescription was? Maybe it wouldn't be too far off to say that Keynes gave Roosevelt and the Congress a theory to justify what Roosevelt and the Congress were already doing anyway!

Remember how that's sort of what Adam Smith did, too, for the industri-

OF SPECIAL INTEREST

FOR AN INTERESTING DISCUSSION AND EVALUATION OF THE LASTING IMPACT OF THE THEORIES OF KEYNES AND MARX, SEE: DUDLEY DILLARD, "KEYNES AND MARX: A CENTENNIAL APPRAISAL," JOURNAL OF POST KEYNESIAN ECONOMICS, VOL. VI, NO. 3 (SPRING, 1984): 421–432.

alist capitalists? He gave them a theory to justify what they were already doing.

It's interesting that the two men sometimes referred to as the greatest economists of all time—Smith and Keynes—did not make their contributions by refining and making more precise the theoretical models of economics. Instead, they conceptualized and explained previously unexplained (or inadequately explained) real-world conditions. Both left many of the refinements to the generations of economists who would follow.

DID THE KEYNESIAN PRESCRIPTION WORK?

Did the Keynesian prescription work during the 1930s depression? To some extent, maybe. Many people got government jobs. But the prescription wasn't really tried. Not *really*. There were lots of anti-Keynesians around in the 1930s!

The depression lingered on until the government began its massive military spending program for World War II. When the wartime spending began, the depression came to a rapid end. Almost immediately the problem became *too much* total spending. So the government had to start working on the opposite problems: shortages, and inflation. During World War II, tight controls were established on wages and prices. Most consumer goods and industrial products were placed under direct government allocation and carefully rationed among the competing, high-priority uses.

ECONOMIC CONDITIONS AFTER WORLD WAR II

After the war the economy kept on booming. What about the widely expected postwar depression? It never came. During the 1950s and '60s there were a few periods of economic slowdown (recession) but never a threat of serious, prolonged depression. Technological progress was phenomenal—from propeller planes to trips to the moon in only about *two decades*—and from account books to modern electronic computers in less time than that. Truly phenomenal.

The late '40s and the '50s and '60s were generally good years in the U.S. and world economies. Not flawless, but not bad. Much progress was made. Most people were living better and better, having more things all the time.

Quietly, mostly unnoticed, some serious problems were ready to erupt and force themselves on the attention of the world. And so they did. The chapters in Book Two (which follows) give the highlights of how it all happened. Also those chapters tell about what the economists were doing and thinking as they tried to keep up with this explosively changing world as we come to the end of the twentieth century.

REVIEW QUESTIONS

1. What is the basic focus of Keynesian economics? Is it primarily micro- or macroeconomics? Explain.

2. Explain the Keynesian "spending and income" equation and explain how it is used.

3. Explain the Keynesian concept of the "savings gap." What solutions does Keynesian economics prescribe to offset the effects of this gap? How are the recommended policies supposed to work?

4. What is government fiscal policy? And monetary policy? What role does each play in Keynesian economics?

5. If you had been the President of the United States back in the 1930s, who would you rather have had as economic advisers—neoclassical economists or Keynesians? Explain why. (*Note:* There is no "right" or "wrong" answer to this question.)

BOOK TWO

THE RAPIDLY CHANGING WORLD AND CONFLICTING THEORIES OF MODERN TIMES

PART SIX

RECENT DEVELOPMENTS AND CURRENT CONTROVERSIES IN ECONOMIC THEORY

The further evolution of Keynesian economics, the ascendency of the monetarists, rational expectations theory, and supply-side economics.

16 THE FURTHER EVOLUTION OF KEYNESIAN ECONOMICS

After World War II, the economy just kept on booming. The government cut back its spending, but consumers and businesses spent enough to more than make up the difference.

PEOPLE SPENT THEIR WARTIME SAVINGS AND THE ECONOMY BOOMED

During the war years, consumers were making good incomes. But they couldn't buy the consumer goods they wanted because the goods weren't available. The nation's resources were being allocated to the war effort—not to the production of consumer goods.

After the war, people's savings (mostly in government bonds) were huge. The people cashed their bonds and bought the things they wanted—new houses, new automobiles, appliances, everything. Businesses invested in new plants and equipment and hired workers and tried to meet the strong consumer demand. This created a strong business demand for new capital and for raw materials and labor. Total spending in the economy was high. Inflationary pressures were great. When the wartime price controls were removed, prices moved up fast. Inflation!

The Federal Reserve bought the bonds that the people, businesses, and banks were cashing. This poured money into the economy. The new money went into the banks, creating new reserves and permitting the money supply to expand rapidly. Then in 1949 demand slacked. This lessened the inflationary pressures. But in 1950 the Korean War caused government spending to increase, and prices again began increasing rapidly. So what happened? Price and wage controls were imposed. The controls were kept on until the end of the Korean War.

THE ECONOMY WAS SLUGGISH DURING THE LATE 1950S

During the eight years of the Eisenhower administration (1953–1960) the economy experienced three recessions. Growth was not as rapid as many economists thought it should be. During much of that period, unemployment was higher than many economists considered necessary.

As the Eisenhower administration was coming to an end, the economy was suffering a fairly serious recession—the worst of the postwar era. It was in this setting that John F. Kennedy defeated Republican candidate Richard Nixon and was elected president. Nixon said it was the recession that cost him the presidency.

KEYNESIAN ECONOMICS AFTER WORLD WAR II

Kennedy entered the White House with the pledge to "get the economy moving again." During the Kennedy-Johnson era the theories of Keynesian economics were used for the first time to guide public policy. But before you get into that you need to know about how the Keynesian ideas were evolving in the years following World War II.

THE KEYNESIAN PRESCRIPTION: UNBALANCE THE BUDGET

The basic idea of the Keynesian prescription for overcoming unemployment and depression was to unbalance the government budget. The government would reduce its "tax withdrawals" from the income stream at the same time that it would increase its "spending injections" into the income stream. The government would create more money to finance its expenditures and push new money into the spending-income flow of the economy.

OF SPECIAL INTEREST . . . _____

THE TERMS "POST-KEYNESIAN," AND "NEO-KEYNESIAN" ARE ALSO USED TO REFER TO THE IDEAS AND THEORIES OF KEYNES AS FURTHER DEVELOPED AND REFINED DURING THE FIVE DECADES SINCE KEYNES' DEATH IN 1946. IN THIS BOOK WE JUST USE THE WORD "KEYNESIAN" TO REFER TO ALL OF THE IDEAS AND THEORIES BASED ON THE ORIGINAL IDEAS OF J. M. KEYNES.

How was this idea of "unbalancing the budget on purpose" received following World War II? Many economists accepted the Keynesian prescription in the 1940s and '50s. But *public policy* did not reflect this attitude.

Many political, Congressional, and business leaders—and ordinary citizens too—had strong "balance the budget" attitudes. During the sluggish years of the 1950s there was no *purposeful* budget unbalancing to try to speed up the economy.

THE KEYNESIAN PRESCRIPTION: THE "NEW ECONOMICS" OF THE 1960S

It was not until the early 1960s—actually, not until 1963, the year of President Kennedy's death—that Keynesian economics was explicitly stated as public policy. It was stated by President Kennedy in his speech at the Harvard graduation in June 1963. This is the basic idea of what he said:

> *Even though we are already running a government deficit, we are going to cut tax rates and even further unbalance the budget. The economy will be so stimulated by the tax cut that soon people and businesses will be making so much more income that they will be paying much more to the government in taxes. The extra tax revenues will bring the budget into balance.*

A radical idea! Cut tax rates in order to collect more tax revenues? (The idea was that *raising tax rates* to try to balance the budget—which was what the Eisenhower administration had done—would only slow the economy even more and make the deficit *larger!*)

What had happened during the years following World War II to prepare the nation to accept such a radical idea?—the idea that *cutting* tax rates will produce more revenue? Such a policy would have been considered nonsense only a few years earlier. What brought about the change in thinking?

THE SYNTHESIS OF KEYNESIAN ECONOMICS INTO NEOCLASSICAL ECONOMICS

Perhaps the most important influence was the synthesis, or integration, of Keynesian economics into the general body of accepted economic principles. As time went on, most economists (and apparently most people) came to accept Keynesian economics—not as a substitute for, but as a necessary complement to neoclassical economics.

But *note this well:* Not *all* economists accepted Keynesian Economics into their "theoretical models" of how the economy functions. Milton Friedman was the leader of the "anti-Keynesian school" of economic thought. He and his followers held out and ultimately emerged with the powerful "monetarist challenge" to Keynesian economics. You will be reading about that soon.

How did it happen that Keynesian economics became acceptable to most economists?—and integrated into their thinking, and their economic models? Probably the greatest influence was Professor Paul Samuelson's *Principles of Economics* book.

PAUL SAMUELSON'S ECONOMICS BOOK

Samuelson's *Economics* (first edition, 1947) did an exceptionally good job of explaining the ideas and principles of Keynesian economics, not to the *exclusion* of, but *together with* the orthodox principles of evolving neoclassical economics. Samuelson's book was widely used, and soon widely imitated.

During the 1950s and '60s most of the graduates pouring out of the colleges and going into business or public administration or law or politics or most other worldly pursuits had been exposed to Keynesian economics. Most of them had some understanding of the Keynesian prescription for overcoming unemployment and recession and for keeping the economy running along at a proper clip.

See what happened? Many people had come to understand the ideas and principles of Keynesian economics. So it wasn't so mysterious any more! An increasing number of leading citizens were able to understand the Keynesian prescription and to call on the government to apply it to keep the economy going at a healthy pace.

NEOCLASSICAL ECONOMICS AND THE KEYNESIAN SYNTHESIS

Exactly what was this Keynesian synthesis?—this integration, of Keynesian and neoclassical ideas? Quite simple, really.

The neoclassical model was still accepted as a valid statement of the *market forces* which are constantly at work in the society. But the Keynesians emphasized that there were other forces, too—forces *outside* the neoclassical model—some outside of *economics* even—which sometimes would be strong enough to overpower the neoclassical market tendencies to maintain full employment—maybe even carry the world in the *opposite* direction. And when that happened, the neoclassical model would not be the best place to look for an explanation of what was happening and why—and of what might be done about it.

THE FOCUS OF NEOCLASSICAL ECONOMICS. Neoclassical economics is based on a different set of assumptions about the world and how it works, than is Keynesian economics. Neoclassical economics focuses on the forces which, if left free to operate without impediment, will always bring the economy fairly quickly and smoothly into a "long-run equilibrium" of full employment and stable prices.

In this long-run equilibrium, all resources uses will be optimized—that is, all labor, land, and capital will be directed in the most efficient ways toward the true objectives of the society. A beautiful system! But history tells us that it doesn't always work out that way in the real world.

THE FOCUS OF KEYNESIAN ECONOMICS. The Keynesians agree that the neoclassical model is an essential tool for explaining what the market forces are and how they work. But they don't believe those forces always work out in the same predictable ways.

Keynesians don't believe in the "inevitable mechanistic determination" of real-world economic events, as described in the neoclassical model. They don't believe that the normal real-world economic condition always looks like the long-run equilibrium of the neoclassical model. Therefore, when they see high unemployment and other signs that the economy isn't running as it should, they look to the ideas of Keynesian economics to help them to understand what's going on.

Keynesian economics focuses on the spending flow—on what speeds it up and what slows it down—and on what the government can do to influence the spending flow. To the Keynesians, the spending flow is what supports employment, production, and prices. When it slows down, the economy slows down. Recession.

As an economy grows and prospers, people's incomes go up. People with high incomes save a lot. They may pull so much savings out of the income stream that a depression will result. Prices may not easily adjust to end the depression as the neoclassical model says. That's when the Keynesians say the government should *take action:* follow the Keynesian prescription! Spend enough to offset the savings withdrawals. Or cut taxes so people and businesses will be able to spend more. Or promote "easy money" (low interest rates) so businesses and people will borrow and spend more.

Many economists with widely differing views can be grouped together under the Keynesian label. Most economists these days agree with some Keynesian ideas. John F. Kennedy was the first U.S. President to publicly announce his commitment to Keynesian economics.

THE KENNEDY TAX CUT PROPOSAL (1963)

In 1963 President Kennedy called on Congress for a tax cut. But it was not until 1964 that the tax cut actually came. And did it work? The answer to that depends on who you ask—a monetarist or a Keynesian. The economy really did speed up, and tax revenues really did *increase.* The American economy enjoyed increased prosperity and growth.

Some economists were critical. They didn't think the tax cut *caused* the prosperity. It's true that there were many things influencing the economy in the mid-'60s. For one thing, the growth of the money supply was fairly slow and stable—exactly what the monetarists would prescribe for prosperity and growth. Another thing was the Vietnam war. We'll talk more about that soon. But first, here's something else to think about.

THE KEYNESIAN PRESCRIPTION GENERATES CONFIDENCE

Throughout the '50s and early '60s almost everyone who took economics in college learned about the Keynesian prescription. Everyone learned that the government knew how to prevent a serious depression. Perhaps people's *confidence* that the economy was depression-free actually helped to make the economy depression-free. Consider this: As long as people are confident that depression won't come, depression can't come!

Did people's understanding of the Keynesian prescription help to stabilize the economy during the '50s and '60s? Nobody knows for sure, of course. But it's interesting to think about.

THE "SELF-FULFILLING PROPHESIES" OF DEPRESSION OR INFLATION

We know that in general, if people expect times to be good, times will be good. But if enough people *expect* bad times—either inflation or depression—then that's exactly what we are likely to have.

People *spend now,* to protect themselves from inflation. Their increased spending brings shortages, and soon we have the inflation they feared. People *save* to protect themselves from depression. When people save more (spend less), businesses don't sell as much. They cut back production and lay off workers. So what happens? Depression. See how it works? As people try to protect themselves from inflation or depression, they tend to bring on or worsen the inflation or the depression they're worrying about.

Confidence is essential. Yet without *Keynesian economics,* what prescription can the economist offer as "economic stabilization insurance"? Not much. Only that if we leave things alone and wait, eventually the natural market forces will correct the problem.

Without Keynesian economics we are right back where we were before the depression of the 1930s, with no way to prescribe effective action to revitalize the system. So who, pray tell, would throw out Keynesian economics? Milton Friedman and the other *monetarists,* that's who. Why? Because they don't think it's needed. And they don't think it works. They think the Keynesian prescription, although perhaps *seeming* to help to stabilize the economy, actually has the effect of *worsening* the problem of economic instability. You'll be reading about the monetarist challenge in the next chapter.

 REVIEW QUESTIONS

1. Briefly explain what public policy Keynesian economics prescribes for unemployment and depression.

2. Under what presidential administration was Keynesian economics first stated as public policy? Was this public policy successful? Explain.

3. What is the focus of neoclassical economic theory? Of Keynesian economics? Are these theories long-run or short-run theories? Explain.

4. Explain the synthesis of Keynesian economics into neoclassical economics. How did this synthesis occur? What role did Professor Paul Samuelson play in this synthesis?

5. Explain briefly how public confidence can play an important role in influencing macroeconomic events.

17 THE MONETARIST CHALLENGE TO KEYNESIAN ECONOMICS, AND THE "GREAT DEBATE"

In the way the monetarists perceive the world, Keynesian economics is unnecessary, irrelevant, wrong, harmful. If the monetarists' perception of the world is correct, then Keynesian economics *is* wrong and harmful. But if the monetarists' perception of the world is *not* correct, then the monetarists are doing mankind serious harm by discrediting these prescriptive tools which the Keynesians offer for dealing with economic instability, economic stagnation, and depression. So in the real world of today, this issue is very serious business.

THE ANTI-KEYNESIANS: MILTON FRIEDMAN AND THE MONETARISTS

Throughout the period of the 1940s, '50s, and '60s, while Keynesian economics was being integrated into the mainstream of economic understanding, a few economists were speaking out loud and clear against Keynesian economics. They were arguing and building their case against the whole idea of government fiscal policy—of adjusting taxes and spending to influence the economy.

The leading challengers have been (and are) Milton Friedman and his colleagues who make up the "monetarist" school of economic thought.

Friedman and his followers weren't the first monetarists. Far from it! The philosopher David Hume, one of Adam Smith's contemporaries, fairly well explained this idea more than two hundred years ago. Then in the early 1900s the Yale University economist Irving Fisher took up the cause and further refined monetary theory.

IRVING FISHER'S MONETARY ECONOMICS*

Irving Fisher explained in detail how the *quantity of money* influences only the *level of prices* (inflation or deflation) in the economy. In the 1920s the Stable Money Association was formed to push forward Fisher's monetary theory. Here's the basic idea:

A change in the size of the *money supply* is the thing that causes *prices* to change. If the money supply increases, people have more money to spend. So they start buying more things. Soon shortages appear. People have money but can't find the things they want to buy. So they start offering *more* to get what they want. Prices start going up.

The economy can't produce more goods to satisfy the increased demand because it's assumed that the economy is already at full employment. The neoclassical model says so. Remember? So output doesn't change—only prices go up.

This process continues until prices are high enough to bring everything back into balance again. If the money supply doubles, prices will double. It's as simple as that.

THE QUANTITY THEORY OF MONEY

What you've just been reading is called "the quantity theory of money." The theory says that the size of the money supply (always and everywhere) is

---

*Irving Fisher, *The Purchasing Power of Money* (New York: Macmillan, 1911).

the *root cause* of changes in the price level. Other things sometimes may seem to cause inflation—like OPEC's 1400% increase in the price of oil between the early 1970s and the early 1980s—but it's the money supply increase which is really at fault. Suppose the money supply had not been permitted to increase. Then other prices would have *decreased* as oil prices increased. There would have been no net inflation. So say the quantity theorists.

THE EQUATION OF EXCHANGE

The quantity theorists use the "equation of exchange" to illustrate their theory. The equation of exchange is a truism. It says: "The total amount being spent in the economy equals the total amount being spent in the economy." Nobody would disagree with that! Here's the equation:

$$MV = PQ$$

where:　M — is the total number of dollars in existence;

　　　　V — is the velocity of circulation—the number of times the average dollar is spent during a year;

　　　　P — is the "average price" of the "average unit of output" in the economy; and

　　　　Q — is the quantity of output—of goods and services being produced and sold in the economy.

OF SPECIAL INTEREST . . .

THE EQUATION OF EXCHANGE IS ALSO SOMETIMES EXPRESSED AS MV = PT, WHERE T MEANS "TOTAL TRANSACTIONS" IN THE ECONOMY AND V MEANS THE "TOTAL TURNOVER VELOCITY" OF MONEY. THE MV = PQ EQUATION EMPHASIZES NEW OUTPUT BEING PRODUCED AND SOLD AND NEW INCOME BEING GENERATED. THE "Q" IN THIS EQUATION IS MUCH SMALLER THAN THE "T" IN THE OTHER EQUATION. ALSO, THE "V" IN THIS EQUATION ONLY COUNTS SPENDING FOR NEW OUTPUT, SO IT IS MUCH SMALLER THAN THE TOTAL TURNOVER VELOCITY REPRESENTED BY "V" IN THE MV = PT EQUATION.

You can see that M times V equals total spending. Suppose there are exactly 600 million dollars in existence in the economy. And suppose the average velocity is one. Then total spending will be $600 million times one, equals $600 million. Or suppose V = 2. Then total spending will be $1200 million. Obviously.

Also, P times Q equals total spending. Suppose there are exactly 600 million units of goods and services being produced and sold in the economy. And suppose the average price per unit is $1. Then total spending for all this output will amount to $600 million. But suppose P = $2. Then total spending will be $1200 million.

THE QUANTITY THEORY ASSUMES THAT V AND Q ARE CONSTANT

To say that "MV = PQ" is to say that "total spending equals total spending". But the quantity theorists (and modern-day monetarists) don't stop there. They go on and say that:

1. *Velocity* is determined by the spending habits of the people and various built-in institutional factors. It does not usually change much. *Conclusion: V can be assumed to be constant.*
2. *Quantity of output* is determined by the productive capacity of the economy. The neoclassical model tells us that the economy tends to produce at its optimal "full employment" rate, which changes only slowly, and in predictable ways. *Conclusion: Q can be assumed to be constant.*

If both V and Q are constant, then the only variables in the equation are M and P. So the equation becomes, in effect:

$$\Delta M = \Delta P$$

which says that whatever happens to the quantity of money (i.e., to the size of the money supply), that's also exactly what will happen to the level of prices. If M is increasing at a 20% rate, then P also will be increasing at a 20% rate.

OF SPECIAL INTEREST . . .

IF THE OUTPUT OF THE ECONOMY (Q) HAPPENS TO BE GROWING AT A 5% RATE, THEN A 20% RATE OF INCREASE IN M WILL RESULT IN A 15% RATE OF INFLATION—SO SAYS THE QUANTITY THEORY.

Now you can understand why the monetarists say that the way (the *only* way) to control inflation is to limit the growth of the money supply. You'll be reading more about all this in the sections coming up.

ECONOMIC CONDITIONS ARE DETERMINED AUTOMATICALLY

The equation of exchange and the quantity theory of money provide an additional example of the way in which the monetarists view the functioning of the economic system. To the modern neoclassical monetarists, macroeconomic conditions are to a large extent determined by the natural forces of the market mechanism (the forces of demand and supply and price) which are illustrated in the neoclassical model.

The natural laws of economics determine what result will follow from each cause. And what if the government tried to alter the results? That would interfere with the natural forces and would be doomed to failure. So say the "modern neoclassical monetarists."*

PUBLIC POLICY IMPLICATIONS OF MONETARIST ECONOMICS

The public policy implication of the basic monetarist idea is obvious: Keep the money supply growing at the rate of output growth. Then everything will be all right. A more rapidly expanding money supply brings rising prices. A contracting money supply brings falling prices. It's inevitable!

---

*Milton Friedman, "Money-II: Quantity Theory," *The International Encyclopedia of the Social Sciences* (New York: Macmillan and Free Press, 1968).

THE MONETARIST PRESCRIPTION: HANDS OFF!

So what do Milton Friedman and the monetarists have to say about the Keynesian prescription for influencing the economy? They disagree strongly. The monetarists insist that neoclassical economics is all we need. If the growth rate of the *money supply* is properly adjusted, spending and prices and employment will adjust automatically and the economy will run properly.

To the monetarists, there's just no need to get involved with the Keynesian prescription. To do so would do harm, and no good. The government's *only* economic policy should be to control the size of the money supply and its rate of increase. As total output and trade increase, the money supply should be permitted to increase enough to finance the increased trade. But that's all.

The government's role should be to keep taxing and spending in proper balance, to work out flexible international exchange rates so international trade can come into natural balance, and to keep the money supply expanding enough to allow for growth. Those are the *only* economic stabilization policies the government should have. Beyond that, the policymakers should just relax and let nature take its course.

Even the monetarists admit that the neoclassical model doesn't work out *exactly right* in the real world. But they think it comes out close enough. And they think that if public policy follows the Keynesian prescription to influence the economy, things will be made worse—not better.

THE MONETARIST CREED: KEEP YOUR EYE ON THE MONEY SUPPLY

According to Milton Friedman and his followers, the government should never take any kind of discretionary action to influence employment or spending or wages or prices. A 4 or 5 percent limit on the expansion of the money supply will take care of the problem of inflation; automatic price adjustments and automatic market forces will take care of unemployment and depression. The government shouldn't do anything to try to make the economy run better than it runs naturally.

"Keep your eye on the money supply. Let everything else alone. If times are bad, there's nothing the government can do. If the government tries to do something it will only interfere with the natural adjustments and further destabilize the economy." So say Milton Friedman and his colleagues, the monetarists.

THE EFFECTS OF MONETARIST ECONOMICS ON PUBLIC POLICY

What effect has "Friedman economics" had on U.S. public policy? Perhaps a little during the Eisenhower administration. But certainly none during the Kennedy-Johnson administration.

During the mid to late 1960s the Johnson Administration tried to deal with the mounting inflationary pressures by direct government influence. Wage-price guideposts were set up and the power of the presidency was used to coerce big businesses and labor into going along with these guideposts. This general approach came to be known as "jawboning"—an unofficial but usually quite effective technique of arm-twisting to prevent labor and businesses from getting big wage or price increases.

Then, when President Nixon took office in January of 1969, the scene changed. President Johnson's economic advisers were replaced. President Nixon and his advisors spoke out strongly against any kind of direct controls—jawboning or otherwise.

The Congress passed a law giving the president legal powers to establish direct controls on wages and prices. But Nixon vowed that he would never use those powers. He vowed, right in the beginning and repeatedly thereafter, that as long as he was President no direct controls would be imposed. His "more-monetarist-than-Keynesian" advisers assured him that holding down the growth rate of the money supply would solve the inflation problem and that no direct controls would ever be necessary.

President Nixon was very slow to change his mind. But as it turned out, he did change his mind. You'll be reading all about that later. But for now, here's another idea in the Keynesian-monetarist argument.

HOW DOES THE ECONOMY ACHIEVE "STEADY MONEY-GROWTH?"

One question which the monetarists have not answered to the satisfaction of their Keynesian critics, is this: "Exactly how do we get the money supply to stabilize, and grow at a gradual, constant rate, year after year?"

The growth of the money supply depends mostly on the rate at which businesses and individuals are borrowing money and repaying their loans. Borrowing depends on "the desire to spend"—either for consumer goods, or for investment. Keynesian economics says that this depends a lot on people's *present* economic conditions and their *expectations* about *future* economic conditions.

Suppose the economy is in a serious depression. And suppose the money supply isn't growing at its "specified 4 or 5 percent" annual rate. Money may be very easily available for loans. Because of the available supply and slack demand for money, interest rates would be very low. So people and business-es "should" be enticed to borrow more. That would cause the money supply to resume its expansion at the prescribed rate. But suppose the people *don't* borrow more, even at the very low interest rates? What then?

WHAT IF THE MONEY GROWTH RATE DOESN'T RESPOND TO INTEREST RATE CHANGES?

Experience has shown that sometimes "borrowing and spending" deci-sions are not very sensitive to interest rate changes. During the very high interest rate environment of the late 1970s and early 1980s, businesses contin-ued to borrow and spend. But during the depression of the 1930s, even though interest rates were very low there was no rush by businesses or con-sumers to borrow and spend.

If people don't borrow and spend, then the money supply will not expand by the "steady annual rate" which the monetarists prescribe. That is, the money supply will not expand *unless* the government takes some "Keyne-sian-type" fiscal policy actions—such as reducing taxes, or creating new money and increasing its own spending.

Most Keynesians would agree that the monetarist objective of keeping the money supply growing at a slow and steady rate is (under "normal" condi-tions) a desirable objective. But the Keynesians don't think it can be achieved under all circumstances without some "Keynesian-type" fiscal policy actions on the part of government. The Keynesians don't believe that the money sup-ply will always maintain its slow and steady growth as an "automatic result" of the operation of the natural forces of the market.

SHOULD WE FOCUS ON THE LONG-RUN?— OR THE SHORT-RUN?

One basic question which explains a lot of the disagreement between the Keynesians and the monetarists, is this: Does the economy in the real world approximate the long-run results which are described in the neoclassical model? Or does the economy operate in each period, in each year, *partly* as a result of the influences described in the neoclassical model, but *also* partly as the result of various short-run influences?—shocks, and short-run fluctua-tions—which government stabilization policies *can* be used to compensate for and help to overcome?

The monetarists agree that shocks and short-run influences do have an impact on the functioning of the economy. But they say that the natural market forces will work out these shocks and short-run fluctuations by themselves in the best possible way. They say that any attempt by government policy to "help the process along" will not succeed, but instead will result in *further destabilizing* the economy.

Why do the monetarists believe "Keynesian-type" action will be destabilizing? And what do the Keynesians have to say about that? And how have recent public policies been influenced by these conflicting theories? These are things you will be reading about in the following section. But from what you already know, you can see why the monetarists are arguing *for* a "hands-off" policy by government—and *against* the use of any Keynesian-type actions to try to overcome recession or inflation.

KEY ISSUES IN THE KEYNESIAN-MONETARIST DEBATE

The very basis, or "root cause" of the disagreement between the monetarists and the Keynesians stems from a basic difference of opinion about how to view the economy, and how the macroeconomic forces in the economy actually operate.

THE MONETARIST "LONG-RUN" VIEW

The monetarists take a long-run view, and assume that the short-run ups and downs of the economy—inflation, unemployment, etc.—are just that—short-run conditions which the natural market forces will work out in due time.

The monetarists assume that the economic forces of competition and price adjustments described in the neoclassical model will work things out soon enough—and much more effectively than would any government program!

Because of the great power and effectiveness of the "natural market forces," these forces should be allowed to control the economy. The government should never try to offset or overthrow market forces in order to achieve short-run price-level or employment or output objectives.

THE KEYNESIAN "SHORT-RUN" VIEW

The Keynesian view of the economy is different. The Keynesians accept the proposition that the natural market forces are powerful, even as they work in the "impure" real world. But they believe that much of the time these forces *will not* be sufficiently powerful to force the economy to "approximate the long-run equilibrium conditions" described in the neoclassical model.

The Keynesians agree that if we waited long enough—and if there were no additional short-run "shocks" or developments which would push the economy away from the long-run equilibrium situation described in the model—then ultimately the long-run condition described by the model *might arrive.* But the Keynesians focus on the fact that the world operates all the time in the short-run.

Keynes said it this way: "In the long-run, we are all dead!" So according to Keynesian economics, whether or not *in the long-run* the equilibrium conditions (of full employment and stable prices) described in the neoclassical model *might arrive* is irrelevant—and certainly should not be used as the *only guide* to government economic policy!

KEYNESIANS EMPHASIZE "UNRESPONSIVE PRICES"

The Keynesian position is that actual conditions in the modern economy are quite different from the *assumed conditions* in the neoclassical model—that the model therefore cannot be relied on as the "complete guide" to appropriate public policy. Keynesians emphasize the condition of *inflexible prices,* and the constant upward pressure on prices from business and labor organizations, many of which have enough power to sometimes succeed in pushing their prices up.

The Keynesians would agree with the monetarists that if spending in the economy slows down *enough*—so that surpluses in markets are widespread and unemployment is very high—then it isn't likely that very many prices will be going up. They aren't likely to go up under such depressed circumstances unless perhaps some prices are "shocked upward" by uncontrollable cost increases such as what happened in the world oil markets in the 1970s.

Keynesians also would agree that when the economy is in a depression, some workers would be willing to take jobs for less than their previous wages, and some businesses would be willing to sell their products for lower prices. But the Keynesians hold that in order for these conditions to arrive, the economy must be in a *serious* depression.

The Keynesians don't believe that such suffering and misery are necessary. And they don't believe that such misery should be forced on the people—not when appropriate Keynesian-type government policies and programs are available to overcome such depressed conditions.

KEYNES EMPHASIZED FISCAL POLICY

Those who accept the Keynesian view of the economy and of the macro-economic forces at work, see an important role for government in economic stabilization. They focus on the flow of spending, and they prescribe government action to try to adjust this flow of spending as near as possible to the "full employment and stable prices" level.

The government is supposed to maintain a stable, growing economy. In the original Keynesian model the government was to achieve this objective primarily through using fiscal policy—taxing more and spending less to hold down excess demand; taxing less and spending more to speed up spending when the consumer and business sectors are not spending enough to maintain full employment. The government is supposed to support its fiscal policies with appropriate monetary policies—tightening money and raising interest rates to help to hold down excess demand; easing money and lowering interest rates to speed up spending when the economy is depressed.

FISCAL POLICY STABILIZATION IS NO LONGER FEASIBLE

Back in the depression years of the 1930s, the Keynesian model gave a pragmatic approach for overcoming the depression. Using government spending to stimulate the economy made sense. It was politically appealing. But by the 1990s it was obvious that this "fiscal policy" approach to economic stabilization was not a realistic option.

By the 1990s we had seen several decades of huge government deficits. The national debt had soared to more than $5 trillion. Annual interest payments on the debt had risen to more than $330 billion.

By the 1990s the focus had to change to: <u>Cut the budget deficit!</u> Stop the growth of this monstrous national debt! Stop the bleeding from this constantly increasing outflow of interest payments! And the idea of stabilizing the economy by adjusting taxes and spending? No way!

Only if the economy was threatened with serious depression would fiscal policy once again become a feasible tool for economic stabilization. You'll be reading all about that in Chapter 22. But first you need to know more about the monetarist position.

THE MONETARIST FEAR OF "OVERKILL"

The monetarists hold that if the government tries to follow the Keynesian prescription, not only will it be unsuccessful, it will *worsen* the fluctuations in employment and prices. The monetarists say that whenever the economy has problems of either unemployment or inflation, the government should maintain a slow and stable rate of increase in the nation's money supply. Then the problems soon will be corrected through natural market forces.

The monetarists say that if the government tries to come in and offset a "too fast" or "too slow" rate of total spending, it will be adding its "corrective" influence into the economy *at the same time* that the natural market forces are exerting *their* corrective influence. The total effect will be to *over-correct* the situation and force the economy to overshoot the desired equilibrium. We will wind up with *the opposite* problem!

If the government tries to correct for *too little spending* (to overcome recession and unemployment), soon the economy will find itself with *too much spending*. Serious inflation is likely to result. If the government tries to correct for *too much* spending (to overcome inflation), soon we are likely to wind up with too little spending (recession and unemployment).

THE MONETARIST POSITION: A PROBLEM OF "RESPONSE-LAGS"

The monetarist position is that there is a natural pattern of almost "mechanical relationships of causes and effects" in the economy. ("When you pull this lever, then this result is certain to occur.") But the important problem is this: No one can tell you *how soon* these results will occur.

The monetarists say that when we have inflation, if you bring down the rate of growth of the money supply, you will bring down the rate of inflation. They agree that the reduced money supply will result in reduced spending and some increased unemployment—a recession—but they are absolutely certain that the inflation rate will come down. But there are "lags"—some time delay—between the slowing of the money supply growth rate and the slowing of the inflation rate. The monetarists believe that in general these lags are not very long—no more than a few months—so we should hold tight on the money supply and wait.

EMPIRICAL EVIDENCE (REAL-WORLD FACTS), COMING UP LATER

Later on, you'll be reading about what happened in the past in the U.S. economy. You'll find out about what happened with money supply changes, inflation rates, interest rates, unemployment rates, and other economic variables. And you'll get a chance to see which theories seemed to do the best job of explaining what happened.

But first, there are some other theories you need to understand. Then you'll be able to use the U.S. economic experience to test those theories, too. What theories? Rational expectations, and supply-side economics. That's what you'll be reading about in the next chapter.

REVIEW QUESTIONS

1. Briefly outline and explain the key issues in the monetarist-Keynesian debate. What is the "real-world" importance of these issues?

2. Briefly explain Irving Fisher's monetary theory. Why is it called the quantity theory of money? How is this theory related to neoclassical economics? And to the modern monetarist position?

3. State the assumptions of the quantity theory of money. What would the Keynesians say about these assumptions?

4. What is the monetarist prescription for influencing the economy? What is the role of government in the monetarist prescription? How do the monetarists defend their position?

5. What influences money supply growth? And why is it sometimes not easy to keep it growing at a gradual, constant rate?

6. Discuss the "long-run vs. short-run" issue. What do the monetarists say? The Keynesians? What is the "real-world" importance of this issue?

7. Discuss the political feasibility of using fiscal policy for economic stabilization. Have their been times when such policy was politically appealing? Politically infeasible? Explain.

18 RATIONAL EXPECTATIONS THEORY, AND SUPPLY-SIDE ECONOMICS

During the 1970s and early 1980s two new theories were gaining increasing acceptance: the theories of "rational expectations," and of "supply-side economics." Both of these theories work within the basic assumptions of neoclassical economics, and both challenge the theoretical propositions of Keynesian economics. You'll be reading about these two theories throughout this chapter.

THE "NEW CLASSICAL" THEORY, BASED ON "RATIONAL EXPECTATIONS"

During the 1970s a new attack by neoclassical economists was mounting against the Keynesians. This group of anti-Keynesians put forth the "new classical" theory, based on "rational expectations." This new theory leads to the conclusion that any stabilization policy which the government might decide to undertake (and which the spending units in the economy—businesses, consumers, financial institutions, etc.—might have "rationally expected" the government to undertake) would be doomed to failure.

The basic idea of the "rational expectations" theory is this: When economic decision-makers (consumers, businesses, etc.) expect the government to initiate a certain economic stabilization policy, then these decision-makers will take action to protect themselves—to "maximize their own positions" in the light of the "rationally expected" effects of the government policy. As they do this, they will make it impossible for the government's stabilization policy to work as planned.

THE LOGICAL STEPS OF THE THEORY

The theory of "rational expectations" is quite complex. But the basic outline of the theory can be summarized in the following steps:

1. First, we must assume the truth of the old saying, "Everybody makes mistakes but only a fool makes the same mistakes over and over." Not many people would disagree with that.
2. After this first basic premise, the theory goes on with a series of steps with which not everyone would agree. The second step is that when government takes Keynesian-type actions to try to stabilize the economy, that tricks people into doing things which ultimately will worsen their economic condition.
3. After the government has done its "Keynesian-type stabilizing tricks" once or twice, people catch on. The realize that if they do what the government policymakers expect them to do, they will wind up being hurt again, just as before.
4. Since people (and businesses, financial institutions, etc) "rationally expect" to be harmed if they respond to the government policies in the way that the government policymakers *expect* them to, they look at the situation differently now. They *do not* do what the government stabilization policymakers *wanted* and *expected* them to do.
5. Because people's "rational expectations" tell them not to respond to government stabilization policies in the "expected way," the government stabilization policies are doomed to failure. The only significant effect of stabilization policies under these circumstances would be to interfere with the efficient operation of the economy.

   In the case of anti-recession policies the only effect would be to cause inflation—not to increase production and employment which was the objective of the policies in the first place. So any attempt to use Keynesian-type stabilization policies to overcome recession would not help at all— would only make matters worse.
6. Following these logical steps, the conclusion is obvious: Government should *never* introduce any Keynesian-type stabilization policies. Instead,

government should make it quite clear that it is *never going to use* any Keynesian-type stabilization policies.

> *The government should emphasize that its only "stabilization policy" will be to permit the money supply to expand by a slow and constant rate (four or five percent per year). Then the economic decision-makers (consumers, businesses, etc.) will make their decisions based on this assurance that the government will not "meddle" in the economy to try to overcome or lessen the effects of any recession which might appear.*

The "rational expectations" theorists (led by Robert Lucas of the University of Chicago) put forth the hypothesis that when everyone in the economy knows that the government will maintain slow and constant money growth, then they will know that they have no cause to "rationally expect" continued inflation. In this stable environment they will be able to make proper decisions. They will follow the "natural laws" of the neoclassical model and thereby ensure that the economy will be as stable as it ever could be—that any recessions which may occur will be short-term and self-correcting.

Recessions are thought to be a natural part of the functioning of the market system. People should learn to accept them as that. They should not call on government policy to try to do anything about them because active government stabilization policies can't help and will make matters worse.

RATIONAL EXPECTATIONS, AND THE TRADITIONAL MONETARIST POSITION

You can see that the rational expectations theory as currently developed leads to exactly the same government policy recommendations as Friedman and the monetarists have been advocating all along. But rational expectations theory arrives at the same conclusion in a different way.

The logic of the more traditional monetarist position is this: The natural market forces for overcoming recession and inflation are *powerful*, and *effective*, but they operate with *time lags*. The economy *ultimately* will correct itself—but not *immediately*. If the government undertakes any stabilization policies to try to achieve a *more immediate* correction of either recession or inflation the *ultimate* result will be overkill. When the government's corrective actions are added to the already powerful corrective forces of the market, the economy will overshoot the objective of long-term stability and growth. Government anti-inflation efforts will cause recession; anti-recession efforts will cause inflation.

The rational expectations theory doesn't focus on the effect of these "time lags." It focuses on the way in which people's *expectations* of the effects of government stabilization policies cause them to behave differently—and how this "change of behavior" renders the government's stabilization policies not only ineffective but also destabilizing. The following section gives some examples so you can see how the rational expectations theory explains this.

EXAMPLES OF "RATIONAL EXPECTATIONS" AT WORK

Exactly how do the "rational expectations" of people and businesses prevent government stabilization policies from working? This section gives two examples of ways in which Keynesian-type stabilization policies are *supposed* to work. Then for each it explains the way in which the new theory says that people's "rational expectations" will prevent these policies from working.

EXAMPLE 1. One way government tries to overcome unemployment and recession is to create new money and increase its own spending. It spends on such things as public works projects and it buys products from businesses. This stimulates businesses to hire more labor and buy more material inputs and increase their outputs.

The Keynesian theory says that as the government does this, the spending flow in the economy will increase. The newly-employed workers will spend more money, and demand throughout the economy will increase. Soon the recession will be overcome as production and employment speed up. The "rational expectations" theory says this won't happen. Here's how the theory explains why not:

1. Suppose government increases its spending to try to induce production and employment to increase. Businesses will respond by producing and selling more to government. They will do this because their "rational expectations" tell them that government spending will cause their output prices to go up *faster than* their costs will go up. Workers will be working for wages which don't go up as fast as prices go up. So businesses will make more profits. This is what stimulates businesses to expand their operations, employ more workers, and speed up the economy.

   Note: Keynesian economists would argue that this is not a true picture of the real world—that in the real world, businesses will sell more as government stimulates demand even if prices do not rise—or even if wages rise as rapidly as do prices. In the Keynesian model, more demand creates more supply. Remember?

2. The "rational expectations" theory says that after the government has used its "increased government spending" approach two or three times, labor catches on. Workers soon come to realize that when the government starts creating new money and spending more, prices soon will rise. They realize that unless they get wage increases right away (at least as much wage increase as the "rationally expected" price increase) soon they will wind up as losers.

   So workers demand (and get) higher wages. This chokes off the possibility for increased profits by businesses and prevents businesses from expanding their outputs and employing more workers as the Keynesian theory predicts. In this case it's the "rational expectations" of labor which doom the government's anti-recession policy to failure.

   Note: Keynesian theory argues that this also is a distorted view of the real world because:
   A. Wage rates are not under such complete control of labor—that it isn't realistic to assume that labor would get higher wages just because they decided that's what they wanted and what they deserved; and
   B. Depressed businesses would be happy to produce and sell more output even if their output prices did not rise, or if their labor cost increased as rapidly as their output prices might be increasing.
3. The conclusion of the "rational expectations" theory, again, is that the government's attempt to overcome recession won't work. It will only succeed in forcing prices up—causing inflation.

The theory says that only if the government could count on "catching people by surprise" (so they wouldn't have any "rational expectations" about the policy) would it be possible for the policy to work. But the theory says that "catching people by surprise" usually isn't possible. People are too sharp and have too much information about what's going on. So the obvious conclusion, again, is that the government should not try to overcome recession or depression by creating money and increasing government spending—so say the rational expectations theorists.

EXAMPLE 2. Another "Keynesian stabilization policy" designed to speed up the economy and overcome recession or depression is the "easy money" approach. It's supposed to work like this: The Federal Reserve buys bonds from banks, businesses, and individuals, and pays for the bonds with newly created money. This increases the money supply, pushes down interest rates in the money markets, and provides banks with more money to lend.

Banks with more money to lend offer loans at lower interest rates. At the lower rates, businesses are more willing to borrow and invest. With lower interest cost, more investment opportunities become profitable. Also consumers are more willing to buy houses and durable goods (automobiles, appliances, etc.) because the interest cost is lower. As businesses borrow and spend more, the economy begins to speed up. Businesses hire more people and generate more income, so people spend even more. This is the way the "easy money" policy is supposed to overcome the depression. This process continues until the economy reaches full employment.

The "rational expectations" theory demolishes this Keynesian scenario in one sentence: "Banks will not make loans at low interest rates because their 'rational expectations' tell them that the 'easy money' policy will cause *inflation*, which will push interest rates up and make low-interest loans unprofitable." Certainly banks don't want to make loans on which they expect to wind up losing money! So the "rational expectations" theory concludes that the government should not try to use "easy money" policy to try to stimulate a depressed economy. The policy would fail and would only cause inflation.

NOTE: It is generally recognized by economists and other informed people that widespread *inflationary expectations* do in fact influence people's economic decisions and therefore also influence the functioning of the economy. For example, since the high inflation period of the 1970s and early 1980s, banks and savings and loan institutions have been making loans with floating rates. If interest rates go up after the loan is made, the rate on the loan also goes up.

The fact is that, in general, businesses and consumers and governments do borrow more when rates are low, and less when rates are high. Look what happened in the mid-1980s and again early in the 1990s when there was a sharp drop in interest rates. There was a great surge in new bonds issued and sold by businesses and by state and local governments. All were borrowing more and taking advantage of the lower rates.

IS THE RATIONAL EXPECTATIONS THEORY VALID?

Now you know the "bare bones" of the "rational expectations" theory. And you know what some of the Keynesian and other non-monetarist economists have to say about it. So what do you think? Is it valid? Is it a significant contribution to our understanding of how the economy works? Or is it no more than a "spoiler attempt" by the monetarist school of thought to destroy Keynesian economics? The answer to that question depends on who you ask. It depends on the view one takes about how a real-world market-directed economic system works—about how close it comes to approximating the long-run conditions of the neoclassical model.

As one recent article says: ". . . the prevailing models of rational expectations share with neoclassical models the undesirable feature of suppressing all dynamical and short-run disequilibrium phenomena. What happens during this period of adjustment to equilibrium is of considerable interest."*

Economists on both sides of the "rational expectations" controversy have analyzed data going back several years. But their findings so far have been conflicting.

One positive thing that economists can agree on about the "rational expectations" theory is this: It reemphasizes the importance of *expectations* in economic decision-making, and it offers us a new idea about the way in which some expectations are formed. Expectations have always played an important role in Keynesian economics. Most economists would agree that *expectations* will always play an important role in influencing the functioning of the economy.

RATIONAL EXPECTATIONS THEORY AND KEYNESIAN ECONOMICS

The Keynesians focus on the *short-run changeability* of expectations as an important factor influencing economic decisions, contributing to the *short-run instability* of the economy (recession and inflation). The rational expectations theorists focus on the *long-run rationality* of expectations—based on the expected long-run effects of government policies—as an important factor influencing economic decisions and (assuming government policies are appropriately stable) contributing to the *long-run stability* of the economy.

So again, the basic difference in the "mental set" between the Keynesians and the neoclassical economists carries on into the basic difference between Keynesian economics and the rational expectations theory. That is, Keynesian economics is concerned with understanding and explaining the *dynamic short-run changes* which occur in the economy—the process by which the economy gets itself into recession or inflation and the process by which it gets itself out. The rational expectations theory concentrates on *long-run equilibrium* conditions. It doesn't focus on the dynamic process of causes and effects which move the economy to (or away from) this long-run equilibrium position.*

---

*Anthony M. Santomero and John J. Seater, "The Inflation-Unemployment Trade-Off: A Critique of the Literature," *Journal of Economic Literature*, Vol. XVI, No. 2 (June, 1978): 533.

{*Malcom Rutherford, "Rational Expectations and Keynesian Uncertainty: A Critique," *Journal of Post Keynesian Economics*, Vol. VI, No. 3 (Spring, 1984): 377–387.

The theory of rational expectations received considerable attention by some academic economists during the late 1970s and 1980s. But the theory didn't have any influence on the non-academic (business) economists who work in the "real world" and focus on what is actually happening in the economy day-to-day, month-to-month, year-to-year. These real-world economists generally dismissed the theoretical model of rational expectations as irrelevant to the understanding of how the economy actually operates.

And by the mid-1990s the rational expectations theory had lost much of its appeal, even among academic economists.

Another development in economic thinking which occurred during the 1970s and 80s was the new emphasis on "supply-side" economics. This also was to some extent an attack on Keynesian economics. But it was a different kind of attack than either the monetarist or the rational expectations attack.

The monetarist attack says that Keynesian economics has always been basically wrong about the economy and about what the government can (and should) do to stabilize the economy. Keynesian economics prescribes stabilization policies, and monetarist economics prescribes "hands-off" policies. "Supply-side" economics doesn't focus primarily on this controversy.

WHAT IS "SUPPLY-SIDE" ECONOMICS?

The basic idea of "supply-side" economics is this: If we want to slow inflation, we need to generate *more output*—more supply of products in the market. If we can succeed in doing that (assuming nothing else changes to upset the results), then the *increased supply* will keep prices from rising and that will solve the inflation problem.

How do we increase the total (aggregate) supply of output in the economy? Primarily by increasing the *productivity* of the average worker in the economy. So "supply-side" economics focuses its attention on *increasing worker productivity*, and on ways to achieve that.

When workers are receiving more income but their outputs are not increasing as much, prices must go up enough to cover those higher wages. Whenever people's incomes are going up faster than their outputs are increasing, there's no alternative. Prices must go up. The solution? Either slow the rate of increase in people's incomes, or increase the rate of growth of output. That's simple enough.

In a few minutes you'll be reading about some conflicting ideas about how to achieve these objective of increasing the rate of growth of output. But first, how does supply-side economics relate to the Keynesian-monetarist debate?

"SUPPLY-SIDE" ECONOMICS AND THE KEYNESIAN-MONETARIST DEBATE

Where does "supply-side economics" fit in the Keynesian-monetarist controversy? It doesn't, really. But it makes the Keynesian prescription somewhat irrelevant.

Keynesian economics focuses on "demand-side" economics. Keynesian economics is concerned with the forces which determine total spending (total, or "aggregate" demand) in the economy. It's concerned with the ways in which government actions can adjust this total spending or aggregate demand flow to achieve full employment and stable prices. "Supply-side" economics looks at the *other side* of the question.

Supply-side economics recognizes that the economic circumstances which exist in the American economy today are greatly different than they were back in the depression of the 1930s—back when Keynes was offering his stabilization policy recommendations.

During the depression the economy was glutted with supply. The demand to buy the output just wasn't there. It made sense, both pragmatically and in Keynesian theory, to concentrate on the demand-side problem. The question then was: "How do we increase the spending flow enough to get all these surplus products in this supply bought up and get the economy back into production again?"

In the American economy of the early 1970s and 80s the situation was very different. A slow rate of productivity growth throughout most of the 1970s, together with constantly increasing incomes of the people, had clearly led to a "supply-side" problem. So by then the question had become: "How do we increase output per worker (supply) enough so that these higher incomes won't keep on pushing prices up?"

CONFLICTING IDEAS ON HOW TO INCREASE PRODUCTIVITY

In the early 1980s everyone seemed to agree on the *need* for a new focus on supply-side economics—on doing something aimed at increasing the productivity of the American economy. But everyone *did not* agree on how this might be best achieved. Almost everyone can agree that increasing productivity requires *increased efficiency* in the production process—that more efficient technology, machinery and equipment, resource management, and a more highly skilled labor force, are required. But how do we achieve that?

Here are some suggested approaches which were being put forward by various individuals and groups in the late '70s and early '80s:

- A reduction of cost-increasing government regulations;
- Reduced taxes on businesses to provide more incentive and more cash flow for investment in more and better capital;
- More emphasis by corporations on long-run productivity improvement and less emphasis on "maximizing profits in the present quarter";
- Improved education and training programs and personnel policies for employees;
- Changing the "reward structure" to reward *productivity* more than seniority;
- Stimulating and rewarding truly innovative activities of any kind by anybody, either labor or management;
- Eliminating government prohibitions to competition and letting the less efficient businesses fall by the wayside to make room for more efficient ones;
- Reduced concern about "equal opportunity" and "consumer protection" and more concern with increasing productivity and competition and "let the devil take the hindmost";
- Eliminating productivity-reducing "job rules" required by some labor-management contracts which slow the introduction of high-technology production techniques;
- Reducing welfare, unemployment, and other kinds of payments which "reward people for not working";
- Developing lower-cost energy sources and reducing the dependence on high-cost imported oil;
- Eliminating government restrictions on (potentially environmentally harmful) energy developments and uses, such as nuclear power, high sulphur coal, strip mining, etc.;
- Increasing the rewards for invention and innovation;
- Convincing the labor force and the general public of the "basic truth" of the "work ethic" and that the "good life" for an individual and for the society comes from increasing productivity;
- Working out "social contract" arrangements between management and labor in each industry and firm (with government's assistance and support) so that management and labor will become partners (not adversaries) in working for increased productivity;

- Establishing government "targets" for productivity increases in each industry and providing rewards and imposing penalties to induce businesses to meet their established targets;
- Establishing government "labor force plans" and inducing people to take training and to move into high productivity occupations;
- Nationalizing the big corporations and establishing government management teams to plan and manage the activities of these businesses for maximum increases in productivity;
- And the list could go on and on.

THE CHOICES ARE NOT EASY

As you look at this list of possible approaches you can see why there would be much disagreement about what should be done. Nobody would suggest that *all* of the possible approaches should be tried. Obviously not. Several of the approaches conflict with each other. And as you can see, some of them would involve basic changes in the nature of the American economic system. You'll be reading more on this issue in Part Eight.

PRODUCTIVITY GROWTH PICKS UP AFTER 1982

Following three years of almost zero productivity growth, in the third quarter of 1982 output per worker-hour showed a significant increase. In the quarters after that, the healthy growth of U.S. worker productivity was becoming increasingly evident. Then in the fourth quarter of 1983 in U.S. manufacturing industries there was a phenomenal productivity increase of 5.7 percent.

The title of the cover story of the February 13, 1984 *Business Week* is "The Revival of Productivity." At that time (early 1984) some experts were predicting that annual growth rates of U.S. output per worker-hour could be as high as 3 percent per year for the forseeable future. Why? Several reasons:

New technological advances. More and better capital to work with. Stable energy prices. Fewer governmental regulations. Labor-management cooperation to increase worker productivity. And supply-side economics tax cuts designed to encourage savings and investment.

During the 1981–82 recession (which you'll be reading all about soon), both labor and management learned a useful lesson in economics. They found out: "We must work together, work harder, and work smarter if we're going to survive in this new world of international competition."

By early 1984 this revival of the growth of productivity was being hailed by some observers as the best economic news of the past decade. Increased output per worker-hour brings more output per person. That permits higher wages and higher incomes, with no inflationary pressures. Increasing productivity can bring years of prosperity without serious inflation.

After 1984, throughout the remainder of the 1980s and on into the 1990s, worker productivity in the U.S. economy continued to increase at an average rate of about 2 percent per year. That's enough to support real, non-inflationary income increases of about 2 percent per year.

Then in the latter part of the 1990s the rate of productivity increase picked up even more. That was a very important factor supporting the "storybook economy" which existed as we entered the new milennium. You'll be reading all about that in the final part (Part 8) of this book.

IN WHICH DIRECTION SHOULD THE ECONOMIC SYSTEM CHANGE?

As you were reading through the list of possible approaches to increasing the productivity of the American economy you probably were aware that many of the suggested approaches reflect the same basic ideas as classical economics—ideas that go as far back as Adam Smith's *Wealth of Nations* in 1776. Even in the American economy in *modern times* there is much sentiment for moving toward more *laissez-faire,* increased competition, and increased reliance on the "productivity principle of distribution."

Most modern-day economists who have any faith in the neoclassical model (and that means *most* economists—including Keynesians) would agree with that. But not *all* economists agree with that.

There are some economists—some dissenters and some so-called "radical" economists—who think that our approach to increasing productivity should be in the *opposite direction*—that the government should get *more involved* in planning and directing the economy. These economists don't believe that the industrial structure which actually exists in the modern-day American economy is directed and controlled "as though by an invisible hand" to respond to and fulfill the wishes and needs of the society. They believe that the kinds of productivity improvements which will best meet the social needs can be brought about only by some kind of government planning arrangement.

These dissenting economists think there should be some basic changes in the nature of the American economic system. Specific suggestions have been offered as to what ought to be changed, and why. You will be reading about some of these recommendations in Part Eight of this book.

Before you go on with any more discussion of the recent development of economic ideas, you need to know more about how our macroeconomic problems evolved during the turbulent years of the late 1960s, the 1970s, the 1980s and on into the 1990s. That's what you'll be reading about now in Part Seven.

REVIEW QUESTIONS

1. Explain the basic idea of rational expectations theory. How does the theory conclude that the public's rational expectations render government stabilization policies useless?—even destabilizing?

2. What is supply-side economics? What questions does this theory address? And what prescription does it offer for the economy?

3. How does supply-side economics compare with Keynesian theory? With monetarism? With rational expectations theory? Discuss.

4. Discuss some reasons for the "revival" of increasing productivity in the 1980s and 90s. How would the supply-siders interpret this increase in productivity? Explain.

PART SEVEN

THE EVOLUTION OF ECONOMIC CONDITIONS SINCE THE 1960S

The "New Economics" of the 1960s, stagflation of the 1970s, wage-price controls, changing Fed policies, Reaganomics, the huge federal budget deficits and foreign trade deficits, and the renaissance of Keynesian Economics.

19 EVOLUTION OF THE INFLATION CRISIS OF 1979–80

Back in the 1950s after the Korean War ended (1953), the wartime wage-price controls were abolished. There was a minor recession; inflation didn't seem to be a problem. But then as the years went by, prices began to creep upward. When prices were increasing at about 2% a year, money was "tightened up" to hold down the rate of inflation. But when money was tightened, the economy slowed down.

When the economy slowed down, the government budget automatically went into a deficit. (Tax payments drop when total income falls, of course.) In 1957–58 the economy went into a recession. The Eisenhower administration tried to balance the budget—to hold down public spending and keep tax collections high. But the budget deficits continued and the economy stayed in recession. There was some improvement in 1958–59, but in 1960–61 things got worse again. In January 1961 when President Kennedy took office, unemployment was approaching 7%—considered unusually high and a very serious problem at that time.

WALTER HELLER AND THE "NEW ECONOMICS"

Not until the early years of the Kennedy administration (1961–62) did the economy begin to pick up. But still, unemployment was high. In 1963, Walter Heller, Chairman of President Kennedy's Council of Economic Advisers (CEA), persuaded Kennedy to apply the Keynesian prescription to try to speed up the economy. Thus, for the first time since the depression of the 1930s, Keynesian economics began to play an important role in influencing economic policy for the nation. Walter Heller was the chief spokesman for this Keynesian approach, which came to be called the *new economics.*

One idea of the "new economics" was that if the government tries to raise taxes to balance its budget when the economy is running too slowly, then the economy will be prevented from reaching full speed. When the economy is underemployed, the government *should* run a deficit. It should set tax rates at that level at which the budget will come into balance *automatically* whenever the economy gets up to full employment. If the economy gets "overheated"— too much spending and inflation—tax revenues will increase automatically, the budget will run a surplus, and that will hold down the excess spending and prevent inflation.

A TAX CUT TO INCREASE TAX REVENUES!

In 1958 when the economy slowed down, the U.S. government ran the biggest peacetime budget deficit in history. When the Eisenhower administration tried to balance the budget, the economy just stagnated and the budget still didn't balance. But in 1964 when the deficit was more than $8 billion, the Kennedy administration *lowered* taxes. (President Kennedy asked Congress for the tax cut back in the summer of 1963. It was slow in coming. As you very well know, Congress doesn't always jump and run just when the President asks!)

What happened after the Kennedy tax cut of 1964? The economy sped up. Unemployment dropped. Incomes rose. Tax revenues increased enough to reduce the deficit from $8 billion in 1964 to $5 billion in 1965. Why? Individuals and businesses were making higher incomes, so they were paying more taxes.

The booming economy helped almost everybody. State and local governments received more tax revenues, so they could do a better job of providing public services. Monetary policy was "easy"—interest rates were low and the money supply was allowed to expand to finance the boom. Everything seemed to be going just fine. Then suddenly there was a new problem: the Vietnam war.

SPENDING FOR THE VIETNAM WAR BROKE THE BALANCE

U.S. involvement in the war expanded slowly, then more rapidly, until soon the war was making heavy demands on the economy. Government spending poured into the nation's income stream. As the government demanded more war goods, shortages developed in some markets. When the economy is "fully employed" and the government uses more of the nation's labor, resources, and products, the people must do with less. Taxes should be raised to get the people to buy less. Otherwise: Shortages. Inflation.

President Johnson and his Council of Economic Advisers urged Congress to increase taxes to pull some of the money back out of the economy to hold down total spending. But Congress did not act. Voting to raise taxes is not ever a very popular thing to do. When President Johnson called for tax increases to finance the unpopular Vietnam war, Congress said, "No!" But the government kept spending. So what happened? Prices began to rise. Inflation.

How much extra spending was the government pumping into the economy? In 1967 the deficit approached $9 billion. In 1968 it was $25 billion! What to do? Antiwar sentiment was growing. Congress continued to refuse to pass legislation to increase taxes to finance the war. Finally, in 1968, there was a tax increase. But it was too little and too late. The inflation fires were already ablaze.

PRESIDENT NIXON'S ECONOMIC POLICIES

Prices had been increasing for several years at a rate of around 3 percent a year. The inflation rate picked up a little in 1968, but it wasn't until 1969, the first year of the Nixon administration, that prices began to break loose and run. In 1969 prices were increasing at an annual rate of about 6 percent. Nixon vowed that he would bring inflation under control. What did his "Friedmanesque" economic advisers prescribe? Tight money, of course.

Remember the slogans? "Keep your eye on the money supply." "When inflation threatens, hold tight on the money supply." "If the money supply is not permitted to expand too much, then it follows as the night the day, prices cannot rise too much." That's what the economic advisers prescribed; and that's exactly what the Nixon administration did—at least that's what it started out to do, and tried to do.

NIXON'S "TIGHT MONEY" POLICY DIDN'T WORK AS EXPECTED

The Federal Reserve (Fed) held back on credit. The Fed refused to let the money supply continue to expand. Soon there was such a shortage of money that interest rates rose to levels higher than they had been in the United States for more than one hundred years. The stock market collapsed—the worst tumble in stock prices since the depression years of the 1930s. And what about prices? Did tight money stop inflation? No.

Prices kept on increasing faster and faster. Also unemployment increased—from 4% to 5%, then, in 1971, to more than 6%. Tight money, plus some slowdown in government buying, forced the economy into a recession. But prices kept on rising. Inflation kept getting worse.

More and more, people were criticizing the Nixon administration's economic policy. Many urged Nixon to stop relying entirely on his indirect, "theoretical" approach. They urged him to go beyond the monetarist approach and beyond the Keynesian approach—to take some *direct* action to break the wage-price spiral. Many suggested direct controls on wages and prices to break the inflation, after which perhaps more normal policy tools could be used to keep things stabilized.

CONGRESS AUTHORIZED WAGE-PRICE CONTROLS

In 1970 Congress passed an Act giving the President the power "to impose such orders and regulations as he may deem appropriate to stabilize prices, rent, wages, and salaries.. . . " But the President repeatedly asserted that he would never use this authority—that he would never use the power of his office to force direct controls over wages and prices. But as everyone knows, history was to prove him wrong.

Early in 1971 it appeared that things were beginning to get better. The economy seemed to be picking up a little and Nixon's economic advisers kept assuring everyone that the tight money anti-inflation policies were just about ready to take hold. But then in the summer of 1971 things took a dramatic turn for the worse.

CONDITIONS KEPT GETTING WORSE

Unemployment had continued to hover around 6%. Consumer spending was slow and was not picking up. Prices just kept on increasing faster and faster. During the early part of 1971 wholesale prices were rising at a record rate. The stock market (which had recovered somewhat) went back into a tailspin. It was clear that economic conditions were getting worse, not better.

The deficit in the U.S. international balance of payments kept getting worse. More and more dollars were pouring into the bank accounts of foreigners. And more and more of those dollar holders began to try to get rid of their surplus of dollars. But no one wanted to hold *more* dollars. The international value of the dollar seemed almost certain to go down.

For more than two years President Nixon and his advisors had been promising repeatedly that the economy was going to correct itself very soon. But as the weeks, months, and years passed and none of the promises came true, people began to suspect that the Nixon economists really didn't understand as much as they said they did. The medicine they kept applying seemed to be doing much harm and no good.

It was in the spring and summer of 1971 that the business and financial community and many of the political leaders, both in the United States and throughout the world, lost confidence in Nixon's economic policy. The problems were getting rapidly worse, threatening serious domestic and international consequences. Something had to be done.

NIXON'S ABRUPT SHIFT IN POLICY

In his historic television address on Sunday night, August 15, 1971, President Nixon announced one of the most sudden shifts of economic policy that has ever occurred in this country. He placed an immediate freeze on wages and prices, announced his recommendations to Congress for tax cuts and other actions to stimulate spending, and announced that the dollar would be devalued—that is, sold cheaper to people in other countries.

Why this absolute reversal in policy? It was obvious that something had to be done. Quickly. Regardless of Nixon's philosophical leanings and the continued urging of most of his advisers (some of whom had deserted the Nixon "game plan" before he did), he knew that something immediate, direct, *dramatic*, had to be done—Nixon the pragmatist, the opportunist, realized this. When he moved, he moved decisively.

Most of the world applauded his decisive intervention. Most of his critics criticized him not for what he did, but because he had waited so long, had "let so many horses out of the stable" before taking any direct action.

THE PHASES OF NIXON'S WAGE-PRICE CONTROLS

The wage-price freeze of August 15, 1971, was an absolute freeze for ninety days on all wages and prices. When the freeze (Phase I) ended, Phase II began. Under Phase II, wage and price adjustments were permitted, but only within the limits of established guidelines. As the months went by, it became clear that the inflationary spiral indeed had been broken. Wages and prices were rising moderately. Confidence in the economy was being regained.

Milton Friedman, leader and most steadfast of all monetarists, criticized the control program, saying that the inflationary spiral *really* had been brought under control by the delayed action of the administration's tight money policies. Friedman said that if the controls hadn't been put on conditions would be *even better!* Of course not everyone believed him.

What about President Nixon? Did he believe Friedman. Maybe so. In January of 1973, fourteen months after the beginning of Phase II, Nixon lifted the Phase II controls. So what happened? In the months that followed, the American economy experienced the worst inflation since 1946. There was a massive rush of foreigners to get rid of their dollars. Soon the dollar was devalued two more times.

Exactly what did Nixon do in January 1973? He announced the beginning of Phase III—the ending of mandatory controls. He wanted to move to voluntary guidelines. People didn't believe it would work, and it didn't. So what did Nixon do next?

In June of 1973 the President announced another freeze. We were almost back again to Phase I—back to August 1971—except now in a much worse position. Monetary and fiscal policies had been expansive most of the time since the freeze in 1971, and inflationary pressures were strong. Prices were much higher, and confidence in the government's ability to cope with the situation was much lower than before.

In addition, the Watergate scandal was eroding domestic and international confidence in the Nixon administration, and the energy crisis and shortages of other basic resources were beginning to push upward on prices. So this time the freeze didn't work. It was "phased out" over several months.

In 1974 the wage price controls were removed and money was made very tight. The economy suffered its worst recession since the 1930s. This was the first year of quadrupled oil prices. There were worldwide grain shortages and soaring agricultural prices. The inflation rate reached 12%.

PRESIDENT FORD'S WIN PROGRAM

The year 1975 started off bad but then got better. Unemployment peaked at about 9%, but after that employment and production picked up some. President Ford called for a voluntary effort by business and labor to hold down prices and wages. He urged everyone to wear a "WIN" (whip inflation now) button to show their pledge to help fight inflation—but it wasn't quite clear what these concerned citizens were supposed to do. The "movement" never caught on. The inflation rate slowed some in 1975, but not much. It averaged about 9% for the year.

The Carter-Ford election year (1976) was not much better. The inflation rate dropped to less than 6%, but the unemployment rate was almost 8%. More than 7 million people were unemployed. The Federal government deficit for the fiscal year ending June 30, 1976, was more than $66 billion—up from $45 billion in 1975. In January of 1977 President Carter took office with a commitment to reduce inflation and unemployment.

PRESIDENT CARTER'S INCREASING USE OF DIRECT CONTROLS

At first the Carter administration didn't make any basic changes in the Ford administration's game plan. Money was kept tight, the budget deficit was held down to $45 billion, and there were some programs to generate employment. But there were no direct controls, either "voluntary" (jawboning) or compulsory.

In the first half of 1977 the inflation rate was high—about 10%. Unemployment was still high—more than 7% of the labor force. But in the last half of 1977 the inflation rate slowed to less than 5% and unemployment was down a little—to about 6.7%.

In January of 1978, President Carter announced that the first domestic priority of his administration would be to reduce unemployment. There was talk of tax cuts to stimulate more spending to generate more employment. But then in the first quarter of 1978 the inflation rate picked up again—up to 9%.

CARTER'S VOLUNTARY RESTRAINTS

In April, President Carter announced a major policy shift. He said that *inflation* (not unemployment) had become the nation's number one problem, and that, effective immediately, his administration was imposing "voluntary" wage-price guidelines. Labor and businesses were asked to limit their wage and price increases to *less than* their average increases over the past two years.

Did the voluntary restraints do any good? Apparently not much. The government did succeed in "talking down" the size of announced price increases in the steel industry. But the inflation rate for the second quarter (April, May, June) was back up to more than 10%. By mid-summer of 1978, President Carter and his economic advisors were planning stronger moves to try to slow down the inflation.

CARTER'S "PHASE II" ANTI-INFLATION PROGRAM

In October 1978 President Carter announced Phase II of his anti-inflation program: tighter money, reduced government spending, and firmer direct controls on wages and prices. New "voluntary" guidelines were announced. Businesses which ignored the guidelines would not be eligible for government contracts, and several other "jawboning penalties" were threatened against those who did not comply with the guidelines. Workers who accepted the guidelines would be eligible for tax rebates if the inflation rate exceeded the wage increase guideline rate of 7%.

Money was made very tight, interest rates rose very high, and Carter announced a major cut-back in planned government spending. The planned government deficit was cut to $29 billion for the fiscal year ending in 1980, down from a planned deficit of over $60 billion for fiscal 1979. (*Note:* Planned deficits and realized deficits don't usually come out in the same place.)

For the year 1978 the inflation rate averaged about 9% and the unemployment rate, about 6%. Entering 1979 the Carter administration appeared determined to slow inflation and to do it without too much recession—that is, without too much increase in unemployment. How did they plan to do that? By using monetary policy (tight money), fiscal policy (spending cuts), and direct wage-price restraints (guidelines, backed up with penalties for noncompliance).

THE RESULTS OF CARTER'S "PHASE II" PROGRAM

How well did Carter's Phase II Program succeed? That's impossible to say, for sure, because no one knows how bad things might have been without that program. But in terms of achieving the objectives of slowing the rate of inflation, it was a failure by any measure. The average inflation rate for 1979 was about 4 percentage points above the average rate for 1978—up to 13%.

Then in the beginning of 1980 prices were spurting upward at the unbelievable annual rate of almost 20%! Why?

The rapid inflation of early 1980 certainly couldn't be blamed on "easy money." Money was tighter and interest rates higher (much higher) during early 1980 than ever before.

THE FED'S NEW POLICY OF OCTOBER, 1979

In October of 1979 the Federal Reserve Board had announced a new decision about how it was going to control the money supply. Until that time, the Fed had looked more at *interest rates* as an indicator of "the tightness of money." But in October 1979, the Fed began to target and try to control the "monetary base"—that is, the reserves available to banks. If the monetary base is not permitted to expand, this cuts off the ability of the banking system to make new loans.

The significance of this shift in Fed policy was this: By controlling the monetary base, the Fed can *absolutely prevent* the money supply from expanding. When it does this, if the demand for money goes very high, then interest rates are pushed up very high. That's what happened between October 1979 and April 1980. But even with the tight money and very high interest rates, inflation continued to speed up just the same.

SOME CAUSES OF THE INCREASED INFLATION RATE

With tight money, and very high interest rates, why did the inflation rate speed up? There are various reasons, some of which you already know. This section talks about some of them.

THE EFFECT OF EXPECTED INFLATION

One very important inflationary influence was the *existence* of inflation, and *expectations* of continued inflation. No one wants to buy a bond or to lend money when they think the value (purchasing power) of money is going to decrease by about 15% per year, *unless* they can earn interest of *more than* 15%—more than enough to make up for the loss from inflation. So in this environment of high inflationary expectations, interest rates had to be high.

Also, businesses and consumers will continue to borrow money and buy things even when interest rates are high if they expect the prices of the things they are buying to be going up at a higher rate than the interest rate. And that was happening with many products during 1979–80. You wouldn't mind paying 15% interest to borrow the money to fill your fuel oil tank if you thought the price of fuel oil was likely to go up by maybe 50%! That's the kind of thing that was happening in the oil markets in 1979.

THE EFFECT OF INCREASED COSTS

In 1979 there was another big jump in the price of imported oil. The higher price of oil quickly worked its way into the prices of gasoline and other petroleum products—and into the costs of production (and ultimately the prices) of most other products also. The very high interest rates (higher than 20% for many borrowers) made borrowed money very expensive. This added significantly to production costs in business and agriculture. Ultimately, output prices must reflect these cost increases.

Workers pushed hard for wage increases. They realized that their *real wages* were decreasing as the value (purchasing power) of their dollars was going down faster than their incomes were going up. But the wage increases even further contributed to increased costs and helped to push prices up even more.

THE SLOWDOWN IN PRODUCTIVITY GROWTH

Another contributing factor was the slowdown of *productivity* growth in the American economy. You already read about this problem in the last chapter. The basic problem is that when workers are receiving *income increases* and their *outputs are not increasing*, there's more income to be spent, but no more output to be bought. That's inflationary. The *supply* of output is inadequate to meet the *demand*. This problem has been partly responsible for the recent emphasis on "supply-side" economics.

THE DECLINING SAVINGS RATE

In 1979–80, most consumers and businesses seemed to be trying to spend as much as they could—either with money, or credit. The "average savings rate" of consumers dropped to its lowest point ever.

THE CREATION OF NEW "MONEY SUBSTITUTES"

With money so expensive to borrow, businesses and banks and other financial institutions were working out all kinds of ingenious techniques for financing transactions without actually using "money." During early 1980 the Fed considered this problem to be so serious that it redefined the money supply so that some of the ingenious new "money substitutes" would be included in the new definitions of the "money supply."

When you consider all of the factors at work in the situation, it isn't too surprising that the inflation rate in early 1980 was very high.

DID CARTER'S WAGE-PRICE GUIDELINES HELP?

What was the effect of the Carter administration's wage-price guidelines? Did they help? The answer to that depends on who you ask. The President's Council of Economic Advisers (CEA) says "Yes." The CEA estimated that during 1979 the guidelines reduced the wage inflation rate by between 1% and 1 ½%. And they said that the guidelines succeeded in holding down some price increases by big businesses.

But not everyone agrees with this. It's obvious that both big business and labor organizations can announce larger price or wage increases than they really expect to get, and then reduce these under government pressure to "appear to be" responding to the government's stabilization efforts. So it's not easy to say, for sure.

WHAT ABOUT IMPOSING WAGE-PRICE CONTROLS

During the last half of the 1970s and on into the 1980s as inflation roared on, there was continuing controversy on the question of whether or not legally-imposed *direct controls* should be placed on wages and prices—perhaps a wage-price freeze—to try to stop the inflation. The argument about whether or not to impose legal restraints on wages and prices is not strictly a "monetarists vs. Keynesians" argument. It's clear that monetarists, because of their view of how the economy operates and responds to the "natural economic laws" would oppose any such government intervention, even as a short-run "emergency action."

THE KEYNESIAN VIEW

People who hold the Keynesian view of how the economy operates would be more inclined to accept the possibility that direct wage-price controls could help as a short-run "emergency action." The Keynesian view holds that sellers—of both *products* and *labor*—have enough economic power to push their prices up. And they believe that a properly designed and administered system of wage-price controls sometimes might be effective in preventing them from doing that. But even so, not all Keynesians are in favor of wage-price controls—even as a short-run emergency action.

Economists in general agree that wage-price controls distort the operation of the price mechanism, reduce the efficiency of the allocation of resources in the society, and impose unjust disadvantages on some buyers and sellers while granting unjust advantages to other buyers and sellers. But this is not the only problem.

It is very difficult (many say, impossible) to design and administer a workable wage-price control system. This would be a most difficult task even if it were done by the nation's most brilliant economists and administrators—and even if there were no political pressures to contend with. But in the real world of limited perception by economists, and strong political pressures, it takes a lot of courage and faith to embark on a wage-price control program, even as a short-run emergency measure. Nevertheless, some kind of government controls designed to limit wage-price increases have been imposed many times, both in this country and in other countries.

A BRIEF HISTORY OF WAGE-PRICE CONTROLS

Over the past four decades, in most countries much of the time there has been some attempt to use *direct restraints* to hold down wages and prices. The United States has been no exception.

In the United States, as you know, wage-price controls were imposed in August, 1971. That was the first time wage-price controls had been imposed since the early 1950s during the Korean War. It had happened during World War II also, and during other wars. But what about the period from the mid 50s to August of 1971? Were wages and prices completely free to seek their own levels? Sometimes, yes. But most of the time, no.

PRESIDENT KENNEDY'S "GUIDEPOSTS" AND "JAWBONING." You know that in the early 1960s, President Kennedy set up wage-price guideposts spelling out the "appropriate conditions" for wages or prices to be increased, and by how much. Both President Kennedy and President Johnson used the power of the presidency to "twist some arms," to convince some businesses and labor leaders to go along with the guideposts.

The "jawboning" policies of the Kennedy-Johnson era were continued until the beginning of the Nixon administration in 1969. Then Nixon abolished all "voluntary controls" and relied on the limited growth in the money supply to bring down the inflation rate. So there was no attempt to apply direct pressure to hold down wages and prices during the period from 1969 until August of 1971, when Nixon announced the wage-price freeze.

"VOLUNTARY" RESTRAINTS HAVE BEEN USED MUCH OF THE TIME. From the end of the Nixon administration's price controls in the early 1970s, on into the early 1980s, there were not any nationwide, legally-imposed controls on wages and prices. But "voluntary restraints," and "jawboning" have been used much of the time. To some extent during the Ford administration in the mid-70s, but even more in the Carter administration, the government was applying direct pressure to try to limit wage and price increases by big business and big labor.

The government's "Council on Wage and Price Stability" tried to identify "unjustified and inflationary" price or wage increases. Then the government tried to induce the offenders to retract and "roll back" the increases.

IN THE EARLY 1980S THE "WAGE-PRICE CONTROLS" ISSUE WAS STILL ALIVE

In the late 1970s President Carter asked Congress to pass legislation giving him "standby authority" to impose a nationwide system of wage-price controls. But the Congress chose not to do that.

In the high-inflation Presidential election year of 1980, Senator Edward Kennedy came out strongly in favor of wage-price controls. Public opinion polls showed that there was much support for Senator Kennedy's position. So in the early 1980s the issue was still very much alive. But then, the inflation rate slowed dramatically. No need to consider direct controls! You'll be reading all about that, and about the policy shift to "Reaganomics," and then what happened after that, in the chapters coming up.

 REVIEW QUESTIONS

1. Explain how, according to the "new economics" of the early 1960s, a tax cut will lead to increased tax revenues. Was the Kennedy-Johnson administration's attempt to use this approach successful? Explain.

2. What was the Fed's new policy of October 1979? Why did the Fed shift policy at that time? Explain.

3. In 1979–80, even with tight-money policies and very high interest rates, inflation continued to rise. Explain some of the factors which contributed to this increasing inflation rate.

4. From the early 1960s in the Kennedy-Johnson era through the Carter administration, some forms of wage-price controls were used much of the time to try to control inflation. Briefly describe what was done, then try to evaluate the successes or failures of these efforts.

5. How does the concept of wage-price controls fit in with Keynesian theory? With monetarism?

20 REAGANOMICS 1981–84: SUPPLY-SIDE TAX CUTS, DEFICITS, RECESSION, AND RECOVERY

The years of the 1970s and early 1980s are referred to as the period of "stagflation" in the American economy. There was stagnation—very little growth of productivity, output, or employment—and continuing, increasing inflation.

THE CARTER VS. REAGAN ELECTION YEAR: 1980

The campaign speeches of 1980 were filled with economic ideas. And promises? Of course.

The federal government deficit was running at the highest level since World War II. Unemployment was high and increasing. Foreign competition in American markets was intense. Several businesses and some financial institutions were on the verge of bankruptcy. The inflation rate, although beginning to come down, was still in the double-digit range—extremely high by historical standards. It was in this setting that presidential candidate Ronald Reagan offered his prescriptions for overcoming the nation's economic ills. His prescriptions have come to be known as "Reaganomics."

REAGANOMICS IS CONSERVATIVE, NEOCLASSICAL ECONOMICS

The main tenets of Reaganomics are:

Cut back the role of government in the economy. Reduce taxes and regulations and controls which are costly to businesses and are stunting the growth of businesses and therefore are retarding the growth of employment and productivity in the economy.

Cut back on spending for welfare and social programs and ultimately shift the burden of paying for these programs to the state and local governments. Limit the major spending thrust of the federal government to national defense spending—to keep the nation strong and free. Design the tax and spending system to encourage savings, investment, increased productivity, and economic growth.

You can see that Reaganomics is conservative economics. It strongly endorses supply-side economics, and is clearly based on neoclassical economic theory.

THE "SUPPLY-SIDE TAX CUT" CONTROVERSY

Republican Senators Jack Kemp of New York and William Roth of Delaware first introduced and tried to pass their supply-side tax-cut bill in July of 1977—the first year of the Carter administration. The bill called for a reduction in income tax rates, from the (existing) 14% to 70% range down to an 8% to 50% range. But the bill didn't pass.

The bill's sponsors said that the proposed tax cut would stimulate savings, investment, increased productivity, economic growth, and higher incomes for individuals and profits for businesses—so much higher, in fact, that soon the government would be receiving more tax revenues than before the tax cut. A tax cut which would increase tax revenues? Yes. That was the idea. When have you heard anyone express an idea like this before?

THE KENNEDY-JOHNSON (KEYNESIAN) TAX CUT

During 1963 President Kennedy proposed "a tax cut to balance the budget." Remember? And in 1964 under President Johnson, taxes were cut significantly. The economy prospered and tax revenues in subsequent years did, in fact, increase.

Was the Kennedy-Johnson tax cut "supply-side economics"? No. It was demand-side economics. The purpose was to stimulate *aggregate demand* which was supposed to bring more production, employment, output, and income—and therefore more tax revenues. That was pure Keynesian economics. It seemed to work. But monetarists and Keynesians will be forever arguing about whether or not it was the tax cut that did the trick—and if so, if it really worked out the way that Keynesian theory said it would.

THE KEMP-ROTH (SUPPLY-SIDE) TAX CUT

The idea (neoclassical theory) underlying the Kemp-Roth tax-cut bill is exactly opposite from the Keynesian idea underlying the Kennedy-Johnson tax cut. The Kemp-Roth bill is supposed to generate more *savings* which will generate more *investment*. More and better capital—more efficient and highly productive factories, machines, and equipment—will be generated. There will be much more output per worker, so more goods will be supplied to the market.

It is this *increased supply of goods and services in the market* which will relieve inflationary pressures and bring stable prices. And the increased incomes and profits generated by the increased productivity will generate increased tax revenues. In subsequent years the increased revenues will eliminate the deficit and bring the government budget into balance.

The very last thing in the world that the supply-siders would want would be for their tax cuts to result in an increase in *aggregate demand!* That would create even more inflationary pressures.

A TAX CUT TO STIMULATE SUPPLY—NOT DEMAND

Supply-side tax cuts are designed to try to increase *savings* and *investment spending*—not consumer spending. Less taxes are collected on *income saved* than on *income spent*. This rewards saving and discourages consumer spending. Also taxes are reduced more for businesses and for individuals in high income brackets because these income recipients save and invest more than do those in the lower income brackets.

Some (perhaps Keynesian) economists question whether it is really possible to cut taxes and increase *aggregate supply* without also increasing *aggregate demand*—perhaps as much as (or more than) the increase in aggregate supply. Perhaps it was this concern which led Dr. Walter Heller, former Chairman of the Kennedy-Johnson Council of Economic Advisers, to comment that the outcome projected for the Kemp-Roth tax bill "stretches both credulity and facts."* And George Bush in his 1980 campaign against Ronald Reagan for the Republican presidential nomination referred to the Kemp-Roth tax cut idea as "voodoo economics."

CANDIDATE REAGAN ENDORSES THE KEMP-ROTH IDEA

During his campaign for the presidency candidate Ronald Reagan endorsed the Kemp-Roth tax-cut plan. Then after his election this supply-side tax cut became the centerpiece of "Reaganomics"—of the Reagan prescription for solving the nation's economic problems.

THE REAGAN ECONOMIC RECOVERY PROGRAM

President Reagan submitted his proposed economic recovery program to Congress in February 1981. The major emphasis was on changing the structure of the federal budget. The President suggested (1) supply-side tax cuts, (2) reductions in non-defense spending, and (3) increased spending for defense. The President's program called for a major shift in the tax structure, and in the priorities and emphasis of the federal government.

REAGAN'S PROPOSED BUDGET: ZERO DEFICIT BY 1984

Reagan's proposed budget was projected to reduce the size of the federal deficit. The deficit was $59.6 billion in the fiscal year ending September 30, 1980—the last full year of the Carter administration.

The projections President Reagan offered for his proposed budget were based on the assumed rapid success of (1) his supply-side tax cuts, and (2) the reduction of productivity-sapping regulations on business. The deficit for the fiscal year ending in 1981 was projected to be $54.5 billion; for 1982, $45 billion; and on down to zero (a balanced budget) for fiscal year 1984.

THE ECONOMIC RECOVERY TAX ACT OF 1981

The President and his supply-side advisors touted "supply-side economics" as the wave of the future. They lobbied forcefully and succeeded in get-

---

*Walter Heller, "The Kemp-Roth-Laffer Free Lunch," *The Wall Street Journal*, 12 July 1978.

ting the Congress to go along with most of the proposed budget changes. The *Economic Recovery Tax Act of 1981*—the biggest tax cut in history—was signed by the President on August 13, 1981.

- Personal income taxes were cut by 25% over a three-year period: 5% effective October 1, 1981, and an additional 10% on July 1 of both 1982 and '83.
- The highest-bracket tax rate was reduced from 70% to 50%, effective in 1981. This cut was designed to leave more money in the hands of the relatively wealthy and thereby to stimulate saving.
- Taxes on businesses were reduced mostly by providing investment tax credits and faster depreciation write-offs—tax cuts designed to stimulate investment.

THE GROWING GOVERNMENT DEFICIT

As it turned out, the 1981 through 1984 budget projections of President Reagan and his supply-side advisors were far from the mark. The fiscal '82 budget deficit was $111 billion—the largest in history. Then the fiscal 1983 deficit was almost twice as large: $195 billion! The fiscal 1984 budget projected a deficit almost as large: $185 billion.

On February 1, 1984, the Reagan administration released its budget document for fiscal 1985. The projected deficit? Almost $200 billion. And deficit projections for the following years didn't look much better.

PUBLIC OPINION TURNS AGAINST HUGE DEFICITS

An article in *Business Week* magazine (February 20, 1984) refers to the events in Washington and in the financial markets following the February budget release, as "chaotic." The stock market did a nose dive. The Dow Jones industrial average was down 64 points during the next six trading days. Clearly, there was much discontent with (and fear of) the huge continuing federal deficits. But what could be done?

THE "GUNS OR BUTTER" ALTERNATIVES.   An obvious way to cut deficits is to cut spending. The Reagan administration was in favor of that all along. The President's budget initiatives were for *more military spending* offset by *cutbacks in domestic programs*. But Congress wasn't willing to go very far in that direction.

THE "TAX INCREASE" ALTERNATIVE.   Another obvious way to reduce deficits is to *collect more taxes.* But the administration steadfastly refused to go this route. Supply-side economics says: "Cut tax rates and stimulate growth and the deficits will go away by themselves." Remember?

DEFICIT-REDUCING INITIATIVES OF 1984

In an election year, candidates don't ignore the public opinion polls. In early 1984 the news media (and Fed Chairman Paul Volcker and Council of Economic Advisers Chairman Martin Feldstein) were hammering away at the dangers of continuing huge deficits. So in March, President (and candidate) Reagan called for taxincreases and more spending cuts to try to reduce the size of future deficits. Later you'll be reading about the painfully slow process of deficit reduction during the last half of the 1980s. But first, a look at the economy in the early 1980s.

WHAT WAS HAPPENING IN THE ECONOMY?

Now you need to know about some other very important things which were going on in the economy during this first five years of the 1980s—especially about the most serious recession and the most rapid economic recovery since the Great Depression of the 1930s. Also you need to know about the role of the Fed's changing monetary policies in influencing the economy during this period.

You need to know why some economists look at the events of 1980–84 as a clear illustration of the accuracy of Keynesian economics—and the inaccuracy of neoclassical, monetarist, and supply-side theories—in analyzing and projecting macroeconomic conditions in the economy. And you need to know why the monetarists and supply-siders and other anti-Keynesians say that the 1980–84 period was not a fair test of their theories. That's what's coming up now.

THE TURBULENT YEARS OF THE EARLY 1980S

The cover of the March 24, 1980 *U.S. News and World Report* shows a whirling tornado of dollars. The title of the cover story is "Economy Out of Control."

In September of 1980 the prestigious Committee for Economic Development (including American economists and business leaders) issued the report: *Fighting Inflation and Rebuilding a Sound Economy.* The first sentence of that report says: "The American economy is in a perilous state."

The American economy in 1980 was facing serious inflation, an energy crisis, a productivity crisis, huge government deficits, a national debt exceeding one trillion dollars, and our highest interest rates in more than 50 years.

THE SERIOUS RECESSION OF 1981–82

During the period 1980 through 1982 the American economy experienced the most serious recession since World War II.

The unemployment rate increased from 7.4% in January 1981 to 8.6% in January 1982 and to 10.8% in January 1983—the highest rate in more than 40 years. In January 1983 more than 12 million Americans were unemployed.

- Real gross national product (GNP)—the rate of flow of real output in the economy—was 1.8% lower in 1982 than the (already low) year of 1981. This was the worst year-to-year decline in GNP in 36 years.
- Average percentage utilization of industrial capacity in December of 1982 was at a post-war low of 67.3%.
- Rates of capital spending for new plant and equipment began to decline in the fourth quarter of 1981 and continued to decline (by 4.5%) in 1982. The decline continued on into the first quarter of 1983.
- Throughout 1982 manufacturers were reducing their inventories—using up more inputs than they were buying, and selling more outputs than they were producing and replacing. In December 1982, inventory reduction was going on at an annual rate of $38.5 billion—a post-World War II record. The *inventory liquidation continued* and set a new post-war record (annual rate) of $39 billion in the first quarter of 1983.

THE PHENOMENAL RECOVERY OF 1983–84

The economic recovery which began to pick up speed in the early spring of 1983, was nothing short of phenomenal. Even the most optimistic economic forecasts were far below the mark.

- Consumer spending increased greatly in 1983 supported by (1) increasing personal income, (2) increased disposable (after-tax) income from unusually large income tax refunds and from the mid-year "supply-side" 10% income tax cut, (3) a low rate of savings by consumers, and (4) increased consumer borrowing and buying on credit.

It was the increased consumer spending (aggregate consumer demand) in 1983 which was the main force responsible for thrusting the economy forward, stimulating business profits and turning the tide toward increased business investment and inventory accumulation (aggregate investment demand).

- Corporate profits revived rapidly. During the first half of 1983 operating profits of all nonfinancial corporations were increasing at an annual rate of 60%. Cash flow margins (how much the company gets to keep from each dollar of sales) reached a 16-year high. Operating profits continued to increase throughout 1983 and on into '84.
- Business investment spending began to increase in the second quarter of 1983, ending a five-quarter decline. By the third quarter of '83, business investment spending was growing at an annual rate (in real terms) of 18.7% and in the fourth quarter, at the phenomenal rate of 29.0%.
- Industrial production was increasing throughout 1983. In December '83 it was 16% higher than in December '82, and was still rising. In early 1984 the Fed was estimating an additional 10% increase in the rate of industrial production during 1984.
- The real rate of GNP growth in the first quarter of 1983 (on an annual basis) was 2.6%. Then the second quarter came in with an astounding 9.2%, only to be topped by the 9.7% rate in the third quarter. The average real GNP growth rate for the entire year (1983) was 6.1%. These high growth rates continued on into 1984 with a first quarter growth rate of 8.3%. Such GNP growth rates in the American economy hadn't been seen in the four decades since World War II.
- Unemployment dropped from a high of 10.8% of the labor force in January 1983, to 9.5% in July, 8.4% in November, and down to 8.0% in January 1984. This unemployment drop was more rapid than in any other economic recovery period in the past three decades.

WHY THE RAPID RECOVERY?

You already know that the rapid recovery resulted from booming consumer spending which triggered booming investment spending. All this led to expanding employment, production, and output—and to the higher personal incomes and corporate profits needed to fuel the continued economic expansion. That's all very easy to see, in retrospect.

But why did it happen when it did? Why not sooner? Or later? Or maybe never? To answer these questions, you'll need to know about some other con-

OF SPECIAL INTEREST . . .

BEFORE 1991 THE U.S. DEPT. OF COMMERCE REPORTED OUTPUT FIGURES FOR THE AMERICAN ECONOMY IN TERMS OF GROSS NATIONAL PRODUCT (GNP). SINCE 1991 IT HAS BEEN REPORTING FIGURES IN TERMS OF GROSS DOMESTIC PRODUCT—GDP. GNP REPORTS THE VALUE OF OUTPUT PRODUCED BY AMERICANS, NO MATTER WHERE IN THE WORLD THAT OUTPUT IS PRODUCED. GDP REPORTS THE VALUE OF ALL OUTPUT PRODUCED WITHIN THE BORDERS OF THE UNITED STATES, REGARDLESS OF WHETHER THAT OUTPUT IS PRODUCED BY AMERICANS OR BY FOREIGNERS. IN GENERAL, AMERICANS ARE PRODUCING ABOUT AS MUCH OUTPUT IN FOREIGN COUNTRIES AS FOREIGNERS ARE PRODUCING IN THE UNITED STATES, SO THE GNP FIGURE AND THE GDP FIGURE ARE ABOUT THE SAME SIZE. BOTH MEASURE THE SIZE OF AND CHANGES IN THE VALUE OF TOTAL GOODS AND SERVICES PRODUCED DURING THE YEAR.

ditions and events of the early 1980s. Specifically, you need to know about the Federal Reserve's *monetary policy*, about what was happening with *interest rates* and why, and about how all this was affecting the economy during this first half of the 1980s.

When you understand all these things, then you'll be able to see the events of the early 1980s in perspective. And you'll be able to understand the conflicting theoretical explanations offered by (1) the supply-side economists, (2) the monetarists, (3) the rational expectations theorists, and (4) the Keynesians. You'll be reading about all that in the chapters coming up.

But first, here's a quick look at the Humphrey-Hawkins Act, and at the Reagan administration's projections for the last half of the 1980s.

ADJUSTMENTS TO THE HUMPHREY-HAWKINS TIMETABLE

In 1978 the Congress passed the *Full Employment and Balanced Growth Act* (known as the Humphrey-Hawkins Act). This Act provided specific target rates for *unemployment* and *inflation.* The administration is legally bound to take the necessary steps to try to achieve these targeted rates.

The targeted unemployment rate was set at 4%. The targeted inflation rate was set at 3%. The Act says that these rates were supposed to be achieved by the end of 1983—but it says that the President could amend this timetable if necessary.

PRESIDENT CARTER'S PROJECTIONS (1980)

In his January 1980 *Economic Report*, President Carter amended the timetable. He set 1985 as the target year for achieving 4% unemployment, and three years later (1988) as the target year for lowering the inflation rate to 3%. It was clear that the Carter administration did not expect to succeed quickly in bringing down either the unemployment rate or the inflation rate. And as you know, after January of 1980, conditions got worse, not better.

PRESIDENT REAGAN'S 1982 PROJECTIONS

In his February 1982 *Economic Report*, President Reagan amended the timetable. The *Report* also amended the target figures, saying (page 215): "The Federal Government cannot fully anticipate the course of the economy; neither can it direct economic outcomes precisely." Then it goes on to give the projections.

President Reagan's 1982 projections show *unemployment* in 1985 of 6.4% and 1987 of 5.3%. The *inflation* rate was projected to be, in 1985, 4.6% and in 1987, 4.4%.

PRESIDENT REAGAN'S 1984 PROJECTIONS

In 1984, President Reagan's *Economic Report* presents a table (page 197) showing projections of unemployment and inflation rates for each year, 1984 through 1989. The *Report* says ". . . the table does not project realization of the Act's unemployment and inflation rate goals, but substantial progress toward them."

The table shows the unemployment rate declining each year, from 7.8% in 1984 down to 5.7% in 1989. The inflation rate also is projected to decline slightly each year, from 4.4% in 1984 to 3.6% in 1989.

Is that really what happened? You know it didn't. There are too many unforeseeable factors which prevent economic forecasting from being precise. Look how far the Carter (1980) and previous Reagan (1982) projections missed the target!

Before long you'll be reading about what really did happen after 1984. But first you need a close look at inflation rates, interest rates, and the Fed's monetary policy during the turbulent years 1979–84. That's coming up in the next chapter.

REVIEW QUESTIONS

1. Outline the main tenets of Reaganomics. In general, how does Reaganomics compare to Keynesian economics?

2. Explain the theory behind the Kemp-Roth (supply-side) tax cut. How does this theory compare with the ideas behind the Kennedy-Johnson tax cut of 1964? Explain.

3. *The Economic Recovery Tax Act of 1981* was designed to bring economic recovery by (1) stimulating personal savings and (2) stimulating business investment spending. Is that what happened? Discuss.

4. Describe the changing economic conditions in the United States during the 1980–84 period. Discuss some of the reasons for these fluctuations.

21 INFLATION RATES, INTEREST RATES, AND MONETARY POLICY, 1979–1984

 KEY TERMS

- prime rate
- nominal interest rates
- real interest rates
- inflationary psychology
- U.S. inflation rate trends
- "tight money"

- Consumer Price Index (CPI)
- Producer Price Index (PPI)
- "crowding out"
- monetary policy
- the M1 money supply

From the mid-1960s to the late 1970s, the average rate of inflation in the U.S. economy was accelerating. You have already read about that. But it wasn't until 1979 that the real crisis arrived.

In 1979 the inflation rate moved up to over 10 percent. Foreigners who were holding dollars began dumping them in the international exchange markets. Nobody wants to hold dollars when their value is falling by a rate of more than 10 percent per year! Drastic action was called for.

In the fall of 1979 the action taken was: Establish tight money. Very tight money. Clamp a tight lid on the size of the money supply. Don't let the money supply grow sufficiently to support the continued rise in prices. Then something will have to give!

TIGHT MONEY AND SEVERE RECESSION: OCTOBER 1979 TO OCTOBER 1982

It was in the fall of 1979 that Fed Board Chairman Paul Volcker met with central bankers and other governmental representatives of the major trading nations and discussed the international problems of the dollar. Then in early October Volcker and other Fed Board members participated in a secret week-end meeting at the White House with President Carter and his advisors.

THE EMERGENCY ACTION OF SATURDAY, OCTOBER 6, 1979

Following the meeting on Saturday, October 6, Volcker announced the strong money-tightening measures—and that, effective immediately, the money supply would no longer be permitted to expand to keep interest rates from going "too high." And what happened after that? Interest rates soared. The stock and bond markets tumbled.

THE HIGHEST U.S. INTEREST RATES IN MODERN TIMES!

By April of 1980 the "prime rate"—the interest rate banks charge their most credit-worthy short-term borrowers—had risen from "more normal levels" of less than 10%, to more than 20%. And corporations wanting to raise money by selling bonds were having to pay interest rates of more than 15%. Business investments would have to be very profitable to justify paying such high rates! Not surprisingly, the economy went into recession.

REAL RATES AND NOMINAL RATES

Why were interest rates so high? The fact is that in *real* terms they weren't so high. In fact, in real terms they weren't high at all! Would you believe they were *negative?* Less than zero? That's right.

The *nominal rates*—the rates actually quoted—the rates you have to pay—had gone up very high. But the *real rates*—the nominal rates *adjusted for inflation*—were negative. Why adjust for inflation? Here's why.

The *nominal interest rate* you earn on your money is the nominal rate of *increase* in the value of your money assets over time. The inflation rate is the rate of *decrease* in the value of your money assets over time. If you're earning 10% nominal interest and the inflation rate turns out to be 15%, that's a *negative real rate* of 5%. You're losing money!

For a brief time in early 1980 the U.S. inflation rate reached a peak of 20%. So at that time, a prime rate of 20% really wasn't so high after all. And would you believe that real interest rates had been negative in the money markets of this country (with a brief exception in 1975–76) all the time from mid-year 1972 until the end of 1980? It's true.

But regardless of the *real* rates, the high *nominal* rates did discourage business investment. The economy slowed down and went into recession. Eventually the inflation rate began to slow down and real interest rates became (and remained) positive.

By mid-1980 the economy was moving rapidly into recession. Unemployment increased from the less than 6% rate in 1979 to about 8% of the labor force by mid-1980. As the economy slowed down, the rate of inflation dropped. The inflation rate (the annual rate of increase in prices as measured by the consumer price index) began to drop from the high of 20% in early 1980. The average rate for the year (1980) was down to 12.4%.

THE LOWEST INFLATION RATES IN A DECADE

For 1981 the inflation rate was down to an average of 8.9% for the year. But prices were rising much more slowly at the end of the year than they were at the beginning of the year. The inflation rate was going down.

By the first quarter of 1982 the inflation rate was down to less than 5%, and it kept slowing down throughout the year. The average inflation rate for the entire year (1982) was only 3.9%—the lowest since the price-controlled year of 1972.

Both the tight money policies of the Federal Reserve and the declining prices of energy were given credit for slowing the inflation. But 1982 was a year of serious recession. Many economists expected inflation to accelerate as the economy began to recover in 1983. But that didn't happen.

THE 1983 RECOVERY DIDN'T REIGNITE INFLATION

For 1983 the Consumer Price Index (CPI) registered an increase in inflation of only 3.8%—slightly lower even than in 1982. And the Producer Price Index (of wholesale prices) increased by only 0.6%—the lowest increase in two decades!

In the years that followed, the money supply grew rapidly and monetarist economists repeatedly warned that a surge of inflation was likely to erupt soon. But in fact, the inflation rate remained low—at less than 5%—throughout the remainder of the 1980s. Fantastic!

INTEREST RATES REMAIN HIGH

The financial markets of early 1980 were unstable and widely fluctuating. They settled down some during the last half of the year, but not much.

Nominal interest rates eased somewhat during the summer, but then climbed again and stayed high. By the end of 1980 the prime rate stood at 21.5%. In early 1981 it eased some, but throughout the summer of 1981 the prime rate fluctuated between 20% and 21%.

It was during this period (beginning in the fall of 1980) that a positive real rate of interest reappeared in the U.S. economy. This initiated the first sustained period of positive real rates of interest in this country since 1972.

THE INFLATION RATE AND REAL INTEREST RATES

The year 1982 was a "turnaround" year in the U.S. money and financial markets. By mid-year 1982 we had the highest real rates of interest in the history of the country!

The prime rate remained between 15% and 17% throughout the first half of 1982. But the inflation rate kept coming down. So the real interest rate kept going up.

The real interest rate remained strongly positive throughout the remainder of the 1980s, supported by the low rate of inflation.

REAL RATES AND NOMINAL RATES IN 1982

As the inflation rate dropped, real interest rates climbed. Why? Because nominal rates stayed the same. Why didn't nominal rates drop? Partly because the money markets didn't believe the good news about inflation.

Who would be so naive as to think that inflation rates were going to remain in the 3% to 5% range? Anyone who thought that would be forgetting the experience of the 1970s and 1980. During those years almost all of the time the inflation rate was higher than expected, and the depositors and lenders wound up receiving negative real rates of interest on their money.

So in late 1981 (when the inflation rate dropped sharply) and until mid-year 1982, real rates soared. (All of us should have put our money into long-term, non-callable 15% or 16% bonds at that time to "lock in" a real return in excess of 10%! Not many times in a lifetime does a person have a chance to do that!) But then, as the inflation rate stayed low, nominal rates began to fall. The following table tells the dramatic story.

WHY DID NOMINAL RATES FALL?

The table shows that nominal rates came down by about 30% during the last half of 1982. Why? There were several reasons. The financial markets

THE BIG DROP IN NOMINAL INTEREST RATES DURING THE LAST HALF OF 1982

	JUNE 1982	DEC. 1982
Treasury Bills	13%	8%
The Fed's Discount Rate	12%	8.5%
Prime Rate at Major Banks	16.5%	11.5%
High-Grade Corporate Bonds	15%	11%
Home Mortgages	17%	13.5%

began to believe that (1) the days of double-digit inflation really were behind us—at least for a while, and (2) the Fed wasn't going to do anything drastic to shock the money markets and force nominal rates back up again. As it turned out, the financial markets were right.

Also, during the last half of 1982 there was a continuing slowdown in inflation, slack business and consumer demand for borrowed money (the recession), and, last but not least, easier monetary policy announced by the Fed in October. All of these conditions helped to push market interest rates downward. But even though nominal rates dropped precipitously, *real rates* remained at or near historic highs throughout 1982, 1983, and on into 1984, and remained strongly positive throughout the 1980s.

WHY DID REAL RATES STAY SO HIGH?

Real interest rates remained high for several reasons:

1. Throughout 1981 and until the fall of '82 the Fed kept a very tight rein on the money supply, thus supporting high interest rates.
2. Not many people believed that the inflation rate could be held in the 4% to 5% range. Lenders were (and are) very reluctant to make fixed-rate loans on the assumption that a 4% to 5% inflation rate will continue for several years into the future.
3. The rapid recovery and economic expansion of 1983–84 brought increasing borrowing demands by both consumers and expansion-minded businesses. The increased demands for money put upward pressures on interest rates. In fact, rates (both nominal and real) did rise moderately in 1983 and early '84.
4. The financial markets exhibited fear of the effects of the huge deficits projected in the budgets of the Reagan administration. Why fear? Because the

government must sell securities (borrow some $200 billion!) in the money markets to finance those deficits. Private businesses tend to be "crowded out" of the money markets by government borrowing. So businesses must pay more interest to get the money they need to finance their operations.

Fear of this "crowding out" effect of government borrowing tends to keep interest rates high. It did not appear likely that interest rates (either real or nominal) would come down very much until some progress was made in reducing the size of the federal government deficit. That's one reason why the President and Congressional leaders were working hard on legislation to try to reduce the size of the deficit.

THE ECONOMIC EFFECTS OF HIGH INTEREST RATES

High interest rates have a profound impact, both on the domestic economy and on the international position of the dollar. High interest rates tend to discourage borrowing and spending by consumers, by businesses, and especially by home-buyers.

IMPACT ON THE DOMESTIC ECONOMY

The high interest rates of the early 1980s had a devastating effect on the housing construction industry, on real estate firms, and on new home ownership. Several savings and loan associations and some banks were forced into near bankruptcy and had to merge with someone else to protect their depositors.

High interest rates forced corporations (and some municipal and state governments) to delay projects needed for modernization, cost-cutting, and growth. High interest rates discouraged investment and played the significant role in forcing the economy into recession—pushing the unemployment rate to 10.8% in early 1983.

In early 1982 some people were talking about the possibility of a serious depression brought about by the very high interest rates. Several utility companies were cancelling plans to build new power plants because of the high interest cost. Some of the airlines were cancelling orders for new aircraft because of the prohibitively high interest cost.

What about the impact on the Reaganomics supply-side economics program? How much more investment spending can we expect when interest costs are so high? And when there is already widespread excess capacity in industry because of the high-interest-rate-induced recession? Not much new investment will be going on, right?

THE INTERNATIONAL IMPACT

The high interest rates in this country have had a detrimental impact on some domestic producers, on some of our trading partners, and on U.S. export industries. Foreigners can trade their money for dollars and then invest the dollars in the United States and get high interest.

As foreigners trade their money for American dollars, that pushes up the international value of the dollar. And that's what happened in the early 1980s. So Americans could buy foreign goods cheaper. But foreigners couldn't afford to buy as many American goods. Some of our export producers were forced to cut back production and lay off workers.

Another problem is that oil prices in world markets are quoted in American dollars. So when the international value of the dollar goes up, all of the oil-importing countries must pay more for their oil.

HIGH INTEREST RATES ARE CONTAGIOUS

When interest rates are high in the United States, that forces up interest rates in other countries. The other nations must push their interest rates up to protect and stabilize the international value of their money. But high interest rates discourage investment, remember? And that fosters recession and increased unemployment. So you can see why the European nations were calling on the Reagan administration to do something to bring down interest rates in this country.

As you already know, nominal rates did fall significantly during the last half of 1982. And rates continued to ease downward until the late 1980s when inflation fears began to nudge them upward again.

MONETARY POLICY AND MONEY SUPPLY GROWTH RATES

The Fed's *monetarist approach* to monetary policy—targeting and strictly limiting the growth of the money supply—was rigidly followed from October 1979 until the fall of 1982. That was the reason for the very high interest rates. And it was the major cause of the serious recession of 1980–82.

CONGRESS TRIES TO "INSTRUCT" THE FED

By summer of 1982 there was much strong opposition to the Fed's monetarist policies—to the very high interest rates which were strangling the economy. Several people in Congress were working on new legislation to amend the Federal Reserve Act and to "instruct" the Fed to let the money supply expand. But before the Congress acted, the Fed acted.

THE FED ABANDONS ITS STRICT MONETARIST POLICY*

It was in the fall of 1982 that the Fed Board abandoned the strict monetarist policy of targeting and controlling the money supply. They decided to ease money—to let the money supply expand and let interest rates fall. And that's exactly what happened.

RAPID MONEY SUPPLY GROWTH IN 1982–83

During the first half of 1982, the U.S. money supply (M1) fluctuated between $445 and $455 billion, with very little increase. But from mid-year '82 to mid-year '83 the money supply increased at the rate of about 15% per year.

 OF SPECIAL INTEREST . . .

> THE M1 MONEY SUPPLY INCLUDES THE TOTAL NUMBER OF DOL-
> LARS HELD BY THE PUBLIC (1) IN CURRENCY AND COINS, (2) IN
> TRAVELERS CHECKS, AND (3) IN CHECKABLE DEPOSITS AT BANKS,
> SAVINGS AND LOAN COMPANIES, AND CREDIT UNIONS.

THE MONEY SUPPLY GROWTH SLOWS

The rapid money supply growth ended in July 1983. From August through November, M1 growth was only 1.6%. Then in December '83 and January '84 the growth rate was up to about 8%. Milton Friedman and other monetarists were criticizing the Fed for permitting the money supply to grow

---

*"Why the Fed Abandoned Monetarism," *Business Week* (December 13, 1982): 92.

so erratically. They were warning of dangers of inflation, and/or another recession.

CHANGING FED POLICIES AND TACTICS

How were Volcker and the Fed responding to such criticism? They were explaining that the *money growth statistics* have been *seriously distorted* by the new kinds of bank accounts (money market accounts, NOW accounts, etc.), and that it is now necessary to look at money market, interest rate, and other economic statistics (in addition to *money supply statistics*) to guide the formulation of *appropriate monetary policy.*

MONETARY POLICY HAS BECOME MORE DIFFICULT

In the next chapter you'll be reading about the apparent failures and successes of various theories—about the question: "Which theories can offer feasible explanations for what happened in the American economy during the turbulent years of 1980–84?"

But first, here's an interesting and revealing quote from Lyle E. Gramley, member of the Board of Governors of the Federal Reserve System. The quote emphasizes the great difficulty of designing and carrying out monetary policy in the rapidly changing money-banking-finance world of today.

I am willing to grant that shifts in money demand over the past seven or eight years have not totally destroyed the usefulness of monetary aggregates as a policy target or guide. But they have certainly made the task of running monetary policy more difficult, and that of explaining what is going on to a skeptical public nearly impossible.

The problems of interpreting the monetary aggregates will get much worse if, as I suspect, we are on the verge of an explosion in the use of EFT (electronic fund transfers). In a world of mature EFT systems, where transactions costs will be much smaller than they are at present, very few large economic entities will have identifiable transactions balances at the end of a business day.

The internationalization of banking and financial markets creates further measurement and interpretational problems for monetary policy. Changes in onshore deposits and domestic private credit flows no longer measure very precisely the amount of money and credit available to finance domestic economic activity.

Developments such as these greatly complicate the life of a central banker. It is not easy to develop new rules of thumb that are robust in a world of rapid innovation, or to estimate new large-scale econometric models that capture the new ways financial variables affect economic activity. Monetary policy-makers will, I am afraid, be operating by the seat of their pants for a long time to come.*

 REVIEW QUESTIONS

1. On October 6, 1979, Fed Chairman Volcker announced an abrupt shift in monetary policy. First, describe the events leading up to this shift in policy. Then explain the new policy.

2. Explain the difference between real and nominal interest rates. During 1980–82, nominal rates were historically high. They finally began dropping significantly in 1982. What was happening with real rates during this period? Why?

3. Discuss the effects of the high interest rates of the early 1980s on the domestic and international economy.

4. Explain some reasons why monetary policy has become more difficult to design and carry out in the modern world.

---

*Reprinted from the Federal Reserve Bank of Dallas, *Voice,* June, 1981.

22

THEORETICAL LESSONS OF 1980–84: THE RENAISSANCE OF KEYNESIAN ECONOMICS

By 1984, economists were looking back and assessing the experience of 1980–84—trying to figure out what had happened and why. What desirable (and undesirable) effects had resulted from the Reagan administration's supply-side tax cuts? And from the massive budget deficits which followed?

And what about the Fed's monetarist "stop money growth" policy of October '79 to October '82? And the astronomical interest rates which followed? And then the rapid money growth during '82–'83? And the erratic growth in the years that followed?

Why was the inflation rate so high? And then why so low in 1982, '83, and from then on?

Why was the 1980–82 recession so severe? And unemployment so high? Why was the 1983–84 recovery so rapid? And why didn't the rapid recovery reignite inflation?

The answers you'll get when you ask these questions will depend on who you ask. The monetarists, the supply-side economists, the rational expectations theorists, and the Keynesians all have different ways of explaining what happened.

SUPPLY-SIDE ECONOMICS: DISAPPOINTING RESULTS

Anyone can look and see that the Reaganomics "supply-side economics" program didn't produce the expected results. The economy was supposed to have been "revitalized" during 1981–82. The federal budget deficit was supposed to have been declining. A balanced budget was due in 1984. Outputs in the economy were supposed to have been expanding so rapidly that inflationary pressures would have been relieved, thereby ending serious inflation.

THE SUPPLY-SIDE PREDICTIONS WENT ASTRAY

As you know, none of the supply-side predictions came true. The serious inflation ended. But not as a result of increased supply.

During 1981–82—the first two years of the Reagan three-year "supply-side" tax cuts—the economy was in serious recession. Investment spending did not increase. In fact, it declined to the lowest level since the Great Depression of the 1930s. And the already large federal budget deficits tripled in size. What went wrong?

The anti-supply-siders said that the supply-side policies were ill-conceived, unrealistic, and doomed to failure from the start. Voodoo economics? Yes. That's what they said.

THE SUPPLY-SIDERS' RESPONSE: WE NEED MORE TIME

The supply-side economists who advised on and supported the Reagan program had a different view. The supply-siders (and President Reagan) said that the very strict monetarist policy, the very high interest rates, and the serious recession during 1981–82 offset the effects of the supply-side program. And they said that later, all of the promised good results would come true.

Now you can understand why in 1984 President Reagan and his supply-side advisors did not want to raise taxes to reduce the size of the federal deficit. They were still sure that, given enough time, the economy would respond to the tax cuts and expand enough to bring the budget into balance automatically.

So who would you believe? That probably would depend a lot on your economic and political philosophy—that is, on what you believed in the first place.

DID LOWER INFLATION SUPPORT MONETARIST THEORY?

Was the Fed's monetarist policy—"target and hold tight on the money supply"—responsible for stopping the double digit inflation? Not entirely. There were some other fortuitous events which helped a lot—declining oil prices, for example. But almost everyone was giving "tight money policy" a major share of the credit.

TIGHT MONEY, HIGH INTEREST RATES, AND RECESSION

It was tight money that caused the very high interest rates and choked off the economy and plunged it into recession. Recession produces surplus products and surplus workers and downward pressures on prices. But does this support the monetarist explanation of inflation? No.

To the monetarists, inflation is a *purely monetary* phenomenon. There's a predictable, almost mechanical relationship between changes in the size of the money supply and changes in the price level. Is that what happened in 1980–84? No. Far from it.

MONEY GROWTH RATES AND INFLATION RATES, 1980–84

In 1981 the money growth rate was the same as in 1980. Then in 1982 money growth accelerated—to an annual rate of 15% from mid-'82 to mid-'83. Then it slowed to almost zero for the last half of 1983.

What was the relationship between these money supply changes and price level changes—i.e., inflation rates? It's hard to see any relationship at all! The average inflation rate for 1980 was 12.4%, for 1981, 8.9%, for 1982, 3.9%, and for 1983, 3.8%.

During 1980–84 the rates of change in the size of the money supply are somewhat related to changes in *employment* and *output*. But the money supply changes do not seem to be related at all to changes in the price level. What did the monetarists have to say about that?

THE MONETARISTS' RESPONSE: THE STATISTICS WEREN'T ACCURATE

Some said that the money supply changes really were related to the price level changes, but that because of "lags" and other factors, the relationships were not easy to see. Some said that because of the serious recession and unemployment, the lags were longer than normal. And some were challenging the money supply statistics.

During this period the banks and thrift institutions (savings and loan associations, etc.) were offering new kinds of (interest bearing) checking accounts. These new accounts were becoming a part of the money supply. The money supply definitions were changing, so the monetary statistics were not very dependable during this period.

Also the velocity of circulation of money—the rate at which the average dollar is being spent—was changing as a result of the new kinds of checking accounts and for other reasons. So, in general, the experience of this period cannot be taken as typical. So said the monetarists.

WHAT ABOUT RATIONAL EXPECTATIONS THEORY?

You remember that according to the theory of rational expectations, government policies designed to produce "Keynesian-type" results will only succeed if the policies catch the people and businesses by surprise. And in the modern world, people and businesses are too smart (their "rational expectations" are too sharp) to let that happen. So Keynesian-type policies should never be used because they are doomed to fail. You were reading all about that back in Chapter 18.

THE PREDICTIONS OF RATIONAL EXPECTATIONS THEORY

Rational expectations theory tells us that a tight money policy will lead to a spending slowdown and recession *only if* the tight money policy is unanticipated—only if it catches us by surprise. Also, easy money will bring economic recovery, expansion, and prosperity only if it comes as a surprise.

According to the theory, any changes in the money supply that are *expected to occur* will *automatically* exert their influence on the inflation rate—i.e., on the price level. For example, an announced policy of easy money and money supply growth would cause inflation *directly*—without any significant increase in employment, production, output, or income. The opposite—an announced policy of tight money and slower money growth—would bring down inflation automatically. There wouldn't be any significant slowdown in the economy—no recession. No increased unemployment.

THE THEORY DIDN'T FIT THE FACTS

How does the rational expectations theory fit with the events of 1980–84? You already know the answer. It doesn't fit very well. In fact, it doesn't fit at all. The events of 1980–84 turned out to be exactly opposite to the results predicted by the rational expectations theory.

As Princeton Professor Alan Blinder wrote in *The New York Times*, Forum Section (February 19, 1984): "The force of events is showing that the new classical emperor (rational expectations theory), though resplendent in theoretical elegance, has no empirical clothes."

THE KEYNESIAN VIEW?—A VICTORY FOR KEYNESIAN ECONOMICS!

Keynesian economists look at the 1980–84 period and see that supply-side, monetarist, and rational expectations theories failed to predict or explain what happened. Proponents of each of these theories give explanations of *why* the theories weren't accurate. "But," say the Keynesians, "the fact remains that those theories failed. Only Keynesian theory can explain what happened in the American (and world) economy during 1980–84."

KEYNESIAN THEORY CAN EXPLAIN WHAT HAPPENED

Keynesian economics says that tight money will bring high interest rates which will cause cutbacks in both consumption and investment spending— reduced total spending (reduced aggregate demand). If money is very tight, interest rates will go very high and serious recession will result. Is that what happened in 1980–82? Yes.

Keynesian economics says that prices in the economy will not respond quickly or directly to tight money policy. But as recession and unemployment persist (and worsen), the inflation rate will begin to respond—to slow down. And that's also what happened in 1980–82.

Keynesian economics says that when the economy is in recession, expansionary fiscal and monetary policies can be used to bring economic recovery and prosperity. And without causing inflation. What policies? Policies to increase aggregate demand. Ease money and let the money supply grow. Cut taxes and run a government deficit. And that's exactly what was happening at the beginning of the rapid recovery period of 1983. And were the fires of inflation reignited? No.

THE RESTORED FAITH OF KEYNESIAN ECONOMISTS

The economic events of 1980–84 seemed to restore the faith of a lot of Keynesian (and former Keynesian) economists. But why had these economists lost their faith in Keynesian economics in the first place? The next section talks about that.

THE SHIFT TOWARD MONETARIST ECONOMICS—1960S AND 1970S

You remember that Keynesian economics grew out of the Great Depression of the 1930s. At first, many neoclassical economists attacked it as false, misleading, dangerous. But by the early 1960s it was widely accepted. Remember the Kennedy-Johnson (Keynesian) tax cut? Apparently it worked. It's hard to argue with success!

Keynesian economics in the early 1960s was very popular. At that time it was not only acceptable, it was fashionable among business and academic economists to be "Keynesian." But then what happened?

A small group of neoclassical economists—the monetarists, led by Milton Friedman—had never ceased their attack on Keynesian economics. But it wasn't until economic conditions turned for the worse in the mid-1960s that the monetarist attack began to become successful and to attract more economists to the monetarist position.

CAUSES AND EFFECTS OF THE INCREASING INFLATION

One important development contributing to the ascendency of monetarist economics was the uncontrolled inflation. To control inflation, Keynesian economics recommends tight money and high interest rates. It also recommends (and emphasizes) the need for higher taxes and less government spending. But during the mid-1960s, political realities rendered this fiscal policy approach infeasible.

Government spending for the Vietnam war kept increasing. The Johnson administration asked the Congress for tax increases, but Congress was unwilling to raise taxes to finance a war that was becoming increasingly unpopular. So the government ran increasing deficits and created new money to finance the war.

It was easy to see what was going to happen. The Keynesians and monetarists (and all other economists worthy of the name) could see that the stage was being set for serious inflation.

You already know what happened after that: serious and increasing inflation, and President Nixon's tight money policies (1969–1971) followed by his wage-price controls (1971–73). But throughout this period the government continued to run deficits—to spend more than it was collecting in taxes.

Throughout the 1970s and on into the 1980s the federal budget continued to run huge deficits. Efforts to bring it toward balance didn't have much success. When the government can't succeed in eliminating its deficit—either by cutting its spending or increasing its tax revenues or both—then this leaves "tight money policy"—holding down the growth of the money supply and pushing up interest rates—as the key element in the anti-inflation program.

The important shift in policy by the Federal Reserve Board in October of 1979 placed increased emphasis on controlling the rate of expansion of the money supply and less on controlling interest rates. This was a move inspired by monetarist economics—which emphasizes the importance of controlling the rate of *money supply growth.* It was a move away from Keynesian economics, which places more emphasis on the effects of *interest rate changes.*

KEYNESIAN ECONOMICS IS BLAMED FOR INFLATION

Would it be accurate to blame Keynesian economics for the unbalanced budgets, the huge deficits, and the resulting inflation of the 1960s and 1970s? Of course not. But some monetarist economists managed to do that. And somehow they managed to make these charges stick in the minds of many economists—in business, in government, and in academia.

Who wants to be associated with the kind of economics which is responsible for causing double-digit inflation? Nobody. So by the mid-1970s it was no longer fashionable to be "Keynesian." Economists deserted the Keynesian camp in droves. They shed their Keynesian labels as fast as they could.

THE SHIFT TO MONETARIST ECONOMIC ADVISERS

Back during the early 1960s, Keynesian economists were chosen by the Kennedy-Johnson administration for the Council of Economic Advisers. During that time, Keynesian economics was having a major influence on government policy.

Since the beginning of the Nixon administration in 1969, however, economists with more "monetarist leanings" have been appointed to the Council of Economic Advisers and to the Federal Reserve Board. So "monetarist" economics and philosophy came to play a more important role in influencing public policy.

MONETARISM CONQUERS ACADEMIA

Monetarist economics was playing an increasing role among university economists. More monetarist theory and less Keynesian theory was being taught at many universities and discussed by economists at their professional meetings. There is no question that with his keen analytical abilities and brilliant persuasiveness, Milton Friedman—the long-time advocate of the monetarist approach and leader of the attack on Keynesian economics—was playing a significant role in this academic victory for monetarism.

Monetarism is very appealing to many academic economists because of its close relationship to (and its reconfirmation of) the neoclassical model. Many (perhaps most) academic economists are better trained to deal with (and are more comfortable dealing with) long-run equilibrium mathematical models of the economy than with the short-run dynamic (day-to-day) economic issues addressed by Keynesian economics.

THE PRAGMATIC APPEAL OF KEYNESIAN ECONOMICS

Even with the ascendency of the monetarists, Keynesian economics continued to have an important influence on public policy. Keynesian economics offers *positive recommendations* for overcoming undesirable short-run macroeconomic conditions. Monetarist economics does not. So Keynesian economics often appeals to pragmatic policymakers as the more *relevant* and *practical* approach in dealing with the economy's problems.

THE KEYNESIAN COUNTERATTACK

As you already know, there were turbulent times (and a lot of surprises!) during 1980–84. Supply-side economics, monetarist theory, and rational expectations theory all appeared to have failed on the basis of the real-world evidence.

As early as 1983 there was evidence that some Keynesian economists were speaking out—reasserting their belief in the accuracy and usefulness of Keynesian economics as a guide to public policy. The following section gives an example of the "rebirth" of Keynesianism.

COMMITTEE ON THE RIGHTS OF CLOSET KEYNESIANS

The Committee on the Rights of Closet Keynesians (CROCK, would you believe?!) was formed in London in 1983. Its objective: Bring back the respectability and acceptability of Keynesian economics. In early 1984 CROCK issued a pamphlet describing how the monetarists and others had created inaccurate impressions of what Keynesian economics is (and isn't) and how the monetarists had falsely blamed Keynesian economics for many of the world's economic ills.

The pamphlet looks at the changing economic conditions of the 1970s and early '80s and concludes that Keynesian theory seems to better explain what happened than do either supply-side, monetarist, or rational expectations theories. The obvious conclusion is that Keynesian economics—as further modified in the light of theoretical developments and real-world empirical evidence—offers the only accurate and useful theoretical framework for guiding real-world economic policy.

THE ANTI-KEYNESIANS WON'T GIVE UP EASILY

None of the events of the early 1980s are likely to convince Milton Friedman and the other monetarists or the rational expectations theorists or the supply-side theorists to roll over and play dead. Or cross over and join the Keynesian camp? Heaven forbid!

All of these other theorists have ways of explaining why the events of the early 1980s did not provide an accurate test of their theories. They will stick to their guns and defend their positions.

THE KEYNESIAN RESTORATION OF THE 1980S AND 90S

Keynesian economics now seems once again destined to play a leading role in guiding public policy. And modern Keynesian economics is incorporating some very significant theoretical modifications. What theoretical modifications? Here are the important ones:

1. The "anti-depression bias" of Keynesian economics—a product of the depression years during which it was spawned—is being balanced by equal emphasis on controlling inflation.
2. Greater emphasis is being placed on the important role played by *money* in influencing macroeconomic conditions, and prices.

---

*The Crock pamphlet is described and analyzed in Alan S. Blinder, "Out of the Closet: Keynesians Regain Some Courage," *The New York Times*, Forum section, Sunday, 12 February 1984.

3. There is new emphasis on the great difficulty (and dangers) of carrying out discretionary economic stabilization policies. Keynesians now know that economic stabilization isn't nearly as easy as early Keynesian z led some people to believe.

THE CENTRAL IDEAS OF KEYNESIANISM WILL NOT CHANGE

Appropriate modifications can be integrated fairly easily into "modern Keynesian economics." But the central ideas of Keynesianism will remain:

- The economy does not always automatically regulate itself smoothly and reliably.
- The monetarist prescription for the slow and constant growth of the money supply does not necessarily guarantee the most desirable economic conditions.
- The government has economic stabilization tools which can—and when conditions warrant, should—be used to fight inflation or to limit recessions.

It is these central ideas of Keynesianism which many economists will never accept. These central ideas challenge a basic tenet of the monetarists and of neoclassical economics—i.e., that the economy is inherently stable, that it adjusts automatically, and that any attempt by government to carry out stabilization policies would only interfere with the natural automatic processes and would therefore be de-stabilizing. So, regardless of modifications in Keynesian theory, among some economists, the battle—the "great debate"—will go on.

THE KEYNESIAN RESTORATION HAS ARRIVED

The events since the early 1980s have significantly strengthened the Keynesian position. In his article, "Keynes Returns After Others Fail" (*The New York Times*, Forum Section, Sunday, February 19, 1984), Professor Alan Blinder of Princeton University says: "It may be premature to declare the Keynesian Restoration is upon us, but someone has to say it first."

In 1994, on the advice of his economic advisors, President Clinton appointed and the Senate approved Professor Alan Blinder to become Vice Chairman of the Federal Reserve Board. A strong and outspoken Keynesian in this key position on the Fed Board? Yes.

And what about the business economists working at the banks, financial institutions and other corporations throughout the economy—economists who are dealing with day-to-day, real world issues? Keynesian economists? Yes. Much of their economic analysis is based on modern Keynesian theory.

The Keynesian restoration has not yet taken over in the hallowed halls of academia. That may take awhile. But economists who are dealing with and interpreting the real world are relying heavily on modern Keynesian theory. Why? Because it's focused on the realities of how the real-world works.

A SUMMARY COMMENT ON PARTS SIX AND SEVEN

In Parts Six and Seven you have been reading a lot about macroeconomics—about the issues of inflation and unemployment and the changing problems, conditions, policies, and theories. But these aren't the only important economic issues and events of the modern world. It's time now to look at some others—at the government budget deficit, the foreign trade deficit, the stock market crash of 1987, and at the issues of giant corporations, environmental destruction, and the way the modern economies of mixed capitalism are evolving as they try to cope with these and other problems of modern society. That's the subject of Part Eight, coming up now.

 REVIEW QUESTIONS ―――――――――――――――――――――――

1. Compare the economic predictions of the Reaganomics supply-side programs to what actually occurred in the economy in 1981–82. How do the supply-siders defend their theory in view of its apparent failure?

2. Monetarism holds that inflation is a purely monetary phenomenon and that there is a direct, predictable relationship between changes in the size of the money supply and changes in the price level. How does this theory fit the "real-world" of the early 1980s? What explanations do the monetarists offer in defense of their theories?

3. How does Keynesian economic theory explain the events (inflation, recession, rapid recovery, etc.) of the early 1980s?

4. List and explain some theoretical modifications to Keynesian economics which have been occurring. Do these modifications change the basic thrust of Keynesian theory? Discuss.

5. In retrospect, do you think the economic events of 1980–84 mean that we should abandon monetarism, supply-side economics, and rational expectations theory in favor of Keynesian theory? Discuss.

PART EIGHT

THE MODERN WORLD: PROBLEMS, ISSUES, DEVELOPMENTS, AND THEORIES

The U.S. budget deficit, the 1987 stock market crash, the collapse of the Soviet Union, the trade deficit, monopoly power and social control, the energy and environmental crises, continuing controversy among economists, and the rapid evolution of economic society.

23 MODERN TIMES: INCREASING PRODUCTIVITY, BUDGET DEFICITS, THE '87 STOCK MARKET CRASH, AND THE TWILIGHT OF COMMUNISM

While the economists keep on building their models and analyzing and trying to explain why things happen as they do, the real world keeps right on growing and changing. Throughout the 1980s and 1990s many revolutionary changes were going on in so many aspects of our economy, and in our lives.

Technology and communications have grown explosively. Computers have revolutionized the workplace. Global competition in both goods and services have had a profound impact. This chapter and the ones that follow discuss these and other developments.

A RECORD-BREAKING PERIOD OF ECONOMIC EXPANSION

From the end of 1982 when the economy was seriously depressed, all the way until the end of the decade of the 1980s, the economy continued to grow without interruption—no recession. Never before had there been a seven-year recession-free period.

It was not until the last half of 1990 that the economy slipped into a relatively mild recession. Then, throughout 1991 and '92 the economy was very slowly recovering.

Before the 1990 recession started, the unemployment rate reached a low of 5.5% of the labor force. But at mid-year 1992 the unemployment rate stood at 7.8%. Then the economy began to speed up. In 1993 and early '94 the rate of economic growth continued to accelerate. Output went up and unemployment went down. Happy days were here again! But then . . .

THE FED TIGHTENS

In early February of 1994 Fed Chairman Alan Greenspan announced that the Fed was going to push up short-term interest rates. This was called a "pre-emptive strike" to prevent the economy from speeding up too much and triggering inflation.

The Fed's money-tightening moves continued throughout 1994 amid much controversy among economists and much criticism by the news media. The question was: "Why slow down the growth of the economy to fight inflation, when there are no visible signs of inflation?"

To answer this question, Dr. Alan Blinder, at that time Vice Chairman of the Fed Board, reminded us that monetary policy operates with some time lags—that when you fight inflation, the Bunker Hill strategy doesn't work. "If you wait until you see the whites of their eyes, you're dead!" Successful monetary policy must be based, not on current conditions in the economy, but on conditions which can be forseen several months down the road.

As it turned out, the Fed was right. The growth rate of the economy was held in check, the economy continued to grow at a moderate pace, and there was no increase in the rate of inflation. The Fed succeeded in achieving its objective: A "soft landing" of a speeding-up economy.

THE EXPANSION CONTINUES INTO THE NEW MILLENNIUM

The expansion of the 1980s was a record-breaker. But the record was eclipsed by the expansion of the 1990s. The little "tap on the brakes" by the

Fed in 1994 turned out to be just what was needed to set the stage for a continuous period of economic expansion.

The economy continued to grow throughout the decade, and the inflation rate remained at record lows, quarter after quarter. The Fed remained "on hold" allowing supply and demand in the financial markets to set interest rates most of the time.

In 1998 in response to economic crisis conditions in Asia, Russia, and elsewhere, the Fed cut short-term interest rated by one quarter percentage point, three different times to provide additional liquidity in the international financial markets. Then in 1999 as the world economy was recovering and the U.S. economy was booming, the Fed took back two of those 1998 rate cuts. The U.S. economy ended 1999 with a rapidly growing economy, very low inflation, and a record low unemployment rate. Alan Greenspan and the other policymakers at the Fed deserve a lot of credit for the masterful way in which they engineered an inflation free, recession free economy——the "storybook economy" of the 1990s.

In January of 2000 as this book was going to press, the economy broke all previous records for a continuous uninterrupted economic expansion. And at that time the end of the expansion was nowhere in sight.

PRODUCTIVITY—OUTPUT PER WORKER HOUR—INCREASES DRAMATICALLY

During the economic expansion of the 1980s, average worker productivity was increasing at less than 1.5 percent per year. Then in the early 1990s output per worker-hour was increasing, on average, at more than 2 percent per year. But by the end of the decade of the 1990s the rate of increase in productivity had more than doubled, to an annual rate of over 4 percent! Why?

Improved techology was playing a major role, as was better education and training of the labor force. Businesses were spending a lot for high-tech, productivity-increasing machinery and equipment.

This "productivity growth" issue is vital. The future of the American economy and of "the good life" for all of us depends on it. Why? Because of the inexorable (powerful and inescapable) laws of economics. It's obvious that the only way the members of the society can have more and better things is for the economy to produce more and better things. What that means is: increased productivity!

Also, expanding outputs increase the supplies of goods available. That helps to hold down inflation. Supply-side economics! Remember?

The Great Dilemma of the Federal Budget Deficit

During the 1950s and '60s the federal government budget ran small deficits from time to time. Then during the 1970s the deficits got larger. But it wasn't until the 1980s that the size of the deficit seemed to become unmanageable.

In fiscal year 1981 (ending September 30, 1981), the federal budget deficit was $38 billion. In fiscal '82 it was $111 billion. For fiscal '83 it was $195 billion. For fiscal '84 it was $175 billion. Then in fiscal 1985? Would you believe more than $210 billion? That's right.

During the summer of 1984 Congress passed and the president signed a $50 billion tax increase and a $13 billion spending cut as a "down payment" on closing the deficit gap. But at that time President Reagan was taking a very strong position against any further tax increases to try to reduce the deficit.

President Reagan's Budget Projections

In 1985 the President's budget projections for future years continued to show large deficits: for fiscal year 1986 $180 billion; for the years following that, still very large but slowly declining deficits.

There was mounting concern in the Congress about the huge deficits. But President Reagan was holding strongly to his position: (1) there should be no tax increases; (2) there should be no cuts in Social Security, either in benefit payments or cost-of-living (COLA) adjustments; and (3) there should be no cuts in planned defense spending.

So the President's position boiled down to this: All deficit cuts must come from spending cuts, and all spending cuts must come from domestic programs such as education, housing, job training, transportation, and others. But the Congress refused to make such deep cuts in spending for domestic programs. So what happened? The deficits just got bigger.

The Gramm-Rudman-Hollings Act of December 1985

It was in this "no compromise" situation that the Gramm-Rudman-Hollings (GRH) Act was passed. This Act set the maximum permissible size of the federal deficit for each fiscal year, 1986 ($172 billion) through 1991 (zero). In any year in which the deficit was projected to exceed the target number, automatic spending cuts would be imposed.

Did the GRH Act achieve its objectives? Of course not. This act tries to force the Congress and the administration to do something they don't want to do. Any such act will always fail.

The size of the actual deficit in the targeted "zero year" under the GRH Act (1991) turned out to be an all-time record: $269 billion! And in the following year (1992) the deficit hit a new high of $290 billion. And the national debt? By 1992 it had gone up to more than $4 trillion!

Obviously these trends could not continue. But what could be done?

PRESIDENT BUSH BREAKS HIS "NO NEW TAXES" PLEDGE

When campaigning for election, George Bush pledged that there would be no new taxes as long as he was president. But when he was in the White House and he saw the exploding national debt and the size of the deficits for the coming years, he broke his pledge. He really didn't have much choice. New tax revenues were clearly essential.

President Bush agreed to work with Congress to try to cut about $25 billion in expenditures and to raise about $25 billion in new revenues. And that's what they did. That was a step in the right direction. But $50 billion doesn't go very far toward eliminating a deficit of almost $300 billion!

PRESIDENT CLINTON'S DEFICIT REDUCTION PLAN

When he assumed the Presidency in January of 1993, President Clinton immediately turned his attention to the deficit problem. He proposed a package of spending cuts and tax increases that would cut the deficit by $433 billion over a 5 year period. Congress passed the package in mid-summer of 1993.

The actual deficit for 1993 amounted to $256 billion. This was down $34 billion from the 1992 deficit. Why the big drop? Partly because of the deficit reduction efforts, and partly because of good luck!

The economy was expanding. Output and employment and incomes were up. More income generates more tax revenues.

Military spending was down because of the collapse of the USSR and the end of the cold war. The price of oil was down, and lower interest rates held down the interest cost on the national debt. Nevertheless, in 1993 we still had a deficit of $256 billion—a long way to go to a balanced budget!

THE REPUBLICAN CONGRESS AND ITS "CONTRACT WITH AMERICA"

In the November, 1994 elections, the Republican Party gained control of both houses of Congress. The new Republican leadership had issued its "contract with America," promising to change many things. A key point was to bring the government budget into balance over a 7-year period.

In pursuing this objective the members of the Congress decided to "play hardball" with President Clinton. They had a powerful tool. To force the President to go along with their plans, they could shut down the government. And, in fact, that's what they did. Here's what happened.

GRIDLOCK SHUTS DOWN THE GOVERNMENT

The Republican Congress would not approve President Clinton's proposed budget for fiscal year 1996, which began on October 1, 1995. So beginning on October 1, '95, all of the operations of the government had to be funded by "continuing resolutions" which permit the government to continue to spend under the previous year's budget. But there was another catch.

There was a law setting the national debt limit for the U.S. government at $4.9 trillion. In the fall of 1995 the national debt was approaching that $4.9 trillion limit. President Clinton asked the Congress to increase the debt limit to permit the Treasury to continue to sell bonds to finance the government's programs. But the Congress refused.

So what happened when the government ran out of money? All national parks and other non-essential functions were shut down. This happened once in the fall of 1995 and again in January of 1996.

On March 21, 1996 the Congress finally increased the debt limit by $600 billion, up to $5.5 trillion. This provided the government with enough borrowing power to carry it through the next 18 months without another "debt limit crisis."

FROM DEFICIT TO SURPLUS: 1997–99

In 1996 there was much public displeasure (disgust?) regarding the gridlock seen in Washington. Both political parties were taking the heat. Nobody was winning. Everyone was losing.

In this hostile atmosphere, predictably, the President and the Congress began to compromise——to work together. They now had a mutually agreed objective: to reduce the monstrous government budget deficit. And so they did. It wasn't all smooth and harmonious, but in the end, tax and spending adjustments were worked out. In 1996 the deficit amounted to only $107 billion-down from $203 billion in 1994 and $164 billion in 1995. Then in 1997 the deficit dropped to $22 billion. And in 1998? Astounding! A surplus of $70 billion! And 1999 was even better: A surplus of more than $120 billion.

Now it was a new economic problem—the problem of deciding what to do with the big government surplus. A more pleasant problem than dealing with the deficit, to be sure! But a problem just the same.

Fed Chairman Greenspan suggested paying off some of the more than $5.5 trillion government debt. Republican leaders in Congress were calling for tax cuts. Some Democrat Congressional leaders were calling for increased spending on education and other domestic programs.

As long as the economy continues to boom, paying off some of the government debt would make good economic sense and would be healthy for the economy. But at the beginning of this new millennium and this Presidental election year, this issue of what to do with the budget surplus was Wasington's big political football.

THE SURPLUS RESULTED FROM THE BOOMING ECONOMY

The revenue and spending legislation worked out by the Congress and the Administration helped some. But the fact is that the government budget surplus resulted from the booming economy of the late 1990s. As the unemployment rate dropped to the lowest level in decades, and as personal incomes increased, much more tax revenues were generated. And that's what generated the budget surplus.

The increased productivity of the economy, the increased output per worker, aided by the computer-technology information revolution, all have contributed to this "storybook economy" which existed at the beginning of the 21st Century.

The meteoric rise in stock prices which occurred during the final years of the 1990s was also playing a significant role in the continuing booming economy, and in the increasing government revenues which generated the budget surplus. But stock prices here moved in unpredictable ways during the 1980s and '90s. The following section talks about a particularly scary time in the stock markets.

THE STOCK MARKET CRASH OF 1987

During the 1980s while the budget deficit was getting worse and worse, what was happening to stock prices? Until midyear 1987, they were going up.

Back in 1982 the economy was in serious recession and stock prices were low. During 1983 and '84 as the economy recovered, stock prices began rising. They continued to rise until August 1987. At that point, the average stock was selling for about three and one-half times as much as in 1982. For example, if you paid $20 a share for stock in 1982, on the average that stock would be worth about $70 a share in August 1987. Why? Demand and supply.

STOCK VALUES GO UP 40% IN 8 MONTHS

Another basic law of economics: For every buyer of stocks (or anything else) there must be a seller. And for every seller there must be a buyer. Otherwise, no transaction! Until August 1987, more people were interested in buying stocks than in selling them. So prices continued to rise.

By mid-August of 1987, average stock prices were about 40% higher than they had been in January. A 40% gain in less than 8 months? That's right! Clearly, during that time the stock market was the place to be! But after that? Not so.

During the summer of 1987 there were indications that inflation might be picking up. Some investors became uneasy and began selling. Between mid-August and mid-September, stock prices dropped fairly sharply. But this was regarded by many as a normal correction in a rising market—a good buying opportunity. And by early October, stocks had recovered more than half of their September losses. Many analysts were declaring that the bull market (rising stock prices) was alive and well and heading for new highs. Then the downtrend began.

On October 6, the stocks of the nation's major industrial corporations lost about 3.5% of their value, in one day. Then on Wednesday, October 14 stocks dropped sharply again, losing almost 4% of their value in one day. Thursday, October 15 wasn't as bad, bringing a value loss of only about 2.4%. But then on Friday the 16th stocks lost another 4.6% of their value. Was this another normal correction? Another good buying opportunity in a rising market?

MANY INVESTORS LOST CONFIDENCE

Over the weekend, people had plenty of time to think about that. Many of them decided that it was time to get out. The managers of billion-dollar-plus portfolios—pension fund managers, big mutual funds, others—decided to sell. Even before the New York stock markets opened on Monday morning, October 19, the handwriting was already on the wall.

When it's Sunday evening in New York, it's already Monday morning in Tokyo and the stock markets are open. And long before daybreak in New York, the markets are open in Paris, Frankfurt, London, and other places in Europe. And what was happening? Stocks were under heavy selling pressure. Prices were dropping fast. Several American stocks trade in these foreign markets. Many portfolio managers and traders in New York were up all night selling stocks on the Far-Eastern and European markets.

OCTOBER 19, 1987: THE BIGGEST ONE-DAY DROP EVER!

When the New York markets opened, prices plummetted. When everyone is trying to sell and no one is trying to buy, prices must fall until someone is willing to buy. And prices did fall. How far? Until the total value of the major industrial stocks had dropped by 22.6%—the biggest one-day percentage drop ever.

More than 600 million shares were traded on that fateful "Black Monday." The previous record number of shares traded in any one day had been about 340 million—and that record had been set on the previous Friday (October 16). Before that, there never had been a 300-million-share day.

The following day (Tuesday the 20th) another 600 million shares were traded. Stocks were sharply up and down all day long. But at the close, some of Monday's losses had been regained. Then in the days and weeks that followed, stock prices jumped around a lot, but for the most part the trend was upward.

Throughout November and December, many forecasters were drawing parallels with the 1929 crash. Some were predicting the next *great depression*. But as the weeks and months went by the statistics on the economy kept looking better, not worse. In December and January unemployment was at the lowest rate since the 1970s. And production, output, and income all were increasing at a healthy pace.

So why did the stock market crash? And what was the effect on the economy? There were many complex causes involved. The sharply falling prices generated panic selling. So the collapse tended to feed on itself. But also, it is generally agreed that prices had gone up too far, too fast. Most stocks were selling for more than their "fundamental values"—based on the assets, earnings, and dividends represented by each share. So the market was poised for a fall.

WHY DIDN'T THE ECONOMY GO INTO A DEPRESSION?

The drop in stock prices from the August highs to the October lows wiped out about $1 trillion of wealth. That was expected to have a severe impact on the economy. But that didn't happen. Why not? Who knows? But don't forget that that trillion dollars in wealth had been created by increasing stock prices between January and mid-August. Maybe that had something to do with it. Maybe the stock owners were saying, "Oh well—easy come, easy go!"

The stock market crash didn't destroy the economy. But it was frightening. The financial system came dangerously close to a breakdown. Quick action by the Federal Reserve to pump funds into the financial system helped to avoid a breakdown.

As a result of the panic selling and program trading which contributed greatly to the 1987 crash, new rules were established for the New York Stock Exchange. If the Dow Jones Index moves more than 50 points either up or down, trading is halted for a "cooling off" period. That's to prevent a cumulative upswing or down-swing from causing the market to do what it did in October of 1987. So far, these "collars" have been used on several occasions and they seem to have had a stabilizing influence.

OCTOBER 1987 WAS A GREAT BUYING OPPORTUNITY!

Looking back to October 20, 1987, that was obviously a great time to buy stocks! By the end of January of 1989, stock prices were higher than they were back on the day before the crash. So, on average, all of the "Black Monday" losses had been regained before the end of January, 1989. And after that? With the exception of a few minor dips, stocks have continued to roar upward. By mid-year 1996 average stock prices were more than 3 times as high as they were on October 20, 1987.

Then the real boom began. During each of the last five years of the decade of the 1990s, stock prices, on average, were up by more than 20 percent per year. As each year ended, the forecasters were saying, "this has been an unbelievable year in the stock markets, but we don't expect next year to be as good." But next year was as good.

The stock markets in the United States and pretty much all around the world ended the 1990s by reaching new highs. And in January of 2000 there was much optimism for the continuation of rising stock prices throughout the year, and beyond.

PROBLEMS, ISSUES AND REVOLUTIONARY CHANGES OF THE 1980S AND '90S

You can see that the modern world has been going through some major changes and facing some difficult problems. But you haven't seen it all. Not yet. Here's a quick glance at some other things.

THE CHANGING POPULATION STRUCTURE

What's happening to the U.S. population structure? It's changing. There are more retired people every year and fewer in the "productive" ages.

This is influencing the directions of the economy: employment, social security programs, education, products produced, housing, recreation—many aspects of the economy. You'll be seeing several important population-induced changes throughout your lifetime.

THE TECHNOLOGY REVOLUTION

A revolution in technology is going on: new telecommunications and computers, and the widespread use of CAD-CAM (computer assisted design-computer assisted manufacturing) and robots.

This technological revolution is making significant inroads in the areas of production, finance, banking, and in the nature of employment and the labor market. And this revolution is just now getting started. Its impact during the coming years will be profound.

THE LABOR MARKET REVOLUTION

There's a revolution going on in the labor markets, and in labor-management relations.

Unions are negotiating give-backs on fringe benefits—sometimes even wage cuts—in exchange for greater job security. There's a new understanding on the part of labor that, for labor to benefit, the industry must survive! And there is a move toward including labor representation on the boards of directors of the corporations.

The "let's all work together and try to survive" attitude is revolutionizing labor-management relations in this country.

THE REVOLUTION IN BANKING

The revolution in banking and in the financial markets has resulted from high interest rates, deregulation, new technology, and some other causes.

New legislation is bringing banks into greater competition with each other, with the savings and loan industry, and with the non-bank financial businesses such as the brokerage firms, insurance companies, credit card companies, and others. The coming of nationwide bank branching is bringing increased competition and increased efficiencies.

As far back as the early 1970s, various studies have been calling for the elimination of the restrictions imposed on banks by the 1933 Glass-Steagall Act. But it was not until November of 1999 that these recommendations were finally carried out by the passage of the Gramm-Leach-Bliley Act. This Act, in the words of Senator Gramm, "knocks down the barriers in American law that separate banking from insurance and banking from securities." This new act was a long time in coming. Eventually it will increase the efficiencies and reduce the costs of banking and financial services for all of us.

THE REVOLUTION IN ANTITRUST POLICY

There has been a revolutionary change in public policy toward big business. In 1982 both AT&T and IBM got settlements of their long-pending antitrust cases.

Several big mergers were occurring. The government has let it be known that the top priority public policy is now concerned with *increasing productivity* and improving the ability of American industry to compete with foreign producers—not with restricting the size of American firms so that they might better compete with each other. Nowadays it is *global competition* (not domestic competition) which is the name of the game.

THE MICROSOFT ANTITRUST CASE

In 1998 the antitrust division of the U.S. Department of Justice charged Microsoft with being a monopoly. Two years later Microsoft was found guilty of using its monopoly power to stifle the growth of its competitors and of illegal practices to extend its monopoly position in the computer software markets. In these "findings of fact," issued in November of 1999, the judge stated that Microsoft had used its prodigious market power and immense profits to stifle innovation and harm both consumers and any companies that dared to compete with it. But there was no indication at that time what the proposed remedy should be. Should Microsoft be split up into separate companies, as was AT&T in the early 1980s? Or what?

The Microsoft case had been going on for two years already when the findings of fact were issued. It will probably be another two years (maybe more) before decisions will be made on what penalties to impose. By the time this case is finally concluded, we will know more about the new direcitons of antitrust enforcement in this high tech world of the 21st Century.

THE UNDERGROUND ECONOMY

The "underground economy" is really the "free economy"—it's the economy which works on its own without the burdens of government regulations or interference or taxes or anything else. It includes everything from the kid down the street who mows your lawn or the plumber who works for "cash only," to the illegal drug trade.

Nobody knows how much economic activity goes on in the U.S. underground economy. But estimates range anywhere from less than $400 billion to more than $800 billion. But by any measure you choose, that's a lot—and it's something to be concerned about.

The underground economy has been growing rapidly. It distorts the overall growth rate and results in an unrealistic view of what's going on in the economy. And it reduces the government's tax revenue. It's already creating some problems. In the future it's likely to create more.

THE TWILIGHT OF COMMUNISM

In the 1970s and '80s the "great economic failure" of Communism as a form of economic system was becoming increasingly clear. Meaning exactly what?

Just this: Centralized economic planning and resource administration as used in the Communist countries has not turned out to be a very efficient way to direct and control a modern economic system.

The movement of the Chinese economy toward using free markets and price and profit incentives began in the late 1970s. Since then, great changes have been made.

In the U.S.S.R. major economic reforms were started more recently. But by the mid-1980s under Gorbachev's leadership the Soviet economic reform movement was moving at remarkable speed, bringing freer markets and greater reliance on the price mechanism.

In both China and the U.S.S.R. *these fundamental economic changes are proving to be one of the most significant economic developments of our time.* It was in the early 1990s that the Soviet Union fell apart and ceased to exist as a political entity. Then in December of 1991, ten of the former Soviet Republics formed the Commonwealth of Independent States (CIS).

Boris Yeltsen became President of the Russian Republic and continued with Gorbachev's policies to move the economy toward private property and a free market economy.

In 1999 the leaders in Chechnya were trying to break away from Russia, and in the beginning of 2000 that war was still going on. On New Years Eve, December 31, 1999, Yeltsin announced his resignation as President of the Russian Republic, and appointed Vladimir Putin as his interim successor, pending elections in the spring. Putin vowed to continue the reforms leading to a free-market economy. Stay tuned . . .

Why are all these free market changes going on in China and the CIS? You might say that the *basic laws of economics* caught up with them. They're learning the hard way about market forces and how they work—and about the *powerful price mechanism.* If they learn it well, the future of their people will be much brighter.

ALL THESE CHANGES ARE BRINGING IN A "NEW WORLD"

How different the world is now from the way it was only a few short years ago! This globalized one-world economy is all tied together with instantaneous communications and transfers of funds and assets everywhere, worldwide. All economic systems are being influenced by this "new world" we find ourselves in.

And mark this well: The rate of change isn't slowing down. It's speeding up! The world of tomorrow will be more different from the world of today, than the world of today if from the world of yesterday. So hang on!

In the chapters coming up you will be reading more about the changing conditions and times in our "globalized modern world."

 REVIEW QUESTIONS ────────────────────────────

1. Give the highlights of changing macroeconomic conditions in the American economy during the 1980s and '90s.

2. What is so important about an increasing rate of productivity (output per hour for the average worker) in the economy?

3. Explain the dilemma of the federal budget deficit, and how the Gramm-Rudman-Hollings Act was supposed to guarantee a solution to this problem. Why did it fail? Discuss.

4. Discuss the continuing budget deficits of the 1990s and President Clinton's budget predictions for 1996–2002. Do you think those predictions are accurate? Explain.

5. Discuss the short-run and long-run seriousness of the stock market crash of October, 1987.

6. Many important (sometimes *revolutionary*) changes have been and are going on in the U.S. and world economy. Mention and explain some of these.

24

INTERNATIONAL FINANCE, DOLLAR EXCHANGE PROBLEMS, AND THE FOREIGN TRADE DEFICIT

🔑 KEY TERMS

- exchange value of the dollar
- U.S. international balance of payments
- balance of payments deficit
- fixed international exchange rates
- dollar crisis of 1971
- floating international exchange rates

- U.S. merchandise trade deficit
- dollar crisis of 1978
- roller-coaster dollar of the 1980s
- foreign investment in the 1990s
- U.S. trade deficit in the 1990s
- J-curve effect
- debtor nation
- G-7 countries

The American economy (whether we like it or not) is closely tied into the world economy. What happens to the money supply, interest rates, and other economic conditions in this country will reflect—*must* reflect—the relationships between the U.S. economy and the rest of the world. Truly, we live in a world of "international interdependence."

AMERICAN POLICIES MUST REFLECT INTERNATIONAL CONSIDERATIONS

American policies these days are often influenced by the position of the U.S. dollar in the international money markets. When interest rates in this country go down, foreigners who hold dollars exchange their dollars for other kinds of money—marks, francs, yen, or something else—so they can invest the money in other countries where they can earn more interest. But when interest rates in the United States go up, foreigners are more likely to hold dollars because they can invest the dollars here and earn more interest than in other countries.

FOREIGN HOLDERS OF DOLLARS CAN AFFECT THE U.S. ECONOMY

Suppose the American economy slows down. There is not so much demand for money in this country, so interest rates tend to fall. The lower interest rates should stimulate more borrowing and spending and continued growth of the money supply. That should help to achieve a healthy and growing economy.

As our interest rates go down, however, foreigners shift their "liquid assets" (money) out of dollars and into other kinds of money. That causes the international value of the dollar to go down. Low interest rates may trigger an "international dollar crisis." (You will be reading more about this, soon).

What about the opposite situation? When businesses and consumers in this country try to increase their borrowing and spending, that pushes up interest rates. The higher interest cost is supposed to prevent the money supply (and borrowing and spending) from expanding too much.

But when interest rates rise in this country, this causes foreigners to shift their "liquid assets" to the U.S. money markets. They want to earn some of the high interest income. When this happens, it increases the supply of available money in the American economy. So that supports borrowing and spending at a higher level than desired. The money supply grows faster than the desired rate because of the injection of foreign-owned dollars attracted to this country by the high interest rates. And the expanding money supply supports inflation? Yes.

U.S. POLICIES "SUPPORTED THE DOLLAR" DURING THE 1970s

Ever since the 1960s, monetary policies in this country have been, from time to time, adjusted specifically for the purpose of stabilizing the international value of the dollar. Our monetary policies (and all other stabilization policies) must take into account the objective of international stability of the dollar.

Now you have a little introduction to the importance of taking an *international view* when considering *domestic* monetary, fiscal, and/or other stabilization policies. So now you're ready to review and analyze some important recent events involving the United States and the U.S. dollar in the international trade and finance markets. That's what most of this chapter is about.

THE EVOLUTION OF THE "DOLLAR PROBLEM" OF THE 1970S

As the trend of inflation in the U.S. economy increased in the late 1960s and throughout the 1970s, what was happening to the "exchange value" of the U.S. dollar in the international money markets? It was going downward—sometimes *sharply* downward.

As prices in this country were spiraling upward, the purchasing power of the dollar was spiraling downward. If prices double, then the dollar will only buy half as much. That means, in real terms, the dollar is only worth half as much as before.

FOREIGNERS BECAME LESS WILLING TO HOLD DOLLARS

Foreigners hold billions of American dollars. Foreign banks, businesses, and individuals have bank accounts in American banks and hold American bonds and other "dollar assets." From World War II until the late '60s the dollar was a very good asset to hold—in fact, "as good as gold." Foreigners could actually use their dollars to buy gold from the U.S. government, so their dollars really were as good as gold.

As long as prices in the United States were going up only slightly (prices in most other countries were going up more rapidly), the dollar was just great as an asset to hold. But when prices in the United States began spiraling upward, it became obvious that the dollar wasn't such a desirable asset anymore. So people holding dollars began to want to get rid of them, to trade them for gold, or for some other kind of money—money less likely to depreciate in value so fast.

Another economic crisis was developing too. As prices of American products spiraled upward, American buyers saw opportunities to buy foreign products *cheaper*. So they did. American consumers began buying more German cars and Japanese cars and tape recorders. Businesses began buying more Japanese steel. As time went on the flood of products from foreign countries increased. Each time an American bought a foreign product, more dollars flowed into the bank accounts of the foreigners.

THE INCREASING U.S. BALANCE OF PAYMENTS DEFICIT

In the years following World War II and on into the 1960s, the United States had been exporting more goods to other nations than we were buying back from them. The foreign producers were not selling enough to us to earn the dollars they needed to pay for their imports from us. So it was necessary through loans and grants of dollars to provide money to foreigners. Otherwise they would not have been able to continue to buy these American exports. But in the 1960s this situation turned around.

As the European and Japanese economies were rebuilt, they began expanding their own outputs. So they bought fewer American products. At the same time, they began to sell more of their products in this country. Americans began buying more VWs and Toyotas and Sonys and other foreign goods—providing more dollars to foreigners. So dollars began piling up in the foreigners' bank accounts.

Then, as the inflation picked up in the late 1960s and on into the 1970s, American goods became more and more expensive. This discouraged foreigners from buying American goods and encouraged Americans to buy more of the relatively cheaper foreign products. More "surplus dollars" poured into the bank accounts of foreigners. All of this was going on at the same time that the U.S. foreign aid programs, overseas military spending, and various other programs of government grants and loans were pouring more dollars into the hands of foreigners.

THE LATE 1960S: TROUBLE BEGINS FOR THE DOLLAR

In the late 1960s it became clear that the dollar was in trouble in the international money markets. The U.S. Balance of Payments was running a deficit—meaning that foreigners were receiving more dollars from us than they were using up. The "surplus supply" of American dollars in the world's money markets kept on increasing.

You know what happens when excess supplies of anything are pushed into any market—the price goes down. That's what was happening to the American dollar. The larger the deficit on the U.S. International Balance of Payments, the greater the surplus supply of dollars which is pushed into the hands of foreigners. So the greater the "downward pressure" on the international value of the dollar.

From just after World War II until the early 1970s, the international value (exchange rate) of the dollar was "fixed." During this period you always knew exactly how many marks or francs or yen (or whatever) you could get for one dollar. But as the Balance of Payments deficits continued and surplus dollars kept piling up in the bank accounts of foreigners, there became increasing pressure for the dollar to be "devalued"—that is, for its "exchange value" in buying other kinds of money, to be decreased.

THE DOLLAR CRISIS OF 1971

During the early part of 1971 the U.S. Balance of Payments was running a deficit *much higher* than ever before. It was obvious that the international value of the dollar could not be held at its "fixed exchange rate" with this flood of surplus dollars pouring into foreign hands.

Everybody who held dollars knew that devaluation *had to come*—and no one wants to hold dollars when they know dollars are going to be devalued. No one wants to hold any asset when they know its value is going to go down! So foreigners who held dollars were trying to sell them in the international money markets—to exchange them for other kinds of money. But who wanted to buy dollars? Nobody.

The rapidly expanding international payments deficit and the rapid gold drain made it absolutely imperative that President Nixon take some action immediately.

THE DOLLAR WAS DEVALUED AND ALLOWED TO "FLOAT"

On August 15, 1971, when President Nixon announced the wage-price freeze he also announced that no longer would gold be sold to *anyone,* and he announced the devaluation of the dollar—that is, that it would be sold cheaper (for less foreign money) in the future. At first the dollar was going to be allowed to "float." That means anyone who wanted to sell dollars would have to sell them for whatever they could get. Official exchange rates for the dollar were temporarily abandoned.

With official exchange rates, American tourists abroad who had travelers checks in American dollars knew just how many francs, marks, pounds, yen, or any other currency they could get for one dollar. But after August 15, 1971, the tourist who went into the foreign bank for currency never knew what the exchange value of the dollar would be—except that it would be lower than before!

What were the effects of the devaluation and other moves to strengthen the dollar? Did they work? To some extent, yes. But as time went on it became clear that the balance of payments problem had not been solved.

In 1972 and 1973 the international problem of the dollar continued, more acute sometimes than at other times. Attempts were made to put together a new system of "fixed" exchange rates, but without success.

UNSTABLE WORLD ECONOMIC CONDITIONS OF THE 1970S

In the early 1970s there were several shocks which disrupted international trade and exchange relationships among the nations of the world. Between 1973 and 1974, prices of imported oil *quadrupled*. That forced up prices of just about everything—fuels, lubricants, chemicals, fertilizers, etc. So worldwide costs of production in both industry and agriculture shot upward.

There were a series of poor harvests which caused worldwide shortages of grain and other food products. So prices for agricultural products went higher—much higher—than they had ever been before. And so did prices of just about everything else. Prices of some raw materials went up sharply. And the prices of some things gyrated wildly from year to year.

The price of sugar shot up from about $200 a ton to more than $1300 a ton, then dropped back to about $600 a ton. The price of copra (for making coconut oil) jumped from less than $200 a ton to about $600 a ton. Then a year later it was down to about $100 a ton. You can imagine the problems of the countries which were depending on sugar and copra for their livelihood! And it wasn't just sugar and copra. Many other products were experiencing similar price fluctuations.

FIXED EXCHANGE RATES WERE ABANDONED

The governments of the various nations worked together to try to do something to meet the various emergency conditions brought about by the "new times" of the 1970s. They tried to work out a new system of "fixed" exchange rates between the monies of the major trading nations. But the international trade and finance markets were too unstable. Finally all attempts to put together a new system of "fixed" exchange rates (between different kinds of money in the international finance markets) were abandoned.

By the mid-1970s, not just the U.S. dollar, but also the money units of all of the major trading nations were "floating." The value of each kind of money (in exchange for any other kind of money) was "set free" to be determined by supply and demand. The exchange rate for each nation's money went up or down from day to day, depending on the supply and demand conditions for that nation's money in the international money markets.

Ever since the mid-1970s, the exchange rates among the currencies of the major trading nations have continued to float—have moved up and down in response to changing supply and demand conditions.

The Dollar Floats Downward

Throughout the 1970s the international exchange value of the dollar kept floating downward. In 1971 the U.S. dollar would buy 3.6 West German marks. By 1976, it would only buy 2.76. In 1971 the U.S. dollar would buy 4.3 Swiss francs. In 1976 it would only buy 2.6.

In 1977 the U.S. "Merchandise Trade" Deficit jumped to $31 billion—by far the largest deficit in U.S. history. The dollar's value in the international money markets dropped sharply. Again, there was serious danger of a "1971-type" dollar crisis.

If people holding dollars rushed to get rid of them, that could bring a total collapse in the international finance markets. If such a crisis occurred, it would cause the international value of the dollar to collapse. That would be disastrous for the world economy. International trade would be disrupted. But not only that—many nations hold their international exchange reserves (their "money to be used to buy foreign goods") in the form of U.S. dollars. Their "international money" reserves would be wiped out.

The Dollar Crisis of 1978

It was during 1978 that the international position of the dollar became really critical. In the 12-month period ending in October 1978 the dollar lost 36% of its value against the Swiss franc, 21% against the West German mark, and 31% against the Japanese yen. The week of October 30 opened with near-panic selling of dollars in the money markets in Europe and Japan. It was obvious that something had to be done immediately to rescue the dollar.

President Carter's "Rescue the Dollar" Package

President Carter called his top monetary advisors to the White House for a secret meeting and worked out a plan. On November 1 he announced the plan—the most dramatic package of actions (and the biggest gamble) the United States had ever taken in international finance. The package included:

- Billions of dollars worth of foreign money to be borrowed by the United States from the foreign central banks to be used to buy dollars in the foreign exchange markets—to increase the demand for dollars, and hold up the price of dollars.

- Sharply higher interest rates in this country (a) to make holding dollars more profitable for foreigners and (b) to let foreigners see that the U.S. was serious about stopping the inflationary decline in the value of the dollar. The Fed immediately raised the discount rate by a full percentage point to 9½%—the biggest single jump and the highest discount rate ever before.
- The sale of 2 billion dollars worth of SDRs (international exchange credits) to Germany, Switzerland, and Japan to get more of their money to be used to buy up dollars.
- The sale of 1.5 million ounces of gold per month by the U.S. Treasury to pull in more dollars out of the foreign money markets.
- Withdrawal of $3 billion worth of marks, francs, and yen from the U.S. reserve account at the International Monetary Fund (IMF)—more money to be used to buy up dollars from foreigners.
- Sale of up to $10 billion worth of high-interest U.S. Treasury securities (denominated in *foreign* money) in the foreign money markets to get more foreign money to be used to buy up dollars.

WAS THE "RESCUE" SUCCESSFUL?

So what happened? The immediate response was overwhelmingly positive. The dollar rose sharply in the money markets all over the world. By mid-November (in only two weeks!) the dollar was up to its highest level in four months. And it continued its upward trend. By mid-April, 1979, the dollar had risen (since November, 1978) more than 10% against the mark, 18% against the Swiss franc, and (would you believe?) 22% against the Japanese yen.

WHY DID THE "RESCUE" WORK?

How did the dollar recover so fast? Many things were involved. For one thing, foreigners found out that the United States was serious and determined about (a) protecting the international value of the dollar, and (b) fighting domestic inflation. Interest rates in the United States were high enough to make dollar-denominated assets good assets to hold. And inflation rates increased in several other countries, making the American inflation rate look not so bad. Also the U.S. balance of payments deficit was going down.

By the end of 1979 it was clear that Carter's "rescue the dollar" package of November 1978 had been successful. But did it permanently solve all of the international exchange problems of the dollar? Of course not. With floating rates, there's no permanent solution. With changing times, new problems will arise.

THE SKYROCKETING DOLLAR AND INCREASING TRADE DEFICITS, 1980–84

In mid-year 1980 the international value of the dollar stopped going down and began to increase. In fact, it increased by an unprecedented 45% during the two and one-half years between mid-1980 and the end of 1982. Then it stabilized for a while. But in midsummer of 1983 the dollar's value surged upward again.

In late July and early August of 1983 the Fed and the central banks of Germany, Japan, Switzerland, and the Netherlands all sold millions of U.S. dollars in the foreign exchange markets *to try to hold down the dollar's rise.* But the stabilizing effect was only temporary. Foreigners were demanding and holding dollars because of the U.S. (1) high real interest rates, (2) low inflation rate, and (3) economic recovery and healthy outlook.

THE HIGH DOLLAR SLOWS EXPORTS AND SPEEDS IMPORTS

American exporters were having difficulty selling in foreign markets because of the high cost of the dollar. And American buyers of automobiles, TV sets and many other products were finding it cheaper to buy imports. Some domestic producers were hard hit by this foreign competition. And the U.S. balance of trade deficits grew larger, year after year.

Between 1980 and 1985 the number of West German marks you could buy with one U.S. dollar increased from 1.8 marks to 3.4 marks. The value of the dollar almost doubled against the mark? Right! That's just one example of what was happening to the international value of the dollar in the first half of the 1980s. Not just in West Germany but in most other countries also, by 1985 the dollar would buy *almost twice as much* foreign goods and services as it would have bought back in 1980.

It works the other way around, too. By 1985 a unit of foreign money would buy only about one-half as much in American goods as it would have bought in 1980. You don't have to know very much about the principles of economics to know what the effect of all this would be on American imports, and on exports. Americans buy more foreign goods? Yes. Foreigners buy fewer American goods? Of course.

THE RECORD TRADE DEFICITS OF THE 1980s

In 1982 the U.S. merchandise trade deficit hit a new record: $42.7 billion. In 1983? Another new record: $69.4 billion. And in 1984? An astounding $107 billion! But that figure was eclipsed by the figures for 1985, '86, and '87, all of which exceeded $140 billion.

What all this means is that Americans were paying out to foreigners billions more U.S. dollars than the foreigners were paying back to buy American goods. So what were the foreigners doing with all of those billions of U.S. dollars? You could guess. Spending them for investments in the good old USA? Right!

They were buying stocks in IBM, AT&T, GM, GE, Exxon, and hundreds of other U.S. companies—buying government and corporate bonds to reap some of those high interest earnings—investing in housing developments, farm land, factories, office buildings, resort properties—just about everything you can think of! During the late 1980s foreigners were investing in U.S. income-earning assets at the rate of about $100 billion a year.

THE TRADE DEFICIT AND FOREIGN INVESTMENTS IN THE 1990s

During the early 1990s when the U.S. economy was in recession, the trade deficits were lower—less than $100 billion. But as the economy expanded after 1992, the annual trade deficits went back up over $100 billion. But they remained considerably lower than the record deficits (more than $150 billion!) of the mid 1980s.

One important reason for the lower trade deficits during the 1990s was the sharp fall in the international value of the dollar since 1985. The international value of the dollar spurted upward throughout the first half of the 1980s. It approximately doubled in value against the currencies of most of the other major trading nations. Then came the crash.

THE DOLLAR FALLS FAST!

During 1985 there was a savings and loan crisis in Ohio. This shook the confidence of some foreign holders of dollars. They began to sell. From mid-year 1985 to December of 1987 the dollar lost about half of its value in the international exchange markets.

In 1985 the dollar would buy 260 yen. In December '87, it would buy only half as many—130 yen. In March of 1985 it would buy 3.4 german marks. In December of '87 it would buy less than half as many—only 1.6 marks.

The "group of seven" major trading nations (the U.S., Canada, Japan, Germany, Britain, France, and Italy) got together and agreed to cooperate in trying to stabilize the dollar. This so-called "G-7" group of nations began working together and have continued to work together to try to stabilize wide swings in exchange rates. But their efforts, in general, have not been very successful.

EXCHANGE-RATE STABILIZATION IS NOT EASY!

The foreign exchange markets trade billions of dollars worth of currencies every day. In order to buy or sell enough currency to influence prices in this market, huge sums of funds are needed.

In fact, the only way a G-7 stabilization effort can be successful is if it succeeds in convincing the other players in these markets—the buyers and sellers of currencies—that the stabilization effort is going to be successful. If the "free traders" in the market believe the stabilization effort will succeed, then they will change their buying and selling to take advantage of the new market direction and the stabilization effort will succeed. But if the traders don't believe it will succeed, then they won't change their behavior and the stabilization effort will fail.

IN 1995 THE DOLLAR FALLS BELOW 80 YEN

In spite of repeated attempts by the G-7 group to stop it, the dollar continued to fall throughout the first half of the 1990s. In late 1995 it touched bottom at 79 yen to the dollar. Then it began to recover.

During the first half of 1996 the dollar was worth about 105 yen, up from 79. The dollar was worth about 1.50 marks—up from less than 1.40 in late 1995.

With continuing trade deficits and so many American dollars pouring into the hands of foreigners, foreign investment in the United States continued to increase. In 1994, annual foreign investment in the United States surpassed $300 billion!

WHY DIDN'T THE FALLING DOLLAR BRING TRADE INTO BALANCE?

The falling dollar makes foreign goods more expensive to Americans and U.S. goods cheaper to foreigners. That should speed up exports and slow down imports. But as the dollar fell, the trade deficit continued to worsen. Why? Partly because of what is called the "J-curve effect."

THE "J-CURVE EFFECT"

As the value of the dollar goes down, we must pay more dollars for each shipload of imports. Also, we receive fewer of our dollars back for each shipload we export. So for any given volume of imports and exports, as the value of the dollar goes down, the dollar value of the trade deficit goes up.

On a graph indicating America's trade balance (surplus or deficit), as the international value of the dollar falls, at first the deficit worsens. The trade balance curve slopes downward. But as time goes on, the lower cost of American goods stimulates our exports and the higher cost of foreign goods reduces our imports. So the "trade balance curve" turns and begins to slope upward. On a graph, this curve resembles the letter J—hence the "J-curve effect." Now look at Figure 24-1 and you'll see an illustration of this J-curve effect.

During 1985, '86, and '87 the United States was on the declining segment of the J-curve. The increasing trade deficit since the third quarter of 1986 has reflected dollar increases, but not volume increases. In fact, the size of the volume deficit actually decreased in 1987.

In constant-dollar terms the trade deficit peaked in the third quarter of 1986 and has been declining slightly ever since. But the physical volume of merchandise exports must expand enough (and imports must slow enough)

After the dollar falls, the "J-curve" shows what happens to the trade deficit as the months go by.

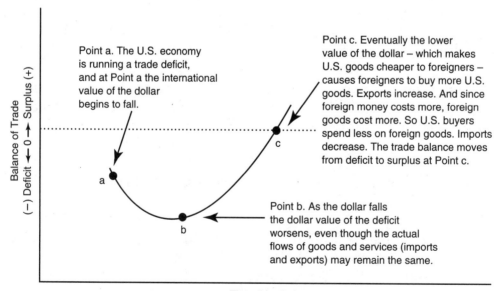

FIGURE 24-1. The "J-Curve" Effect of a "Falling Dollar"

to more than offset the J-curve effect of the lower international value of the dollar. Only then will the deficit come down and the curve go up.

It wasn't until the second quarter of 1988 that Point b of the J-curve seemed to be reached and the turnaround in the dollar-value deficit seemed to be beginning.

THE NEW POSITION OF THE UNITED STATES IN THE WORLD ECONOMY

You can see that not only the American economy but also the *world economy* has gone through a period of great change. The changed position of the United States (and of the U.S. dollar) in the world economy has been one of the most significant developments.

THE UNITED STATES BECOMES A DEBTOR NATION

From World War I to the mid 1980s, the United States had been a net creditor nation. That means that, on balance, Americans had been receiving a *net inflow* of interest, rents, and profits from their overseas investments. But in 1985 the United States became a net debtor nation.

In the early 1980s, as the U.S. economy expanded, as inflation remained under control, and as real rates of interest stayed high, the United States was one of the best places in the world to invest. And these foreign investments helped to finance both the *federal debt* and *private debt.*

Foreigners, by investing their dollar-earnings in the United States, increased the supply of loanable funds in U.S. financial markets. That helped to prevent interest rates from going higher. But the amount of foreign investment in the United States increased greatly. And that is what changed the United States into a "net debtor" in its "investment relationship" with the other nations of the world.

Exactly what does all this mean? Just this: In future years the U.S. "international balance of payments" will show a net outflow of dollars to foreigners to pay the interest, rents, and profits earned on their investments in the United States. It means that American investments overseas are earning less (in total) than foreign investments in the United States are earning (in total). A net outflow of American dollars is required to make up the difference.

NO LONGER THE "BENEVOLENT PROTECTOR"

The 1970s brought to an end the period during which the United States would play the role of "benevolent protector" for the economies of the other nations of the world. The United States has had to become a tough competitor in international markets. For many years the U.S. economy had been so strong that we had been able to get away with "breaking all the rules of prudent international finance." But not now.

Today there are several strong economies in the world. So the United States has learned to be more careful to protect its own position in the world economy.

The United States has learned that it can no longer ignore the international consequences of its domestic economic policies. We know that if the government creates "easy money" and cuts taxes and increases government spending to try to overcome a recession, this discourages foreigners from holding dollars. This could cause a "dollar crisis" in the international money markets. But when the United States follows "tight money" and "tight budget" policies, this supports the dollar. Foreigners holding dollars feel confident about the future value of the dollar when they see strong anti-inflation policies in this country.

THE INTERNATIONAL SITUATION CANNOT BE IGNORED

All of this doesn't mean that the United States must let its domestic economic policies be dictated entirely by international considerations. But it does mean that the international considerations are important enough that they no longer can be ignored. Never again will the United States be able to undertake domestic economic policies without an eye to the impact on the international position of the dollar.

THE OUTLOOK

One important factor which will influence this country's international trade and finance position in the coming years is what happens with *energy production and consumption.* Until our dependence on imported oil is reduced, we will continue to face a built-in tendency to run trade deficits. You'll be reading more about this issue later in this book.

Another important factor will be what happens to *productivity.* If output per worker in this country can continue to increase, this can make American products more competitive in world markets—and foreign products will be less competitive in American markets.

Another vital factor is the *inflation rate.* When prices in the United States are increasing more rapidly than prices in other countries, then American sellers lose their foreign markets to foreign producers. Also they lose some of their American markets to foreign producers. If the inflation rate can be held down to less than the inflation rates in foreign countries, that will strengthen U.S. competitiveness in world markets.

REVIEW QUESTIONS

1. Explain why, after floating downward throughout the 1970s, the international value of the dollar surged so high in 1980–84.

2. Explain how U.S. domestic policies affect the international value of the dollar, and economic conditions in other countries.

3. Write a brief essay outlining the evolution of the international dollar problem throughout the 1960s and 1970s.

4. Explain how the existence of inflation in the United States affects the international value of the dollar and the U.S. balance of payments.

5. Do you think the G-7 nations can successfully stabilize the exchange rate of any given currency? Discuss.

6. Explain what is meant by the "J-curve" effect.

25 BIG BUSINESS, MONOPOLY POWER, AND SOCIAL CONTROL

Remember how the market system is supposed to work? Adam Smith and the other classical economists explained it. Alfred Marshall and the other neoclassical economists explained it. It works through consumer demand, and competition among sellers.

All the sellers try to make more profit by trying to outdo each other in serving the consumer. That way the society's wishes are served, and the producers are controlled by the demands and preferences of the buyers. This is the way the society controls its economy through the *market process.*

DOES "BIG BUSINESS" CONTROL THE ECONOMY?

What happens when big business comes into the picture? Suppose there's only one seller of a product. And suppose the product is one that most people feel is essential. Since there aren't any competing sellers, the seller may not bother to improve the product. The producer may not bother to produce as much as the people would like—may let shortages develop and raise the price and make more profits. A seller with monopoly power can get *rewarded* for doing a *disservice* to society!

This is the point: Competition is essential if the market system is to work right. As businesses get larger and larger and hold larger and larger shares of various markets, they have more and more power to control those markets in their own interests. They don't have to be so careful about responding to the interests of the buyers. Essentially, that is the problem of big business—of monopoly.

THE CONTINUING GROWTH OF BIG BUSINESS

Back in the last century, big businesses were growing by leaps and bounds. The Sherman Antitrust Act was passed in 1890 to try to hold down the growth of monopoly. In 1911 both the Standard Oil Company monopoly and the American Tobacco Company monopoly were split up into several different companies. And since that time there have been several more antimonopoly acts passed, and many court cases.

The laws and the courts have had a considerable effect in limiting the growth and exercise of monopoly power. But still there's a lot of big business around. Is that bad?

Back in the 1930s many people were concerned about big business. A study showed that about one-half of all the corporate wealth in the United States was concentrated in the hands of some two hundred companies. And what has happened since that time? This concentration of corporate wealth has increased even more.

If we look only at *industrial* corporations (eliminating the transportation, utility and other service companies), the pattern of increasing concentration of corporate wealth in the hands of a few is easy to see. In 1929, about one-fourth of all industrial corporate wealth was in the hands of the top one hundred corporations. By the early 1960s that figure had grown to about one-third. By 1970, it had increased to about *one-half.* Today, more than one-half of the industrial corporate wealth is owned by the top 100 industrial corporations. Is that a problem?

Can you see that this concentration of wealth in the hands of a few corporations might be something for economists to worry about? How does a national or world economy made up of a few massive corporations operate? Does it follow the laws of economics as defined in the neoclassical model—a model economy made up of great numbers of small, "purely competitive" businesses? Of course not.

WE HAVE NO ACCEPTED THEORY OF THE "BIG BUSINESS" ECONOMY

Certainly there are advantages of bigness in business: planning and stability, long-range goals, willingness to make long-range commitments for research and development. Some people say that big businesses are good because only big busi-nesses can develop a "social consciousness" and direct some of their energies toward improving conditions in the society. But one thing is certain: These big firms will not operate the way the small, perfectly competitive firms of the neoclassical model operate.

So how do the big firms operate? Does some kind of effective competition keep these corporations moving toward the best interests of society? Is there effective social control over these corporations and their economic behavior, or not? And what does the future hold in store on these questions? These are not easy questions to answer.

We really don't have an accepted theory of how a modern economic system works in the real world. We know that most prices are "administered" (that is, *set by somebody*). And we know that there is a lot of planning and long-range goal seeking, both by governments and by big businesses—much more than would exist in the neoclassical model. But how does it really work? We just don't have a generally accepted theory to answer that question.

Those economists who hold strongest to the neoclassical tradition say that the real world still does approximate the neoclassical model. They say we shouldn't be looking for other ways of explaining the world.

Many economists don't think that the big modern corporations behave very much like the little "typical firms" described in the neoclassical model. So what explanation do most economists give? And what answer do they offer? That's the problem. Most of them don't have an explanation or an answer to offer.

But one economist has: John Kenneth Galbraith. Lets take a look at what Galbraith has to say.

GALBRAITH'S CHALLENGE

It was in 1958 that Galbraith published his widely-read book, *The Affluent Society*. The book attacks much of the "conventional wisdom" of modern-day economists. Nine years later (1967) he continued that attack in his book *The New Industrial State*. Then in 1973 he completed the attack and offered his solutions in *Economics and the Public Purpose*.

Galbraith raises serious questions about the applicability, the realism, and the helpfulness of the conventional wisdom in economics. He doesn't think the assumptions of the neoclassical model are close enough to reality. He thinks the results of the model are more misleading than helpful in understanding what really happens in the economies of the modern world.

Galbraith thinks the neoclassical model and the things conventional economists do and say are more harmful than good, because the effect is to hide the truth about the things which are really *wrong* with the system. In the foreword of his book, *Economics and the Public Purpose*, he says: ". | . | . on no conclusion is this book more clear: Left to themselves, economic forces do not work out for the best—except perhaps for the powerful."

CONSUMER SOVEREIGNTY AND THE DEPENDENCE EFFECT

Galbraith first attacks the idea of "consumer sovereignty"—the idea that the economic system is directed by and responds to the wishes of the people. He says that people's wants are not *independent* of the system, but are a *reflection* of the system. There is a kind of "keeping up with the Joneses" effect: as the economic system produces more things, new desires for those things are generated. So, says Galbraith, the system is responding to wants which it (the system) is *creating*. Galbraith calls this the "dependence effect." (Do you see how this is very close to some of Veblen's ideas as discussed back in Chapter 11?)

If the dependence effect is granted, the idea of "consumer sovereignty" as the driving force in the economic system (as in the neoclassical model) doesn't make much sense anymore. No longer are consumers rational in pursuing their objectives. As they spend, they are responding to the influences of the system. They are not the ultimate source of power. They are not the independent force, choosing the objectives and directing the economic system toward those objectives. Their behavior doesn't control the system. It is *controlled by* the system! So says Galbraith.

THE GIANT CORPORATION AND THE TECHNOSTRUCTURE

Galbraith's second major challenge to the neoclassical model is on the idea that businesses will adjust their behavior to try to get maximum profit. He focuses on the behavior of the giant corporations and points out that the big modern corporation is not run by a risk-taking entrepreneur. The guiding intelligence—the brain of the enterprise—is made up of many people with technical knowledge and many diverse talents. These people influence the *group decisions* which ultimately control the corporation. Galbraith calls this collective intelligence or "brain" of the organization the "technostructure"— certainly not much like the risk-taking entrepreneur of the neoclassical model!

According to Galbraith, the technostructure wants to be a part of a *successful* organization. This means the corporation must *survive.* There must be adequate earnings. Also, it is important that the corporation grow. The first order of business of the technostructure is to avoid risks that might threaten the survival or growth of the company.

What policies and conditions would be favored by Galbraith's "technostructure"? The technostructure:

1. would be in favor of government policies for stability of prices and employment;
2. would not object to labor unions which would provide them a stable supply of labor and assure that labor costs would be more or less the same throughout the industrial system, eliminating the threat of competition from other producers with low-cost labor;
3. would be in favor of high expenditures for education and skill development by the government, thus to be assured an adequate supply of labor; and
4. would be in favor of high government spending in technology-developing activities, such as in defense or the space program.

A GOVERNMENT-INDUSTRIAL-LABOR COMPLEX?

Galbraith's view of the "new industrial state" is quite different from the dog-eat-dog world of maximum-profit-seeking competitive activity. He sees close parallels between the objectives of the industrial technostructure and those of many political leaders and labor leaders as well. All seek reasonable success in pursuing their objectives of stability and growth. He sees businesses and governments alike planning for long-range order and stability and movement toward predetermined objectives—a far cry from the automatic operation of the laissez-faire market system described by Adam Smith, or the neoclassical economists!

Galbraith doesn't see a total elimination of competition, but he sees competition more between *industries* than between firms in the same industry. The steel industry must be careful lest it lose its markets to aluminum, plastics, and other metals and metal substitutes. This is the only kind of competition that effectively operates between the massive corporations in Galbraith's "new industrial state."

Galbraith sees a tendency for the technostructure to over-emphasize *economic* goals. The technostructure wants to increase production, incomes, employment, consumption, and all that. There is no place in the corporate planning process for placing emphasis on *noneconomic* objectives and goals. And Galbraith says these noneconomic goals may be more important in an affluent society than the "economic" or "material" objectives and goals. So what does Galbraith prescribe?

THE GALBRAITHIAN PRESCRIPTION: THE "NEW SOCIALISMS"

In his former books, Galbraith diagnoses the problems. In *Economics and the Public Purpose,* he prescribes. What does he prescribe? A vastly different kind of economic system than the one which exists (or which most economists seem to *think* exists) in the United States today.

Essentially, Galbraith wants (a) the industries which can't perform adequately on their own to be run by the government; (b) the big corporations and technostructure planning to be brought under government planning; (c) the remainder of the economy to be strengthened so that it can operate effectively as a *free market* sector, and (d) more income redistribution by government to reduce "unearned" (rent, dividend, interest, etc.) incomes and to more nearly eliminate poverty.

What about these Galbraithian ideas? Are they feasible? Or too radical to contemplate? Galbraith says, "practical necessity has already forced a measure of practical action" along the lines suggested. He says that what he is really doing is providing "the theoretical justification for what circumstances and good sense have already initiated."

Here again, as with John Maynard Keynes, Adam Smith, and others, we find an economist looking at the undeniable problems in the world— watching what's wrong, seeing what's being done—and then offering an explanation.

Galbraith offers mankind a new way of looking at and approaching the economic issues and problems of the modern world. But the image of the world which Galbraith describes is not the image which most economists or most people are ready to accept. Therefore the Galbraithian prescription is not likely to be taken very soon—certainly not in very large doses.

GALBRAITH, KEYNES, VEBLEN—CHALLENGERS TO CONVENTIONAL WISDOM

Galbraith, like Keynes and like Veblen before him, has walked a path quite distinctly different from that of the conventional economist of the day. All three of these men have broken step with the profession in order to turn their attention more directly to the problems and issues of the day. In so doing, all three lost friends and gained some (perhaps bitter) enemies.

I suppose that everyone who breaks ranks with their colleagues and then mounts an attack on their hallowed beliefs is bound to be criticized. Galbraith (like Keynes and Veblen) has many critics. But judging from what one can find out, neither Galbraith nor Keynes nor Veblen was bothered in the least by the flurries of criticism which their pioneering ideas generated.

THE EFFECTS OF THE GIANT CORPORATIONS? ECONOMISTS DISAGREE

So what can we say about the present and future effects of giant corporations in the U.S. and world economies? And about Galbraith's way of looking at and explaining the way a modern industrial economy functions? And about his recommended "New Socialisms" for changing the economic system to better serve the society? I'm sorry, but we really don't know.

Anyone in touch with the modern industrial society knows there's truth in what Galbraith says. But how much? And what does this tell us about the "social efficiency" of the modern industrial market-oriented economic society? And should we embark on a program aimed toward the Galbraithian prescription?

What do the economists say when faced with these issues? Again, as you might have guessed, what they say will depend on *which economists* you choose to ask and on their philosophical predilections—that is, on what they believed in the first place.

RECENT DEVELOPMENTS, AND THE OUTLOOK

There have always been some philosophers, economists, politicians, business leaders and others calling for changes in the relationship between government and business. On one side, the objective has been to get government to reduce its regulations and controls and permit big businesses the freedom to operate more efficiently—to increase the *productivity* and the *competitive position* of the American economy in the world economy. Others have recommended that we extend *greater government control* over big businesses to ensure that they perform with maximum efficiency from a "social objectives" point of view.

NADER CALLS FOR FEDERAL CHARTERING OF CORPORATIONS

Long-time consumer advocate and critic of big business, Ralph Nader, has called for *federal chartering* of corporations instead of continuing to allow the individual states to approve corporate charters. In Nader's view, Federal chartering would establish more stringent requirements and would permit the federal government to exercise more effective control over corporate activities "for the good of the nation." But business leaders and some economists argued that this move would only result in further bureaucratic interference and result in further slowing the productivity of the American economy.

You already know what Galbraith was suggesting—that the major corporations be brought under the direction of government planners. Several economists (but by no means a majority) have argued that Galbraith's recommendation (or something similar) would improve social control over big business and would improve the performance of the economy. But most business and labor leaders, most economists, and most key people in government express the opposite view—i.e., that the economy will function best if entangling and cost-increasing government regulations on business can be reduced.

THE MOVE TOWARD DEREGULATION

Ever since the late 1970s Congress has been passing "deregulation" acts aimed toward reducing costs and increasing productivity and competition. The first industry to be deregulated and "set free to compete" was the airlines. Then in March 1980 the *Depository Institutions Deregulation Act* called for a phased deregulation of banking, and in November of 1999 the restrictions of the Glass-Steagall Act of 1933 were finally removed by the Gramm-Leach-Bliley Act.

In June 1980, the *Trucking Industry Deregulation Act* was passed. This sets the trucking companies free to compete with each other. More recently, there has been legislation to reduce government regulation of the railroads and of the communications industry.

In addition to deregulation, new regulatory techniques are being introduced to reduce the "compliance costs" which businesses encounter when government regulations are imposed. Some regulations will always be required. But if the costs of complying with these regulations can be reduced, businesses can then operate more efficiently.

It is clear that ever since the 1970s public policy toward business has been shifting toward reducing the regulatory burden on business. The political mood in Washington has been significantly influenced by increasing concern about "supply-side" issues—the productivity of the American economy and our competitive position in the world economy. The majority view in Washington seems to be that less regulation and more competition will stimulate increased productivity and will be healthy for the nation's economy.

MERGERS DIVESTITURES, DOWNSIZING, AND MULTINATIONALIZATION

During the 1980s, and even more in the 1990s, there were revolutionary changes in American "big business." Every day we read about mergers and consolidations, downsizing and "re-engineering," divestitures and spin-offs and other restructuring moves by big businesses. These rapid changes still are going on in banking and financial services, in transportation, utilities, manufacturing—in fact, throughout the economy.

Downsizing, cost reduction, and productivity increases in the past have been "desirable options." By the 1990s these objectives had become essential for survival.

The multinationalization of U.S. corporations has been proceeding at such a rapid pace that by the last half of the 1990s, many American corporations were generating more than half of their earnings in foreign countries. Who would have thought that such "truly American" companies as CocaCola, McDonalds, DuPont, Exxon, and so many others are "foreign" companies as much as they are American. But that's the way it is in the globalized, multinational modern world.

THE DEREGULATION AND PRODUCTIVITY OUTLOOK

It has now become clear to most people—not just business and political leaders and economists, but to the general public as well—that a healthy economy and rising standards of living depend on the success and growth of businesses. It may not be true that "What's good for General Motors is good for the country," but a lot more people seem to be thinking that there might be some truth in it.

More people are beginning to understand the relationships between productivity and inflation, and between our inflation rate and our ability to compete in world markets. More people are becoming aware of the need for productivity growth and for the healthy growth of businesses to support this productivity growth. And public policy toward big business is beginning to reflect these changing attitudes.

There is no question that much government regulation of business will continue. But unless something in American industry takes a serious (and now unforeseen) "turn for the worse," it seems *very unlikely* that any major steps toward increased government planning and control over business (such as suggested by Galbraith) will be taken in the foreseeable future.

It is clear now that by the mid-1990s we had moved into a "new industrial world." The trend for the future will continue to be toward downsizing and increasing efficiency and productivity.

The move toward more efficient industrial and corporate structures will continue—sometimes through consolidation, and sometimes by divestitures in cases where that's the most efficient way to go. And it's certain that there will be continued multinationalization, both of U.S. firms and of big businesses in all other industrial nations throughout the world.

WHAT ABOUT ANTI-POLLUTION REGULATIONS?

As public policy moves toward deregulation, does that apply to anti-pollution regulations? If those are relaxed, won't that harm our environment? Should we let that happen?

These are difficult questions. They involve unpleasant opportunity costs—trade-offs. But that's what economics is all about. Remember? In the next chapter you will be reading about the issues of energy, and pollution, and about the kinds of trade-offs required and the kinds of decisions that must be made.

REVIEW QUESTIONS

1. What are the major advantages of big business in the modern U.S. economy? The disadvantages?

2. What is the basic problem with big business according to classical and neoclassical economics?

3. Explain how Galbraith's concept of the corporate "technostructure" is different from the neoclassical "entrepreneur" concept. How would these different concepts affect a firm's economic behavior?

4. Briefly explain Galbraith's "New Socialisms." What does he prescribe for the economy? Are these prescriptions economically and politically feasible in the present day U.S. economy? Discuss.

5. What factors have brought about the moves toward deregulation in the U.S. economy? How do these moves compare to Galbraith's prescriptions?

6. Why has so much corporate restructuring been going on in recent years in the U.S. economy? Discuss.

26 ECONOMIC ISSUES AND CONFLICTING IDEAS ON ENERGY AND POLLUTION

This book explains many issues and ideas about which most people know very little. But everybody knows that we have had an energy problem and a pollution problem. We all feel some of the effects of changing energy costs, and of pollution. This chapter focuses on the economics of these two issues.

THE ENERGY PROBLEM

In the 1960s the price of a barrel of crude oil was about $1.80. In the early 1970s it was around $2.00.

Then in 1973 the 13 major oil-producing nations got together in their "Organization of Petroleum Exporting Countries" (*OPEC*) *cartel* and raised the price of oil by more than 400 percent—from $2.40 in early 1973 to about $11 a barrel in 1974.

In 1979 the OPEC cartel doubled oil prices again. Then in 1980 they added on another increase. The shock to the U.S. and world economy was profound.

In the 1980 *Economic Report of the President,* President Carter said that the American economy is "dangerously exposed" to the changing supply and price conditions of oil in the world market. Nobody would argue with that statement. Everyone was already aware of the impact on the American economy of the changing supply and price of oil. The effects have touched every one of us.

Everyone is paying higher prices for gasoline and heating oil. But not everyone sees what the greatly increased cost of energy has done—and will continue to do—to production costs of everything. Everything which is produced or constructed or transported requires energy.

Oil is not the only source of energy, of course. But the productivity of the modern American economy depends more on oil than on any other energy source. Also, when the oil price goes up, prices of other energy sources are forced up too. So we experienced a great "shock to the system" as a result of the 1400 percent increase in the price of oil—an increase which occurred over a period of only ten years.

OUR INCREASING "FOREIGN OIL BILL"

In 1970 our "import bill" for imported oil amounted to less than $3 billion. In 1974, following the first big increase in oil prices by OPEC, our "imported oil bill" amounted to about $25 billion. For the year 1980 the total cost of imported oil amounted to about $80 billion.

In 1980 the oil price ranged from about $30 to $40 a barrel, depending on the grade of oil and where you bought it. The increasing oil prices were causing a massive cash drain from U.S. businesses and consumers, and great upward pressures on prices in the United States and worldwide.

Fortunately for the United States (and most other countries in the world), after 1980 oil surpluses developed and prices came down some. Also, we were learning how to get by using less oil. By 1982 the total cost of oil imported into the United States was down from about $80 billion to about $60 billion—a 25% decrease in only two years.

THE CARTER ADMINISTRATION'S ENERGY POLICY

In 1977 the Carter administration established the U.S. Department of Energy and President Carter declared "the moral equivalent of war" on the energy problem. The Carter administration's energy policy had a twofold objective:

1. For the *long run*, to promote an adjustment of the economy to the "new world" of more costly energy supplies, and
2. For the *short run*, to reduce as quickly as possible the nation's vulnerability to further oil supply restrictions and price increases.

THE SHORT-RUN PROGRAM

The government established a "strategic petroleum reserve" which could be used to "tide us over" if the foreign producers decided to reduce or cut off our oil imports. The government promoted energy conservation by promoting more fuel-efficient automobiles and buildings, lower thermostats in winter and higher in summer, and by other means.

The administration also began working with other oil-importing nations to try to get all of them to reduce their oil imports. The idea was that if all oil-importing nations could succeed in cutting back their oil imports, that would reduce the world demand for oil and reduce the likelihood of any more big price increases by OPEC.

THE LONG-RUN PROGRAM

For the long run the administration's policy was aimed toward permanently reducing our dependence on imported oil. The program included (1) government support for energy conservation measures, (2) support for the development of alternative energy sources, and (3) policies to stimulate domestic oil production.

THE ENERGY SECURITY ACT OF 1980

In June of 1980—three years after President Carter had declared "the moral equivalent of war" on the energy problem—the Congress finally passed and the President signed the *Energy Security Act*. This Act—some 400 pages long—spelled out the nation's energy policies and programs for the coming years.

One of the major sections of the Act establishes the "Synthetic Fuels Corporation." This is a government corporation to support the development of synthetic fuels. When he signed the Act, President Carter predicted that the effort to develop synthetic fuels ("synfuels") " . . . will dwarf the combined programs that led us to the moon and built our entire interstate highway system."

The *Energy Security Act* also provided support for solar energy development, alcohol-fuel production, geothermal power plants, energy conservation measures (including weatherizing homes), and for the strategic petroleum reserve.

The passage of this act was a very important event. Nothing approaching its scope had ever been done before in the energy field. As Congressman John Dingle of Michigan said: "This is a major step toward a national energy policy."

Carter's Proposed "Oil Import Tax"

In early 1980 the Carter Administration also tried to impose an import tax on oil which would be passed along (at about 10CS per gallon) to buyers of gasoline. But the Congress defeated that proposal by an overwhelming majority.

The obvious purpose of the proposal was to try to reduce the consumption of gasoline and thereby reduce our dependence on imported oil. But it appeared that the members of Congress (in an election year) did not want to be associated with approving a 10CS price increase on their constituents' gasoline.

The Windfall Profits Tax on the Oil Companies

In the 1970s and early 1980s there was much controversy about the question of what should be our policy toward the giant oil corporations. This question is closely related to some of the issues which were discussed in the last chapter—questions about "big business, monopoly power, and social control." But in the case of the big oil corporations this question was especially important because of the energy crisis.

As world oil prices increased, the big oil companies began earning increased profits. The news media focused on the fact that oil company profits were increasing, and there was strong public sentiment against the oil companies for "taking advantage of the consumers."

The fact is that if oil company profits had been reduced all the way to zero, this would not have reduced the price of gasoline at the pump by more than two or three cents per gallon—but the news media didn't mention that. And it's a fact of economics that if oil company profits went to zero and remained there for very long, soon there wouldn't be any gasoline at the pump!

The Carter Administration, the Congress, and the general public were in favor of a "windfall profits tax" on the oil corporations. So that tax was passed. The Congress tried to design the tax to minimize the negative effect on investments in exploration and development of new sources of domestic oil.

Did the windfall profits tax affect domestic oil production? Any tax that reduces a company's profits automatically reduces both incentives and cash flow for new investments. But of course there's no way to know for sure just how serious this "deterrent effect" of the windfall profits tax may have been.

THE POWERFUL MAGIC OF HIGH PRICES

As it turned out, it was the *powerful price mechanism*—not the government's program—which finally brought the exploding oil prices under control. By the middle of 1981, the basic laws of economics were catching up with OPEC. *High prices* perform powerful magic!

When OPEC jacked up oil prices, increased production by both OPEC and non-OPEC producers became very profitable. Also it became very profitable for people to find ways to reduce their consumption of oil. So *oil supplies* began increasing, while *oil demand* began decreasing.

In 1981, surplus oil was flooding world markets. Many OPEC nations couldn't sell all their oil. Some began cutting prices. By early 1982, American consumers found gasoline prices going down.

By December 1982, when the official OPEC base price was $34 a barrel, some OPEC sellers were cutting their prices. And surplus oil was trading in the "spot market" (free market) sometimes for prices as low as $25 a barrel. In January 1983 OPEC held an emergency meeting to try to pull the cartel back together to reduce outputs and stabilize prices. But the meeting ended (in the words of Saudi Arabia's oil minister) "in complete failure."

Throughout the 1980s the OPEC members tried repeatedly to regain control of the oil markets. But they never succeeded. In July of 1986, for a short period, the oil priced dropped to less than $10 per barrel. But most of the time the price was fluctuating between $15 and $20 per barrel. And that continued right up until the time of the Iraqi invasion of Kuwait.

Then, in early October of 1990, the oil price shot up to over $40 per barrel on the fear that oil production would be disrupted by the Persian Gulf War.

But that didn't happen. In a matter of weeks the oil price was back down to under $20 per barrel.

After 1990, oil prices continued to fluctuate in the $15 to $20 per barrel range right up until the spring of 1996, when prices moved up above $20 per barrel. Oil supplies were reduced by (1) the exceptionally cold winter, and (2) the cutting off of Iraqi oil because of economic sanctions against Iraq. Gasoline prices in the United States spiked upward.

The sharply higher price of gasoline was big news, and a flurry of action was taken. President Clinton announced the release of oil supplies from the nation's strategic oil reserve. Congress passed a temporary repeal of the 4.5% federal tax on gasoline. An agreement was reached to permit Iraq to sell oil on world markets.

Soon oil prices were again ranging between $15–20 per barrel, and they continued to fluctuate in this range until almost the end of the 1990s. In 1999 the oil producing nations—both OPEC members and others—had a little more success in restricting oil supplies, and that, together with the continuing increased demand of a growing world economy, resulted in oil prices moving up into the $25–26 range. That's where oil prices were when this book went to press in January, 2000.

A GOOD LESSON IN BASIC ECONOMICS

Think back over this entire OPEC "episode"—from the early 1970s to the present. It provides an excellent example of one of the most basic principles of economics. Just this: anytime a price is set *too high* it will *discourage consumption* and *stimulate too much production*. The ultimate result will be surpluses which will force the "too high" price to fall. In the case of the OPEC cartel that's exactly what happened.

What was the effect of the 1,400 percent increase in the price of oil between the early 1970s and the early '80s? It was shocking! Both the U.S. and the world economy were profoundly affected. If you dig in very deeply on any one of the major "economic crisis issues" of the 1970s and early 1980s, what will you find? That the high price of oil was a contributing factor? Yes. That's what you'll find in every case.

ENERGY AND PRODUCTIVITY? OR ENVIRONMENTAL PROTECTION?

In recent years, environmental protection programs have become an important influence in the American economy. But these programs have increased costs of production and output prices throughout the economy. Increased *cost* means decreased productivity; increased *price* means inflation.

ENVIRONMENTAL REGULATIONS INCREASE PRODUCTION COSTS

Producers are saying that they could increase productivity and outputs and sell at lower prices if they were not required to follow the environmental regulations. Some of the business leaders in the oil, gas, and coal industries are saying that the government should permit them more freedom to produce by least-cost methods, and should permit them to explore and produce on now prohibited areas of government land. They say that these changes in government policy would enable them to significantly increase their energy outputs. They say that with these policy changes it would be possible to greatly reduce our dependence on imported oil.

But many people take the opposite view. They don't think we should relax our environmental protection requirements—either for the purpose of increasing the productivity of the economy or for the purpose of increasing our energy output.

THE TRADE-OFFS ARE SERIOUS AND BASIC

It is clear that there are some very important, very *basic* trade-offs here. The "economic problem" is staring us in the face. The "opportunity cost" of a cleaner environment may be: (a) lower productivity of the economy, (b) more inflation, (c) our inability to compete effectively in world markets, and (d) continued high dependence on imported oil. But the "opportunity cost" of moving as rapidly as possible to solve these other problems may turn out to be serious environmental destruction!

Which way will we go? Which way *should* we go? You can see that this is a very tough question—one which will continue to generate serious controversy among economists, politicians, business leaders, the Sierra Club and other environmental groups, and the general public.

WHAT ABOUT NUCLEAR POWER?

The controversy about nuclear power—especially following the Three Mile Island accident—has brought this issue into sharp focus for many people.

The American economy could increase its efficiency and reduce its dependence on imported oil significantly by the rapid introduction of nuclear power. Nobody disagrees with that. But whether or not you are in favor of moving in this direction depends on your own personal judgment about the *safety* of nuclear power, and about the *seriousness* of the radioactive waste disposal problem.

People who believe that nuclear power presents a serious danger to present and future society would much prefer to accept the (admittedly unpleasant) alternatives. But those who believe that nuclear power is not a real danger to the society—that the necessary safety and radioactive waste disposal procedures will be worked out—will argue strongly for more use of nuclear power. Many of the people on both sides of this fence are sure that they are right. But the truth seems to be that no one knows—that no matter which road we choose to take, we will not know (until the future tells us) if it was the right one.

THE ENVIRONMENTAL CRISIS— A CLOSER LOOK

Back during the Industrial Revolution, while the very efficient and highly motivating market system was supporting industrial growth by leaps and bounds, the industrial society was coming closer and closer to solving its traditional economic problem—how to provide material necessities for the people. But at the same time, the market system was setting the stage for the creation of this new and serious problem—the problem of the ecological balance between an industrial society and its environment.

As the Industrial Revolution broke loose, outputs expanded. Then population began expanding more and more. As the decades passed, both of these influences—increasing outputs and increasing numbers of people—began to build up the environmental problem. In recent decades that problem has become acute.

HOW SERIOUS IS THE PROBLEM?

Almost everyone these days is aware of some kinds of undesirable pollution or environmental destruction going on around them. But how serious is the problem, nationwide? Consider this:

- The United States has about a quarter of a million miles of rivers and streams in its major watersheds. More than one fourth of that mileage is polluted.

- More than 100 million tons of carbon monoxide are being released into the air every year. Other air pollutants: hydrocarbon, sulphur oxides, nitrogen oxides, and others amount to millions of tons each, per year.
- There's more than 150 million tons of garbage and trash being thrown away every year. And billions of tin cans, billions of bottles, and even *several million junk cars* every year.

It would take a lot of polluting to pollute all the land and water and air of the earth and kill off all the wild life and marine life—and human life. But some scientists say we are moving in that direction at a rapid clip! Everyone knows that the trend can't be allowed to continue. Something must be done. But what? And how? These are tough questions. And some of the trade-offs— the opportunity costs—are difficult to accept.

MARKET FORCES DON'T AUTOMATICALLY PROTECT THE ENVIRONMENT

How did it happen that the market system, which is supposed to direct the society's resources into *desirable* channels, allowed the environmental problem to arise? Why didn't the market system protect society against it? The answer is simple: The environmental problem is outside the market. There is no way that the automatic market process can handle this problem.

These *many* decades since the Industrial Revolution, we have been living high without paying the full costs of what we have been getting from the earth. We have been pulling natural resources from the earth without having to incur the costs of reproducing or recycling those natural resources. We have been dumping wastes into the environment without having to pay the costs of cleaning up the wastes. But now we are in a situation where we can't do as much of that anymore.

Too many resources are being pulled out of the environment and too many wastes are being put back. It is already going too fast to be sustained. To dramatize the problem some people refer to our planet as "spaceship earth." We're flying through space on a finite world; when we use up all of our supplies, then we will all die. Like it or not, that's the way it is.

Economist Kenneth Boulding is one who emphasizes this problem. Boulding says that we must begin to think of recycling *everything*, and replacing *everything* which we take from nature. We must dump *nothing* into the environment which natural forces cannot handle—that is, which nature cannot recycle.

THE "HUMAN HERD" IS GETTING TOO BIG FOR THE RANGE

What about the *population* aspect of the problem of ecological imbalance? At the beginning of this century there were only about 1.5 billion people on earth. Today there are six billion. At current rates of growth, by the middle of the next century there will be about sixteen billion. But there's just no way that so many people can be supported on the earth! Not unless we find a lot of unbelievable ways to recycle things, and to generate something out of nothing.

What's going to happen? Two things will happen, because they *must* happen. (1) Somehow the population expansion will be slowed, and (ultimately) stopped. (2) *All* productive activities will begin shifting more and more energy toward recycling materials and toward protecting and rebuilding the natural environment. The normal processes of life in all the advanced nations must go through some changes. There's no doubt about it.

THE HIGH "REAL COST" OF PROTECTING THE ENVIRONMENT

The recycling and environmental protection efforts are going to cost a lot. Many resources, much energy, much valuable effort will be required. *All* products are likely to cost more in *real* terms—not just in "inflated values" from inflation.

Resources, energy, capital, and labor will be diverted toward environmental rebuilding, recycling, and pollution control. That will mean a lot more energy and resources used up, but without any increase in the quantities of goods produced. So we will get less output for our used-up inputs. That will mean fewer goods for the people.

Will our standards of living actually go *down?* No one knows, of course. But it's quite possible. The inputs used for environmental protection must come from somewhere. Those inputs (including human effort) can't be used to do or make what they were doing or making before.

Somehow the environmental problem must be solved. No question about it. But how fast? and how? What role will the government play? And what will be the role of the forces of the market process? What kind of "economic system" do we need—and what kind will we choose—to cope with this problem?

As our society faces its environmental problem, some very difficult, but very critical decisions must be made. How will we approach it? There is no question that the market process, acting alone, cannot solve this problem for us. The political process—government regulations and controls—must be involved. But to what extent?

There doesn't seem to be any question that stringent environmental protections need to be maintained. But that is a move away from letting market forces work their powerful magic! Every step in the direction of greater governmental control is actually a change in our "economic system."

How easy it is for an economic system to change! But that shouldn't be surprising. Economic systems are changing all the time. That's what you will be reading about in the next chapter.

REVIEW QUESTIONS

1. Explain how higher domestic oil and natural gas prices would reduce U.S. dependence on foreign oil. What role does the "powerful price mechanism" play?

2. Discuss some of the opportunity costs of protecting the environment. Who will "pay" these costs?

3. Explain why the "free market process" does not (cannot) automatically protect the environment.

4. What forces did finally bring exploding oil prices under control? How are these forces affecting the OPEC cartel?

27 THE CONTINUING EVOLUTION OF THE WORLD'S ECONOMIC SYSTEMS

KEY TERMS

- the economic problem
- market process
- political process
- price mechanism
- inequality and income redistribution
- survival of capitalism
- externalities
- "spill-over effects"

- the production question
- the distribution question
- making the economic choices
- implementing the economic choices
- converging economic systems

Throughout history, economic systems have been changing. But it wasn't until recent centuries that the changes began to become big, and cumulative—like a chain reaction, like a row of tumbling dominos.

Feudal society eroded, people were shaken loose from their land and from their traditional roles in life; trade expanded and the *market system* evolved. Remember? Then the Industrial Revolution added much more speed to the progressive changes, and the modern economic systems evolved out of all that.

THE MARKET PROCESS IS A VERY POWERFUL FORCE

The powerful forces of the market process and the price mechanism have been responsible for these revolutionary changes in economics—and in society. These forces are still very powerful in the modern world.

THE PRODUCTION QUESTIONS

Decisions about which resources to use for what purposes (and which to conserve), about which products to produce in what quantities (and which not to produce); and decisions by consumers about which products to consume (and in what quantities) all still are greatly influenced by prices.

- Prices which are relatively high and rising always tend to discourage consumption and to stimulate production. Ultimately, prices which are "too high" result in *surpluses.*
- Prices which are relatively low and falling always tend to encourage consumption and to discourage production. Ultimately, prices which are "too low" result in *shortages.*

These powerful forces of price are still very much alive in the modern world and are exerting their influence on our economic choices every day. But not *all* of the output and input and consumption choices of the society are left free to be determined by market forces.

THE DISTRIBUTION QUESTION

The powerful forces of the price mechanism still play the most important role in answering the distribution question in the "free societies" of the modern world. People who are highly productive—or who own highly productive assets—are the ones who receive the largest incomes. But in modern society, not *all* income distribution is left free to be determined by "impersonal market forces."

Income redistribution—by government programs—is having a significant effect on the way in which the distribution question is now being answered. But it is still true that *productivity* is the most important factor in determining who will be rich and who will be poor.

So the forces of the market process and the price mechanism are still extremely important in the modern world. Anyone who forgets this is likely to make foolish mistakes and wind up *worsening* their economic circumstances. And government policies which fail to consider the great power of the price mechanism are likely to have the ultimate effect of worsening the economic circumstances of the people. But even so—even with all this great power—the market process still cannot solve *all* of the modern world's economic problems.

THE MARKET PROCESS CAN'T SOLVE ALL THE PROBLEMS

The tough problems of this century have battered society from several sides. We have encountered wars, inflation, depression, expanding economic power of giant businesses, a world population explosion, poverty, environmental pollution, crises in the cities, international financial crises, and other difficult problems.

What about all these problems? They all require that some of society's resources be directed toward solutions. Yet how can that happen? The *market system* doesn't automatically direct resources toward wars and environmental protection and urban crises and population explosions and such. So how can the problems be handled? The government must get involved.

The government must play a more important role in the resource-directing process. That is to say: The economic system must change to include more government-directed choices. Is that what's going on in the world? Yes, that's exactly what's happening.

THE PSYCHOLOGICAL IMPACT OF THE DEPRESSION

During the 1930s many people were out of work. Businesses and banks were failing. The economic system was not functioning as the economists said it was supposed to. During this period the self-reliant economic philosophy of many people shifted.

Attitudes changed from the position: "I can always find a job—or do whatever may be necessary to take care of myself!"—to the position: "There are times when economic conditions beyond my control make it impossible for me to take care of myself. So the government must do something *to ensure* that the people have adequate employment opportunities and adequate economic security!"

This shift of the public mood away from laissez-faire and toward more reliance on the government has been reflected in the basic nature of the economic system. The result has been greater involvement by government in making the economic choices for the society.

THE INFLUENCE OF KEYNESIAN ECONOMICS

You remember that it was during the depression that *Keynesian economics* emerged. This provided a theoretical explanation which specifically calls for government policies aimed toward the objective of maintaining a healthy and growing economy. Both the psychological impact of the depression, and the introduction of Keynesian economics (and the wide acceptance of the Keynesian theories) have had the effect of increasing *the role of the political process* in making basic economic choices in the American economic system.

Many people think it is *good* that the government has become more involved in directing and influencing the economic choices. But many other people think it is *definitely not good*. Perhaps the future will tell us who was right. But for now, while we're waiting to find out, of one thing we can be quite sure: The American economic system has undergone some significant changes—changes which now are affecting, and which in the future will continue to affect all of us.

THE INCREASING ROLE OF THE STATE

In all free economies of the modern world during this century, the role of the government (the state) has been increasing. Urgent problems of modern society have required it. Why? Because the market process operating by itself can't deal with some of the problems that must be dealt with.

Governments have become increasingly involved in planning—in setting goals and in directing various activities in the economy. As this has happened, the free market economic systems have evolved into something else—something different from either the model or the reality of traditional capitalism.

As "free market systems" change in response to the emergency needs and crisis conditions of modern society, it's an interesting and suspenseful drama to watch. It makes some people sad, some bewildered. But that's always the way with rapid change. As modern economic systems change, what about capitalism? Will capitalism survive?

WHAT ABOUT THE SURVIVAL OF CAPITALISM?

Questions about the survival of capitalism really don't make much sense. What is capitalism? Capitalism *was* the economic system of the mid-nineteenth century, observed and attacked (and incidentally, named) by Karl Marx. That kind of economic system doesn't exist anywhere in the world. It hasn't for more than fifty years! To talk about the survival of the system Marx called capitalism would be an irrelevant exercise.

THE BANNERS OF OUR WORLDLY RELIGIONS

The names we use for economic systems these days really don't offer very accurate descriptions of anything. Capitalism, socialism, and communism have become words to argue about. The words don't describe any real-world economic systems. These words—creations of nineteenth-century social protest philosopher-prophets—have become the "banners" in a kind of worldly religious struggle.

The whole argument is far more emotional than rational, and far more political than economic. We would all understand economic systems a lot better—and likely the twentieth-century world would be a much more pleasant place to live—if everyone would forget about these worldly religions. Better we should confine our discussions to the *substance* of different economic systems and forget about the emotion-packed names by which they are known.

WE'VE SOLVED THE OLD PROBLEMS AND CREATED NEW ONES

The problems of modern civilization are pressing more and more on all people, everywhere. These problems have been visited upon us by our own progress. We have gone so far toward solving the old problems—hunger, disease, others—that we have uncovered (or permitted to arise) new problems.

The new problems have been allowed to arise only because they have not been held in check by the powerful automatic social control mechanism which brought the great progress. What mechanism? The *market process*, of course!

So now, how does society take charge and take action on these new kinds of problems? By building new kinds of control mechanisms—mechanisms which will be effective over things which the *market process* cannot effectively control.

HAS THE MARKET SYSTEM HAD ITS DAY IN THE SUN?

What powered the great thrust of economic growth which tore the world loose from its traditional past and brought us to this seething modern world of intermittent crises and turbulent change? The market system did it—the market system with its powerful price mechanism.

THE MARKET PROCESS GENERATED THE MODERN WORLD

The high-living, bewildering modern world was generated by the powerful motivating and controlling forces of the market process:

- the harsh law-of-the-jungle system of rewards and punishments, where the productive people are rewarded and the others go hungry;
- the powerful incentive of *profits*, stimulating more production and greater efficiency; and
- the powerful force of prices, conserving and rationing the society's resources, and motivating the production of more of the wanted things.

These powerful forces of the market process were responsible for the economic breakthroughs which generated the modern world.

People, businesses, nations, all were striving, conserving, pushing to get ahead. They wanted the pleasure of having more things. People were highly motivated, working, producing.

As the market system stimulated the production of the things people and businesses were buying, more and better goods were produced. New kinds of goods—both consumer goods and capital goods—became available. There were more and better machines, equipment, factories—things needed to keep productivity increasing.

The market process provided a way to harness *self interest* and to use this powerful force as the *energy* to thrust the economy forward, to speed up production and generate rapid economic growth. We who live in the advanced nations would be able to have only a fraction of the things we now enjoy, were it not for the powerful motivating and controlling forces of the market process. So what now? Is that all over and done with? And if so, what happens next?

THE MARKET SYSTEM (IN ITS PURE FORM) IS NOT SOCIALLY ACCEPTABLE

Throughout the world the modern market-oriented economies have been turning away from the market process. The political process—government direction and control—is making and carrying out more of society's economic choices.

It's happening not only in the advanced nations but in the less-developed countries, too. The less-developed countries are devising government plans and using administrative directions and controls to try to steer their economies toward their longed-for goals of economic development. Why is the powerful market process being pushed aside and overruled by governments? There are several reasons.

THE PROBLEMS OF INEQUALITY AND SELFISHNESS

Many things about the way the market process works are not so acceptable anymore (some never were). Inequality is one problem—great wealth, with things being used lavishly by the rich while the poor go hungry. All modern market-oriented nations have developed programs to lessen this *inequality* generated by the market system.

The modern nations produce enough so that even the poor can be adequately provided for. So governments are overthrowing the "distribution choice" of the market process and shifting more of the output to the poor.

Another problem, to some people, is the emphasis on *selfishness* as the *motive force* which makes the market process work. Some people don't like the idea of giving rewards to those who do selfish things. Selfishness has proven to be a very powerful and highly efficient force for driving the economic system (and also for achieving the survival of most living things). But most people don't consider selfishness to be a "human virtue."

But there is an even more basic problem than inequality or the emphasis on selfishness. Sometimes it is impossible for the freely operating market process to reflect and respond to some of the true wishes of the society. *That's* the *real* problem.

THE MARKET PROCESS CANNOT SET GOALS FOR SOCIETY

The market process directs the society's resources to "flow toward the dollar"—that is, to go where, and to do what the *spenders* wish. The uses of all of the society's things are determined by the ways in which the people and businesses choose to spend their money. So what's the problem? Just that in the modern world, that arrangement can't *always* optimize the use of society's resources—can't *always* make the choices which will work toward the objectives and goals of the society.

Many desired objectives cannot be achieved simply by letting resources be directed into whatever the people spend their money for—and into nothing else. This arrangement would leave many important functions inadequately performed—perhaps not performed at all. What functions? Such things as education, fire and police protection, roads and streets, public welfare, national defense, health and hospitals, perhaps urban housing, perhaps others.

Most people have agreed for a long time that the *political process* must direct some resources into these "public" functions—that the market process acting alone can't look out for the society's best interests in these areas. But now, suddenly (almost overnight!), this *kind* of problem is exploding all over the landscape! Now there are *many cases* where the free market process can't look out for the society's best interests.

What's the problem? Economists call it "externalities." It's the "spillover effect" that happens almost every time anybody does *anything* these days.

THE PROBLEM OF EXTERNALITIES—THE "SPILL-OVER EFFECT"

The free market process just can't control the spill-over effects—the things that happen outside the market—things like air and water pollution that don't influence the *costs* and *prices* of things. The market process would force the producer to use cheap fuel, dirty the air, and sell the product at a low price. But the *true social objectives* would require more expensive fuel, cleaner air, and a higher-priced product.

Before there were such great increases in population and industrialization, there wasn't much of a problem of externalities. But now, all modern societies face the *urgent* and *unavoidable* task of bringing our heavily populated, heavily industrialized modern world into ecological balance with our natural environment. And how can the free market process do that? That's the problem. It can't.

So the society must cope with these problems some other way. And what other way is there? The political process? Government plans, regulations, controls, charges, penalties, subsidies, and such? Yes.

ENTER: THE POLITICAL PROCESS

On some issues these days, the political process must get involved. Governments must overthrow some of the choice-making power of the market process, must define the essential objectives, and must arrange for resources and energy to be used to achieve those chosen objectives.

So has the market process had its day in the sun? Has it "done its thing" in ripping out the social control mechanisms that kept societies stable (and alive) for thousands of years?

In its brief moment on stage, the market process—the price mechanism—has blasted mankind off on this bewildering journey through time. Many people now realize that we must make some changes in the directions of our journey. So, must we push the free market process off-stage after such a short (but brilliant!) performance? Not entirely. But perhaps to some extent? Yes.

THE MARKET PROCESS: FROM MASTER TO SERVANT OF SOCIAL CHOICE?

Throughout the last century and up to the depression of the 1930s the forces of the free market process really were in charge. The market process really was in "master control" over the society's resources. Private individuals and businesses, responding to market forces, determined for the economy *what* was going to happen and *where, when, how,* and *how much.* The free forces of the market process really did provide the avenue of social choice.

THE TEMPERING OF THE MARKET PROCESS

Since World War I (in Europe) and especially since the depression of the 1930s (in the United States), the choice-making power of the free market process more and more has been modified, restrained, and pushed aside.

It isn't that markets and market forces have been abolished. Incentives and rewards still operate. Prices are still exerting their powerful force in conserving things and motivating the production of things. The drive to get ahead and the attractiveness of profits still motivate people and businesses. So what is the nature of this change that's occurring?

It is partly a tempering of the market forces themselves. Taxes on wages and profits change the "incentive force" somewhat; welfare payments and payments to unemployed people reduce somewhat the discomfort of being unproductive. And there are other ways the market forces have been lessened. But that isn't the big issue. Much more important—especially for the continuing long-run evolution of the world's economic systems—is this:

> *The market process for a fleeting moment in history was the powerful, disruptive master* of social choice. Now, to some extent it is being broken to harness—forced into the role of *servant* to carry out the deliberate (we hope, *rational*) resource-use choices of the society—choices made by (and in view of objectives and goals chosen by) the local, state, and national governments—that is, by the *political processes* of the society.

How is it possible for the role of the market process to be changed from master to servant? After you read the next two sections you will understand.

SOCIETY'S ECONOMIC PROBLEM: THE PRODUCTION AND DISTRIBUTION QUESTIONS

Each society faces its economic problem—of dealing with scarcity, of deciding what to do with each of its scarce resources: What to use and what to save? What to do and what to make? Who will get to have how much of what? Those are the choices which, somehow, the society must make. That's the society's *economic problem.*

Usually economists break down the economic problem into (1) the *production* question (deciding what things to produce, in what quantities; using how much of which inputs and what production techniques, and so on), and (2) the *distribution* question (deciding how big a share of the output each person will get).

How does a society get the answers to these questions? Through its economic system, of course. That's the purpose of the economic system—to work out the answers to these questions and to carry out the choices. Each economic system uses some combination of (1) the social process (following the traditional ways of answering the questions), (2) the political process (government decisions), and (3) the market process (letting resources flow to meet the demands of the people). These breakdowns:

- of the *economic problem* into "production" and "distribution" questions, and
- of the *techniques* for the *economic-problem-solving* into "social," "political," and "market" processes,

are helpful. But there's another way these questions can be broken down.

To understand what's happening right now in the rapid evolution of the world's economic systems—for example, to understand the shifting role of the market process from master to servant of social choice—we need a new breakdown. We need a breakdown between (1) economic *decision making* (*choosing* the objectives and goals), and (2) the *implementation* of economic decisions (*directing resources* to achieve the chosen objectives and goals).

SOCIETY'S ECONOMIC PROBLEM: THE DECISION-MAKING AND IMPLEMENTATION QUESTIONS

Solving a society's economic problem involves not one but *two* functions: (1) *making* the choices, and (2) *carrying out* the choices. Why is it so important to separate these two functions? Just this: One process (for example, the political process) may be used to *make* the decision, while another process (for example, the market process) may be used to *carry out* the decision. And that's important.

Now do you begin to see what has been happening to the role of the market process? Of course! Its *decision-making* function more and more is being stripped away; its *implementation* function is being used more and more to carry out *political process decisions!* Is that how the market process has been shifting from the role of *master* of social choice, to the role of *servant?* Of course. The market process has been becoming more of a "servant" to the society's will—as that "will" is expressed by the society's political processes.

Just as the market process can both *make* and *carry out* the economic choices for society, so can the political process perform both functions. The former Soviet Union, the People's Republic of China and other Communist (that is, neo-Marxian socialist) countries have relied very much on their political processes to perform both functions—to make and to carry out the choices. Generally the plans have been implemented by administrators who direct the resources to carry out the plans.

But, as you know, in recent years the countries with planned economies have been discovering the efficiency of the market process as "servant to the political process." They are finding out how easy it is to get labor and other resources to move in the desired directions by offering wage and price incentives. At the same time the market-oriented countries are becoming more aware of the real-world limitations on the ability of the market process, acting alone, to protect the society's resources and to generate optimal levels of social well-being. So they are shifting more of the *decision-making* function to the political process.

THE MARKET PROCESS: STILL MUCH MORE MASTER THAN SERVANT!

Since the New Deal days of the 1930s the U.S. economy has seen increasing planning and huge government budgets, all influencing the allocation of resources in the economy. We have social security and other social welfare programs, massive highway systems, educational systems, military systems, space shuttles and on and on. All these resource-use choices were made by governments—(national, state, and local)—i.e., by the political process.

About one-third of all of the productive activity in the U.S. economy is directed by political-process choices, most of which are implemented by the market process—by the powerful price mechanism. One-third is a lot! But don't lose sight of the fact that, for the other two-thirds the *market process* is still *the master of social choice*.

It wasn't the government that caused the shift of auto production to small cars or housing construction to condos or the big shift to home computers. It was the market process! The invisible hand? Consumer sovereignty? Right!

To be sure, government does get involved in the private market through regulation and taxation and in many other ways. But the bottom line is: It's *consumer choice* which still directs the flow of most of the resources in the American economy. So the decision-making role of the market process— although somewhat bypassed and somewhat restricted and regulated—is still very much alive. The market process shows no sign that it's about to resign all of its decision-making functions to the political process.

THE CONVERGING EVOLUTION OF THE WORLD'S ECONOMIC SYSTEMS

So what's happening? The former Communist countries are changing their economic systems to take more advantage of the highly efficient market process. At the same time, the market-oriented countries have been introducing more government plans, directions, and restrictions—stripping the market process of some of its decision-making role, but usually depending on the market process to carry out the plans.

As the economic systems of the world evolve, it seems inevitable that more of the choices in the market-oriented economies will be made through the political process. But it's likely that the market process will continue to be used to implement the plans. Why? Because the market process is highly efficient. No resource administrator needs to work out each little detail.

People and resources move automatically in response to market-process incentives. And with the market process, people have more freedom of choice. No one needs to be ordered around. Price adjustments can be used to pull more (or fewer) people and resources in each direction.

ECONOMIC SYSTEMS ARE BECOMING MORE ALIKE

While the market-oriented societies are learning more about how to use the political process in setting goals and objectives and designing plans, the leaders in the less-market-oriented economies are learning more about the efficiency of the market system. In most of the less-developed countries too, some political-process planning with market-process implementation often seems to offer the most effective approach for achieving the desired objectives.

THE PHILOSOPHICAL PROBLEMS

So is everyone happy with these changes in their economic systems? No—far from it. Many people in the United States and other market-oriented countries take "capitalism" as a sort of religion and argue against any government goal-setting and planning. (Government planning is communistic!)

Many people in the former Soviet Union and other neo-Marxian socialist countries take communism as a sort of religion and argue against any use of the market process. (Price and profit incentives are capitalistic!) But times are changing. More and more people are changing their minds. It seems that these narrow attitudes are slowly passing into history. As that happens, a major cause of conflict in the world will be removed.

THE TECHNICAL AND POLITICAL PROBLEMS

There are two other kinds of problems. First, it isn't easy for socio-economic planners to figure out exactly how to harness the market process so as to direct the economy toward the desired objectives. It takes a lot of expert economic understanding and analysis to figure out how to do that. And even so it may not come out right.

Second, even if the planners knew exactly what to do, the political realities of *politics* often would prevent them from carrying out their well-designed plans. Still, somehow it's being done—not always done *well*, but being done. There's more planning in the "free" economies, and much more use of the market process in the "planned" economies.

So what does the future hold in store? Will all of the economic systems of the world soon look exactly alike? Of course not. But it's obvious now that in recent years the world's economic systems have been becoming more alike. The 1990s developments in Russia, in the other CIS nations, and in the People's Republic of China certainly seem to confirm this idea. Maybe as this evolution proceeds, all of our economic systems will become more socially and economically efficient. Let's hope so.

DOES THE WORLD NEED NEW SOCIAL CONTROL MECHANISMS?

Back in ancient times and feudal times—and in some societies even today—a structure of "nonmarket-type" social control mechanisms held the society together, prevented things which would have been socially destructive, and made possible the *survival* of the society. But then came the erosion of the traditional societies and the emergence and growth of the powerful market process, pushing all else aside and thrusting forward the explosive development of modern society.

What now? Are we about to go full circle? Throughout most of the time that people have been on earth, the traditional social control mechanisms—the clan, the tribe, the manor, and other such social arrangements—have "kept it all together."

Must *world society* now begin to develop social control mechanisms to try to achieve for all of us what the traditional social control mechanisms achieved for the traditional societies? Has the powerful market process, as *master of social choice,* had its day in the sun—now to be relegated to the role of *servant* to the socio-economic planners? And if so, how do we expect these national and worldwide changes in economic systems to come about? And what effects will these changes have on the future lives of people?

These are interesting and critical questions. The quality and economic conditions of future life on earth—perhaps even the continued existence of human life itself—will be significantly influenced by the way these answers come out. It isn't likely that we—or even you—will be around long enough to know the answers. All we can do at this point is to hope that the decisions we make and the directions we choose will prove to have been the right ones.

REVIEW QUESTIONS

1. It was the rise of the market process which brought the rapid changes from which modern economic systems developed. Why have all modern economies (including the United States) to some extent turned away from (and/or redirected the results of) the market process? Explain.

2. What are externalities? What problems arise because of externalities? How can society deal with these problems?

3. Explain some of the ways that, during this century, the market process has gone from "master" to "servant" of social choice. Does this mean that the "free market process" no longer works?

4. In recent years, different economic systems appear to be becoming somewhat more alike. Why is this true? Do you think this trend will continue? Explain.

NAME INDEX

SUBJECT INDEX

Classical economists, 87, 88
Clayton Act (1914), 104
Clinton administration, budget
deficit, 261
Collars, 266
Command, 13, 19; early civiliza-
tions, 32-33; feudalism, 41;
Roman Empire, 36-37
Committee for Economic Develop-
ment, 226
Committee on the Rights of
Closet Keynesians (CROCK),
250-251
Common land, 44; enclosures of,
44, 53
Commonwealth of Independent
States (CIS), 270, 325
Communism, 317; twilight of, 269-
270
Communist Manifesto, 55, 93-95
Communist Party, 139
Communist revolutionaries, 89
Competition, 290; between indus-
tries, 294; effective, 104-105;
foreign, 221; global, 268; pure
(perfect), 20
Compliance costs, 297
Confidence, Keynesian prescrip-
tion and, 174-175
Conservative economics, 222
Consolidations, 297, 298
Conspicuous consumption, 113
Consumer choice, 324
Consumer Price Index (CPI), 235
Consumer sovereignty, 292, 324
Consumption, present, 21
Continuing resolutions, 262
Contract with America, 262
Conventional wisdom, 292
Cooling off period, 266
Corn laws, 56, 78
Corporate profits, 1983-84, 228
Corporate wealth, 290
Corporations: effect of high inter-
est rates on, 238; federal char-
tering of, 296; giant, 293, 295;
industrial, 290-291; oil, 304-305
Cost-of-living adjustments
(COLAs), 260
Council of Economic Advisors
(CEA), 150, 208, 209, 217;
Kennedy-Johnson, 224, 249;
Nixon, 249

Council on Wage and Price Stabili-
ty, 219
Cradles of civilization, 31
Crowding out, 238
Crusades, the, 42-43

D

Das Kapital, 94, 96, 109
Debt limit, 262
Debtor nation, 285
Decision-making function, market
process, 323
Declaration of Independence, 68
Deficit-reducing initiatives of 1984,
226
Deficits, 208, 214; budget (*see* Budget deficit, federal); planned
and realized, 214; and tight
money policy, 249; trade in the
1980s and 1990s, 282
Demand, directing the economy,
123-125
Demand curve, 118-120
Demand-side economics, 199, 223
Dependence effect, 292
Depository Institutions Deregula-
tion Act, 296-297
Depression, 108-109; in business
cycles, 141; caused by high
interest rates, 238; Great, 135-
143; Keynesian prescription,
161, 162, 170; psychological
impact of, 315; self-fulfilling
prophesies of, 175
Deregulation, 296-298
Devaluation, dollar, 211, 212, 277
Differential rent theory, 78-79
Disposable income, 227
Distribution choice, 319
Distribution question, the, 12, 314,
322
Distributive share, 14-15
Divestitures, 297, 298
Division of labor, 70
Dollar: crisis of 1971, 277; crisis of
1978, 279-281; devaluation, 211,
212, 277; exchange value (rate)
of, 275-278; floating, 277, 278,
279-285; vs. yen, 282, 283
Dow Jones Index, 266
Downsizing, 297

E

Early civilizations, 31-37
Ecological imbalance, population
aspect, 310
Economic behavior, natural laws
of, 70, 71, 75, 109
Economic conditions: in the 1920s,
136; in 1933, 138-139; of the
1970s, 278-279; after World War
II, 162-163
Economic Consequences of the Peace,
155
Economic crises: conflicting ideas,
2, 3; of the early 1980s, 1-2;
improvement since the early
1980s, 2-3
Economic expansion, 258-259
Economic forces: awareness of,
xiv; change fueled by, 3-5
Economic Journal, 155
Economic morality, 35
Economic power, 102
Economic problem, the, 10-12, 322;
solving, 12-14, 323
Economic progress/growth, 20-21,
35; and the command process,
36; during industrial revolution, 52-53, 56-57
Economic questions, three basic,
12-14
Economic Recovery Tax Act of
1981, 224-225
Economic Report: 1980, Carter's,
230; 1982, Reagan's, 230; 1984,
Reagan's, 230
Economic system, 19, 315, 322
Economic systems of the world:
becoming more alike, 325; converging evolution of, 324-326;
philosophical problems, 325;
technical and political problems, 325-326
Economics: classical, 69, 76;
defined, 22; early ideas on, 33-
36; normative, 82; positive, 82;
supply-side, 189
Economics and the Public Purpose,
292, 294
Economy: directed by society's
demands, 123-125; in the early
1980s, 226-229, 238-239; free,
269; underground, 269
"Economy Out of Control," 226